THE CAMBRIDGE COMPANION TO
RELIGION AND TERRORISM

There is currently much discussion regarding the causes of terrorist acts, as well as the connection between terrorism and religion. Terrorism is attributed either to religious "fanaticism" or, alternately, to political and economic factors, with religion more or less dismissed as a secondary factor. *The Cambridge Companion to Religion and Terrorism* examines this complex relationship between religion and terrorism through a collection of essays freshly written for this volume. Bringing varying approaches, from the theoretical to the empirical to the topical, the Companion includes an array of subjects such as radicalization, suicide bombing, and rational choice, as well as specific case studies. The result is a richly textured collection that prompts readers to critically consider the cluster of phenomena that we have come to refer to as "terrorism" and terrorism's relationship with the similarly problematic set of phenomena that we call "religion."

James R. Lewis is Professor of Religious Studies at the University of Tromsø (Norway). A scholar of New Religious Movements, he currently edits or coedits three book series and is the general editor for the *Alternative Spirituality and Religion Review*. Recent publications include *Violence and New Religious Movements* (2011), *Sacred Suicide* (2014), *Cults: A Reference and Guide* (2014), *The Oxford Handbook of New Religious Movements* (2015), and *The Invention of Satanism* (2016).

Other Titles in the Series

(continued after index)

THE CAMBRIDGE COMPANION TO

RELIGION AND TERRORISM

Edited by

James R. Lewis
University of Tromsø

CAMBRIDGE
UNIVERSITY PRESS

CAMBRIDGE
UNIVERSITY PRESS

One Liberty Plaza, 20th Floor, New York, NY 10006, USA

Cambridge University Press is part of the University of Cambridge.

It furthers the University's mission by disseminating knowledge in the pursuit of education, learning, and research at the highest international levels of excellence.

www.cambridge.org
Information on this title: www.cambridge.org/9781316505625
DOI: 10.1017/9781316492536

First published 2017

Printed in the United States of America by Sheridan Books, Inc.

A catalogue record for this publication is available from the British Library.

Library of Congress Cataloging-in-Publication Data
NAMES: Lewis, James, 1949– editor.
TITLE: The Cambridge companion to religion and terrorism / [edited by] James Lewis, University of Tromsø.
DESCRIPTION: 1 [edition]. | New York : Cambridge University Press, 2017. |
SERIES: Cambridge companions to religion | Includes bibliographical references and index.
IDENTIFIERS: LCCN 2017008345| ISBN 9781107140141 (Hardback : alk. paper) | ISBN 9781316505625 (pbk. : alk. paper)
SUBJECTS: LCSH: Terrorism–Religious aspects.
CLASSIFICATION: LCC BL65.T47 C36 2017 | DDC 201/.763325–dc23
LC record available at https://lccn.loc.gov/2017008345

ISBN 978-1-107-14014-1 Hardback
ISBN 978-1-316-50562-5 Paperback

Contents

Contributors

Meerim Aitkulova holds an MA from the Peace and Conflict Transformation Program, University of Tromsø – the Arctic University of Norway. Her areas of interest include new Islamic movements in Kyrgyzstan and security processes in that country.

Scott Atran is Directeur de Recherche, CNRS, Institut Jean Nicod – Ecole Normale Supérieure and Research Professor, Gerald Ford School of Public Policy and Institute for Social Research, University of Michigan; Research Professor, John Jay College of Criminal Justice, City University of New York; Senior Fellow, Harris Manchester College and School of Social Anthropology, University of Oxford, and the author of numerous books, including *Talking to the Enemy* (2010) and *In Gods We Trust* (2002)

William T. Cavanaugh is Senior Research Professor at the Center for World Catholicism and Intercultural Theology, DePaul University in Chicago. His degrees are from the Universities of Notre Dame, Cambridge, and Duke. He is the author of five books and many articles. His books have been translated into French, Spanish, and Polish.

Nicole S. D'Amico is Editorial Director of Academic Publishing. She received her MA in Journalism Studies at the University of Sheffield and is also a media officer for the Italian Politics Specialist Group for the Political Studies Association. She is the coauthor of "Cult Journalism" in the *Oxford Handbook of New Religious Movements, Vol. II*, and "News Media, the Internet and the Church of Scientology" in *The Brill Handbook of Scientology* (2017).

Espen Dahl is Professor of Systematic Theology at the University of Tromsø. He is the author of *Phenomenology and the Holy: Religious Experience after Husserl* (2010), *In Between: The Holy Beyond Modern Dichotomies* (2011) and *Stanley Cavell, Religion, and Continental Philosophy* (2014).

Lorne L. Dawson is Chair of the Department of Sociology and Legal Studies at the University of Waterloo. Most of his research is in the sociology of religion, particularly the study of new religious movements. His work on why some new religions become violent led to research on the process of radicalization in homegrown terrorist groups. He has written three books, edited four, and published over sixty academic articles and book chapters.

Ellen Dobrowolski is currently a graduate student at University in Tromsø – the Arctic University of Norway. She is the author of *The Prophet of the New World: Religious Insanity and the New Religion of Louis Riel*, forthcoming in the Alternative Spirituality and Religion Review.

Lorenz Graitl is Lecturer at the Department of Asian and African Studies at Humboldt University Berlin. He received his PhD in sociology from Freie Universität Berlin. His first book, *Sterben als Spektakel: Zur kommunikativen Dimension des politisch motivierten Suizids* (2012), discusses the historical genesis and communicative aspects of different forms of political suicide, as well as corresponding discourses of legitimization.

Christopher Hartney is a Senior Lecturer in the Department of Studies in Religion at the University of Sydney where he teaches courses in religion and violence, and religion and film. He specializes in the study of new religions in East Asia and Vietnam, and has published extensively on Caodaism, Vietnam's largest indigenous religion. He is a past editor of the *Journal of Religious History and Literature and Aesthetics*.

Mark Juergensmeyer is Professor of Sociology at the University of California, Santa Barbara. He is an expert on religious violence, conflict resolution, and South Asian religion and politics, and has published more than two hundred articles and twenty books, including *Global Rebellion: Religious Challenges to the Secular State* (2008) and his widely read *Terror in the Mind of God: The Global Rise of Religious Violence* (2003).

James R. Lewis is Professor of Religious Studies at the University of Tromsø – the Arctic University of Norway. He currently edits or coedits four book series. He is the general editor for the *Alternative Spirituality and Religion Review* and former editor of the *Journal of Religion and Violence*. Lewis is also the author of over a hundred articles and book chapters, and the author, editor, or coeditor of two dozen monographs and anthologies.

David Miller is Professor of Sociology at the University of Bath and RCUK Global Uncertainties Leadership Fellow (2013–2016). Recent publications include: *The Henry Jackson Society and the Degeneration of British Neoconservatism* (2015, coauthor); *Stretching the Sociological Imagination: Essays in Honour of John Eldridge* (2015, coeditor); *The Web of Influence: The Role of Addictive Industries in Shaping Policy and Undermining Public Health* (forthcoming, coauthor).

Tom Mills is a sociologist and researcher at the University of Bath and Lecturer in Sociology at Aston University. His 2015 doctoral research examined how the end of social democracy and the rise of neoliberalism impacted the BBC, and is the basis of his forthcoming book, *The BBC: The Myth of a Public Service* (2016). He is the coauthor of *What Is Islamophobia?: Racism, Social Movements and the State* (2017); *The Cold War on British Muslims* (2011) and *The Britain Israel Communications and Research Centre: Giving Peace a Chance?* (2013).

Pieter Nanninga studied History and Religious Studies and completed his PhD on the representations of suicide attacks in al-Qaeda's martyrdom videos

(2014). Currently, he is Assistant Professor of Middle Eastern Studies at the University of Groningen. His research focuses on global jihadism (especially al-Qaeda and the Islamic State) and he is particularly interested in the relationship between culture, religion, and violence.

Stephen Nemeth is Assistant Professor of Political Science at Oklahoma State University. He received his PhD from the University of Iowa in 2010. His primary interests are in the organizational and spatial attributes of terrorist violence. He has authored or coauthored several articles on terrorism and conflict management.

Per-Erik Nilsson is a postdoctoral scholar financed by the Swedish Research Council (Vetenskapsrådet). He is working within the Impact of Religion Research Program, Uppsala University, and the CHERPA research center at Sciences-Po, Aix-en-Provence. In his current research Nilsson focuses on secularism, nationalism, and populism in France.

Peter Schalk is Professor Emeritus from Uppsala University. His main areas of research was in Buddhism-Hinduism and religious expressions of social-economic conflicts in present South Asia, especially on the concepts of martyrdom in a cross-cultural perspective. His focus was on non-religious concepts as promoted by the Liberation Tigers of Tamil Ealam (LTTE).

Acknowledgments

As anyone who has written a book or edited an anthology knows, one typically acquires too many debts to be able to adequately acknowledge everyone. So at the risk of offending some individuals I will fail to mention, let me thank a few people to whom I owe the greatest debts.

Above all, let me first thank my wife, Evelyn Oliver, who has patiently borne with me and tolerated the often excessive amount of time I have spent on the computer during this and other projects.

Then let me thank the contributors, some of whom have waited for years to see this collection emerge into the light of day. Among these contributors, let me especially thank Mark Juergensmeyer, who was an early supporter of this project.

I would also like to acknowledge the more general support of the University of Tromsø – The Arctic University of Norway, the Department of History and Religious Studies, and my Religion-Theology colleagues.

Finally, William T. Cavanaugh's chapter originally appeared as "Religion, Violence, Nonsense, and Power," *Patterns of Violence, Christian Reflection: A Series in Faith and Ethics,* 59 (Waco, TX: The Institute for Faith and Learning at Baylor University, 2016), pp. 11–18. It is reprinted here by permission of the publisher.

Introduction

JAMES R. LEWIS

It could be argued that the era of contemporary religious terrorism began (at least in terms of public awareness) on the morning of Tuesday, 11 September 2001, when four passenger airliners were hijacked by members of al-Qaeda. Two of the airliners were rammed into each of the twin towers of the World Trade Center in Manhattan. Another was rammed into the Pentagon. Yet another was en route to Washington, DC, when passengers attacked the hijackers, who subsequently crashed the plane into a field in Pennsylvania. In total, almost 3,000 people died.

In the aftershock of any terrorist attack – especially an attack carried out in the name of religion – it is easy to understand reactive comments that dismiss attackers as mindless fanatics, driven by irrational religious hatred or even by diabolical motives – as if 'terrorists' were minions of the Devil himself. To cite a few of George W. Bush's quasi-theological statements regarding al-Qaeda's leader, Osama bin Laden, spoken shortly after 9/11:

> I consider bin Laden an evil man ... This is a man who hates freedom. This is an evil man.

The President was then asked, "But does he have political goals?" to which Bush replied,

> He has got evil goals. And it's hard to think in conventional terms about a man so dominated by evil.[1]

Again, it is not difficult to understand the feelings underlying this rhetoric – as well as to understand the strong military response that followed. There is, however, a painfully obvious problem here, namely that this kind of emotional evaluation and its accompanying strategic response does not seem to have blunted the phenomenon we refer to as 'terrorism'. If anything, manifestations of this phenomenon only seem to have gotten worse – as if, like the Sorcerer's Apprentice, efforts to destroy 'terrorism' only prompt it to expand and grow.

Given the indecisive consequences of purely reactive military responses, it is clear that (at least to many researchers, including the present author) more time and energy needs to be invested into the less flashy approach of trying to *understand* the complexities that lie behind such attacks – including, when appropriate, the attackers' religious convictions. This is not to say, of course, that analyses have not already been carried out. Thus, for example, in a piece published in 2004, noted terrorism researcher Andrew Silke observed that, on average, a new book on terrorism was being published every six hours.[2] At that time, studies of terrorism were being conducted in the shadow of 9/11. As a consequence, many authors commented, in one way or another, on the religious convictions of the hijackers and on the perpetrators of other violent acts who seemed to be inspired by religious motives.

In the years immediately following the 9/11 attacks as well as in the present period, the great majority of commentators do not have religious studies backgrounds, and are not usually or primarily interested in religion. As a consequence, the religious dimension of terrorism has often been dealt with superficially. Secularist critics with axes to grind against religion have portrayed the imputed irrational fanaticism at the core of religion as the primary cause of terrorism, while analysts with political science backgrounds have tended to downplay if not dismiss the religion factor altogether. Academicians from criminology have examined terrorists as criminals; psychologists have postulated psycho-pathological mechanisms at work in the terrorist mind; and so forth. Voices from religious studies have been relatively few.

There is, however, no such thing as a single religious studies approach. Thus, an additional complexity that needs to be taken into account when discussing religion and terrorism is that, over the past several decades, there has been a revolution within religious studies. As discussed in their *Nytt Blikk på Religion* (*New Views on Religion*), Ingvild Saelid Gilhus and Lisbeth Mikaelsson note that cultural studies is currently supplanting prior approaches to the study of religion.[3] In this emergent approach, religion is viewed as an aspect of culture, and stress is placed on the interaction between religion and other cultural phenomena. As part of this project, the very term 'religion' has been interrogated and critically analysed as an ideological category embodying specifically Western viewpoints and assumptions. Some have even argued that there is nothing essential about religious phenomena that set them apart from non-religious phenomena. From this point of view, assertions that 'religion' (in some abstract sense, distinct from specific traditions) causes anything should be rejected. This makes studies that assign a special status to 'religious violence', such as, to take but one example, Charles Selengut's *Sacred Fury*,[4] problematic. For the most part, contributors to the current collection share the critical understanding that *religion* is a cultural construction rather than a trans-historical force, but without necessarily rejecting the role of understanding specific religious traditions for understanding specific acts of violence.

Additionally, the majority of contributors share – though in varying degrees – the viewpoint that there is an important sense in which terrorism is also a cultural construction. By this I mean that *terrorism* is not an objective phenomenon that we recognise in the same way that we recognise, let us say, conch shells on the beach. At a very basic level, like religion, there is so much variability among the different conflicts that give rise to the incidents of political violence which we label 'terrorism' that it might be better to talk in terms of terrorisms, in the plural.[5] Additionally, the very term carries with it a sense of condemnation, as 'something the bad guys do'.[6] In other words, the term is inherently subjective, as reflected in the familiar expression, 'one person's terrorist is another person's freedom fighter'.[7] Many analysts have been especially guilty of confining the meaning of terrorism to the violent political acts of non-state actors against nation states, especially against Western nations and their allies. In recent years, the terrorist label has also been extended to individuals and military units fighting under the banner of the Islamic State, which has not been regarded as having the status of a legitimate nation state.

Beyond these shared understandings, for the present collection I have intentionally brought together a selection of researchers with widely varying – sometimes bordering on mutually exclusive – approaches and theoretical orientations. Thus, for example, Mark Juergensmeyer, who contributed the introductory chapter to the present collection, was one of the first religious studies specialists to focus on the religion-terrorism nexus. As a consequence, his influential scholarship, particularly his *Terror in the Mind of God* (originally published in 2000[8]), has been a point of reference – and critical reflection – in the works of subsequent researchers. In his *The Myth of Religious Violence*,[9] William T. Cavanaugh, author of the second chapter, takes the cultural approach to its logical conclusion. Explicitly contrasting his work with Juergensmeyer and with a selection of other earlier theorists, he asserts that there is no distinctly religious violence that places it in a separate category from non-religious violence. However, Cavanaugh's and related approaches that downplay the role of religion have, in turn, been used as critical points of reference for subsequent researchers. Thus, for example, in his chapter in the present collection, Lorne Dawson argues against approaches that completely sideline religiosity as a causal factor in understanding terrorist acts.

A relatively recent approach to 'terrorism studies' is Critical Terrorism Studies (CTS). In a manner not unlike Cavanaugh's interrogation of 'religion' and – as the name suggests – CTS critically examines our assumptions about, and portrayals of, 'terrorism.' And while Tom Mills and David Miller would not necessarily place themselves firmly within that particular school, their chapter on religious terrorism in this anthology nevertheless adopts a 'critical' approach in the spirit of CTS, as well as adopting the historical sociological approach of Lisa Stampnitzky's important study, *Disciplining Terror: How Experts Invented 'Terrorism.'*[10]

I had originally conceptualised this collection as falling into two parts, with Part One containing chapters focused on different theoretical approaches. However, because theory and content are so often interwoven, I was forced to abandon that plan. Nevertheless, the collection contains five chapters which emphasise theoretical aspects: Scott Atran, whose work on cognitive-evolutionary approaches to terrorism has been so influential, concisely articulates his thinking about Devoted Actors and violence in his contribution. Espen Dahl examines the controversial but nevertheless resilient thought of René Girard, especially Girard's later thinking about terrorism. Stephen Nemeth discusses rational choice theory, and how this approach has been applied to religion and terrorism. Lorenz Graitl summarises how a variety of different researchers have attempted to apply Emile Durkheim's classic sociological ideas about suicide to contemporary suicide bombings. Finally, the present author offers a partial revamping of older approaches to myth and ritual in terms of studies of 'imitation', through which he interprets select aspects of certain radical subcultures.

The subsequent three chapters offer detailed discussions of the religion-terrorism relationship. Whereas Peter Schalk's essay deconstructs and critiques treatments that portray the Tamil insurgency in Sri Lanka as motivated by religious concerns, Pieter Nanninga's piece on al-Qaeda digs down into the culturally informed meanings of statements by Osama Bin Laden to produce a remarkably nuanced analysis that fundamentally calls into question what it means to say that al-Qaeda's attacks are motivated by 'religion' – or, for that matter, what it means to say that Bin Laden was *not* motivated by religious concerns. Nanninga's second chapter offers a similarly nuanced analysis of how the Islamic State draws, in part, from Muslim traditions in its creation of spectacular acts of symbolic violence.

The collection's penultimate three chapters examine a range of different responses to contemporary non-state terrorism. Per-Erik Nilsson examines the French national response to the attack on the satirical magazine, *Charlie Hebdo*, and the various cultural meanings encoded in that response. Meerim Aitkulova then looks at how the government of Kyrgyzstan utilised an incident that was portrayed as a response to Islamic State terrorism as a way of marshalling support for the government, as well as a pretext for requesting military aid from the United States and Russia. Lastly, Christopher Hartney explores the meanings of screen portrays of terrorism. Finally, James Lewis and Nicole D'Amico argue that the self-sacrifice of Falun Gong practitioners is being encouraged by the movement's leadership as part of a larger strategy to bring pressure to bear on China.

SURVEY OF CONTENTS

Violence in the name of religion, plentiful enough in our time, is an enduring feature of religious life. The history of every religious tradition leaves a trail of blood, though some would argue that the violent images in religion are greatly misunderstood. Yet the fact remains that religion is filled with the symbols and language of violence. Perhaps more to the point, in the modern world dramatic acts of terrorism have been undertaken in the name of religion. In 'Does Religion Cause Terrorism?' Mark Juergensmeyer situates the issue in a middle ground, giving religion some responsibility but not the exclusive role in understanding the terrorist acts associated with certain religious traditions. In the first chapter, he kicks off the collection by discussing the attraction between religion and terrorism in general terms.

In the present collection's second chapter, 'Religion, Violence, Nonsense, and Power', William T. Cavanaugh is particularly interested in examining discourse about 'religion' in Western approaches to terrorism. Religion is generally thought to be a peculiarly virulent source of – or an aggravating factor in – terrorist attacks. The categorisation of ideologies and practices as 'religious' and 'secular', however, is a Western way of dividing up the world. This chapter traces a genealogy of the concept of religion, and shows how the concept is not a neutral analytical tool but rather serves to draw attention to certain kinds of violence and away from other kinds of violence, those labeled 'secular'.

In 'Discounting Religion in the Explanation of Homegrown Terrorism: A Critique', Lorne L. Dawson focuses on the genre of professional literature penned by scholars and certain 'terrorism experts' and finds, in sharp contrast to Cavanaugh, a pervasive pattern of denying that there are any direct causal relationships between Islam and terrorism, and more generally between being religious per se and being a terrorist. To demonstrate this point, he examines studies by a selection of three of the most prolific and influential scholars of terrorism. He concludes by pointing out that much of the primary data available about the motivations of jihadi terrorists are *prima facie* religious, and that if we wish to be effective in countering this kind of terrorism then, at minimum, this self-understanding must be taken into account.

In 'Religion, Radicalization and the Causes of Terrorism', Tom Mills and David Miller offer a number of related perspectives on portrayals of the connection between religion and terrorism. One important contribution is that their chapter provides a concise history of 'terrorism studies', especially the emergence of this inchoate 'field' back when the Soviet Union was portrayed as the driving force behind terrorism, and how this focus was eventually supplanted by a focus on religion in the so-called New Terrorism. Mills and Miller also examine the political leanings of the various individuals and entities involved in terrorism studies (e.g., think tanks), and how such orientations play into the stigmatising of Islam as the source of terror.

Uncompromising wars, revolution, and today's global terrorism are driven, in part, by Devoted Actors who adhere to sacred or transcendent values that generate actions independently from, or out of proportion to, rationally expected outcomes, calculated costs and consequences, or likely risks and rewards. In 'The Role of the Devoted Actor in War, Revolution, and Terrorism', Scott Atran demonstrates how field-based observation, surveys and experimental studies in real-world political conflicts show ways in which Devoted Actors, who are unconditionally committed to sacred causes, and whose personal identities are fused within a unique collective identity, willingly make costly sacrifices including fighting and dying, thus enabling low-power groups to endure and often prevail against materially much stronger foes

Decades ago, the French-American philosophical anthropologist, René Girard, put forward one of the few widely influential theories of violence and religion. Girard's approach has been highly contested, but it has nevertheless had a major impact on current theoretical discussions. From the 1960s and onward, Girard put forward and continually developed his thought in different phases: from his theory of mimetic desire, to its consequences for archaic religion and sacrifice, to his Judeo-Christian deconstruction of sacrificial myths. In 'Girard on Apocalypse and Terrorism', Espen Dahl discusses what he describes as a fourth phase of Girard's thought, in which Girard links religious terrorism and Biblical apocalypse in order to shed light on the structure of violence in the contemporary world.

For social scientists, 'rational choice' refers to what are actually a range of models which posit that individuals are motivated by self-interest and a desire to maximise their sense of well-being or, in the language of economists, their utility. Rational choice theorists assert that their models have been able to impose an element of predictability on human behaviour, allowing for the scientific study of a range of economic, social and political processes – including 'religious' terrorism. In 'Rational Choice and Religious Terrorism: Its Bases, Applications, and Future Directions', Stephen Nemeth discusses the assumptions of the rational choice model, its use in terrorism research, and its applicability to the study of religious terrorism, objections to the model and its future applications.

Many studies on suicide bombing utilise Durkheim's category of altruistic suicide, but often do so in a superficial way, without establishing links to his larger theory of religion. In the field of media studies, Durkheim's theories on ritual and ceremony are frequently used. They are even applied to secular contexts, though not without critique. Acts of terror have also been described as media events; however, they perform a diametrically opposite function due to their disruptive and chaotic nature. Acknowledging the multi-dimensional character of events that are perceived in various ways by different audiences, in 'Terror as Sacrificial Ritual?' Lorenz Graitl asks if extreme violence like suicide bombings or beheadings can really be seen as Durkheimian ritual. Perhaps Durkheim's explanatory framework must instead be modified to adequately answer these questions.

Contemporary approaches to myth (and ritual) tend to emphasise both the differences among myths as well as the embedded character of religion, in part because of a more general revolt against universalising approaches, particularly as these earlier approaches were represented in the work of Mircea Eliade. In 'Imitations of Terror: Applying a Retro Style of Analysis to the Religion-Terrorism Nexus', James R. Lewis utilises a selection of these earlier understandings of myths as the basis for interpreting the mythic/ritualistic characteristics that many terrorist acts seem to exhibit. The later part of the chapter presents a rethinking of this older approach in terms of more recent research and theorising, particularly as old and new overlap in the notion of 'imitation'.

Despite traditionally religious terms sometimes used to describe the movement, in 'The LTTE: A Non-religious, Political, Martial Movement for Establishing the Right of Self-Determination of Īlattamils', Peter Schalk argues that religion is and has been of no concern for the Tamil Tiger Movement in Sri Lanka. A conviction about a universal right of self-determination for a people like the Īlattamils was Vēluppiḷḷai Pirapākaraṉ's explanation for negotiating and fighting for secession. After failed negotiations to establish this right against the will of the Government of Sri Lanka, India and rest of the world, Vēluppiḷḷai Pirapākaraṉ guided his cadres in armed struggle by teaching a non-religious, political and martial martyrology.

The role of religion in al-Qaeda's violence has been strongly debated since the attacks of 11 September 2001. In 'The Role of Religion in al-Qaeda's Violence', Pieter Nanninga provides a nuanced understanding of the role of religion in al-Qaeda's violence by relating the topic to insights from religious studies. Based on the statements of the leaders of 'al-Qaeda Central' – the group around Bin Laden in Afghanistan and Pakistan in the period between 1996 and 2011 – he argues that it is not very fruitful to ask whether religion, as an abstract category, has played a role in al-Qaeda's violence. Instead, Nanninga claims that it is more interesting to examine why the question on the role of religion in jihadist violence has been so prevalent over the last one and a half decades.

In most literature on the topic, the Islamic State's violence has been perceived as a means of spreading terror. However, acts of violence are also expressive actions that embody cultural meanings for the participants and 'say' something to the audience. In 'Meanings of Savagery: Terror, Religion and the Islamic State', Pieter Nanninga examines the cultural meanings of the Islamic State's violence, paying particular attention to the role of religion, which, according to some authors, is especially relevant in cases of theatrical, symbolic violence. Focusing on the videotaped beheadings of journalists and aid workers in 2014 and the Paris attacks of 2015, Nanninga argues that Muslim traditions provide one of the sources that the Islamic State draws upon to create spectacular acts of symbolic violence that are not just a means of terror, but also performances in which the actors display for others the meanings of their social situation.

In the wake of the attacks in Paris on 7 and 8 January 2015 against the satirical weekly *Charlie Hebdo* and the kosher supermarket *Hyper*

Cacher, the hashtag 'I'm Charlie' (*Je suis Charlie*) quickly spread in the news and social media. It soon became a watchword for manifesting adherence to the French national body. In 'Where's Charlie? The Discourse of Religious Violence in France Post 7/1 2015', Per-Erik Nilsson attempts to answer this question by analysing what he refers to as the discourse of religious violence. This means understanding how certain statements at a given period, despite being potentially contradictory and paradoxical, share a common ontological and epistemological groundwork. It also implies stressing the creative, proscriptive, and disciplinary power of discourse: how discourse targets the production of subjects and the performative dissemination of power through them.

In 'Understanding the Threat of the Islamic State in Contemporary Kyrgyzstan', Meerim Aitkulova argues that the problem of religious radicalisation in general and the threat of the Islamic State in particular are exaggerated in Kyrgyzstan to suit the security interests of the government and certain international players. Expert forecasts parroting the same popular international discourses of radicalisation without a more detailed analysis of local realities and disregarding the voices of religious people evokes a *déjà vu* feeling of the Afghan threat that was based on the same narrative about the inevitability of the problem. Yet neither the Taliban's nor other terrorist traces could be identified in Kyrgyzstan's major conflicts in the post-Soviet era that thrice violated the peace and stability in the country, namely two revolutions and a bloody ethnic conflict. However, enhancing the militant secularism of current authorities and the ambitions of certain international powers to plant their own flag in the country may have far more negative consequences than the Afghan problem since the entire growing religious population is under suspicion.

In 'Terror and the Screen: Keeping the Relationship of Good and Bad Virtual', Christopher Hartney seeks to problematise how we approach religion and terror on the screen in light of the work of the recent methodologies developed by thinkers like Fitzgerald, Cavanaugh and Sloterdijk. The terror depicted in such narrative structures reinforces wider mythic understandings of our worldview and the processes by which we conceive of its defence and act to defend it. The 'crossover' point highlights some very dubious political agendas and demonstrates that the relationship between terror, politics and religion can never be clear cut within a modernistic milieu that seeks to confuse narratival and mythic conceptions of the other with 'our' reality – and then obfuscate further that confusion through extremely tight definitions of religion.

Finally, in 'Understanding Falun Gong's Martyrdom Strategy as Spiritual Terrorism', James R. Lewis and Nicole S. D'Amico examine the accusation of 'state terrorism' levelled against the People's Republic of China by members of the Falun Gong, the Qi Gong group banned in China in 1999. Most non-specialists think of Falun Gong as a peaceful spiritual exercise group unjustly persecuted by Chinese authorities. However, the founder-leader, Li Hongzhi, has encouraged his followers to conduct a vigorous public relations campaign against the Chinese government, and simultaneously discouraged them from sharing his apocalyptic teachings with non-practitioners. These inner teachings include an esoteric theory of karma which prompts practitioners of Falun Gong to actively seek persecution and martyrdom, and go a long way towards explaining their persecution in China.

Endnotes

1 Cited in Lisa Stampnitzky, *Disciplining Terror: How Experts Invented 'Terrorism'* (Cambridge: Cambridge University Press, 2013), p. 190.
2 Andrew Silke, 'Contemporary Terrorism Studies: Issues in Research', in *Research on Terrorism: Trends, Achievements and Failures*, ed. Andrew Silke (London: Frank Case, 2004), pp 1–29.
3 Ingvild Sælid Gilhus and Lisbeth Mikaelsson, *Nytt Blikk på Religion: Studiet av Religion i Dag* (Oslo: Pax, 2001).
4 Charles Selengut, *Sacred Fury: Understanding Religious Violence* (Lanham, MD: Rowman & Littlefield, 2nd ed., 2008).
5 Silke, *Research on Terrorism*.
6 Louise Richardson, *What Terrorists Want: Understanding the Enemy, Containing the Threat* (New York: Random House, 2006), p. 19.
7 Gerald Seymour, *Harry's Game* (New York: Random House, 1975), p. 62.
8 Mark Juergensmeyer, *Terror in the Mind of God: The Global Rise of Religious Violence* (Berkeley: University of California Press, 3rd ed., 2003).
9 William T. Cavanaugh, *The Myth of Religious Violence: Secular Ideology and the Roots of Modern Conflict* (New York: Oxford University Press, 2009).
10 Stampnitzky, *Disciplining Terror*.

1 Does Religion Cause Terrorism?

MARK JUERGENSMEYER

In the wake of any terrorist attack, the immediate questions are who and why – who would do such a thing, and why they would want to do it? When religion is a part of the picture, the questions are compounded. This is the case whether the perpetrators are the ISIS activists in the Paris attacks, partisans in the Syrian civil war, Christian abortion clinic bombers in the United States, or violent Israeli settlers whom Prime Minister Ariel Sharon called "Jewish terrorists" during the dismantlement of settlements in Gaza and the West Bank in August 2005.

One of the enduring questions is what religion has to do with this – with them and what they did. Put simply, does religion cause terrorism? Could these violent acts be the fault of religion – the result of a dark strain of religious thinking that leads to absolutism and violence? Or has the innocence of religion been abused by wily political activists who twist religion's essential message of peace for their own devious purposes? Is religion the problem or the victim?

Each case in which religion has been linked to violence is different. So one could be justified in saying there is no one simple answer. Yet this has not stopped the media commentators, public officials, and academics whose generalizations about religion's role abound. Their positions may be found in the assumptions lurking behind policy choices and news media reports, and, in the case of the academics, within the causative theories about terrorism that they propose. Curiously, their positions are sometimes diametrically opposed. An example of the diversity of opinions may be found in two relatively recent and widely discussed books published in 2005, Robert A. Pape's *Dying to Win: The Strategic Logic of Suicide Terrorism* and Hector Avalos' *Fighting Words: The Origins of Religious Violence*.[1]

THE ARGUMENT THAT RELIGION *DOES* CAUSE TERRORISM

Avalos' book, *Fighting Words*, posits that religious terrorism is indeed caused by religion. Or, rather, that religion creates an imaginary supply of sacred resources over which humans contend. Avalos regards all forms of social and political conflict to be contests over scarce resources. The ones who do not have the scarce resources want them, and the ones that have them want to keep them. In the case of religious conflict, the scarce resources are things that religion specifically supplies: the favor of God, blessings, and salvation. By definition, these are things that are not equally bestowed on everyone and must be earned and protected. When Rabbi Meir Kahane challenged Jews to restore God's honor, it was God's favor to the Jews that he wished to restore. Hence, an ordinary battle is a conflict to earn the highest heavenly rewards.

From Avalos' point of view, moreover, the necessity of violence is often built into the very structure of religious commitment. The act of atonement in Christianity, the sense of revenge in Judaism, the martial triumphalism of Islam, all require violent acts to fulfill their religious images of the world. And in each case, the result of violence is to bring the benefits of the scarce resources of spiritual blessings to the grateful perpetrator of the religious violence.

Avalos' position is controversial even in the academic community. Many observers have pointed out that current religious conflicts are seldom about religion *per se* – they are about national territory, political leadership, and socioeconomic control, cast in a religious light. Within the wider public, there is perhaps even less support for the notion that religion in general leads directly to violent acts. Despite the rise of religious violence in recent years, most people still regard religion – at least in the case of their own religion – as something benign. This attitude is prevalent even among members of religious communities from which violence has originated. Most Muslims regard Islam as a religion of peace, and Christians and Jews regard their own religions in the same way. Most of the faithful in these religions refuse to believe that their own beliefs could have led to violence.

Yet when one looks outside one's faith, it is easier to blame religion. In the current climate of Muslim political violence, a significant sector of the American and European public assumes that Islam is part of the problem. Despite the cautionary words of President George W. Bush imploring Americans not to blame Islam for September 11, a certain Islamophobia has crept into public conversation.

The implication of this point of view is the unfortunate notion that the whole of Islam has supported acts of terrorism. The inevitable attachment of Islam to terrorism in the ubiquitous phrase "Islamic terrorism" is one example of this habit of thinking. Another is the vaunting of *jihad* to a place of supreme Islamic importance – as if all Muslims agreed with the militarized usage of the term by unauthorized extremist groups. The most strident expositions of this way of thinking are found in assertions of Christian televangelists such as Pat Robertson and Jerry Falwell that the Prophet himself was a kind of terrorist. More moderate forms are the attempts by political commentators and some scholars to explain – as if there was need for it – why Islam is so political. Even Connecticut's liberal Senator Christopher Dodd, in a television interview in November 2003, cautioned Americans not to expect too much tolerance from Islam, given its propensity for ideological control over public life. He referenced a recent book by historian Bernard Lewis for this point of view, a book that he recommended to the viewers.[2]

The assumption of those who hold this "Islam is the problem" position is that the Muslim relationship to politics is peculiar. But this is not true. Most traditional societies have had a close tie between political leadership and religious authority, and religion often plays a role in undergirding the moral authority of public life. In Judaism, the Davidic line of kingship is anointed by God; in Hinduism, the kings are thought to uphold divine order through the white umbrella of *dharma*; in Christianity, the political history of Europe is rife with contesting and sometimes merging lines of authority between church and state. Violent Jewish, Hindu, and Christian activists in recent years have all, like their Muslim counterparts, looked to traditional religious patterns of politicized religion to justify their own militant stance.

The public life of contemporary America is no exception. It is one in which religion is very much involved with politics and politics with religion. The evangelical professions of faith of President Bush and advisors such as former Attorney General John Ashcroft fuel the impression that U.S. foreign policy has a triumphant agenda of global Christendom. This characterization of religion's hand in U.S. politics is often exaggerated by foreign observers in Europe and the Middle East, but the Christian rhetoric of American political leaders is undeniable and lends credibility to such a view.

Even more troubling are strands of Christian theocracy that have emerged among extreme groups in the United States. Some employ violence in their opposition to secular society and their hatred of a globalized culture and economy. A neo-Calvinist theology of a religious state lies behind the bombing of abortion clinics and the shooting of abortion clinic staff by Lutheran and Presbyterian activists in Maryland and Florida. The Christian Identity philosophy of race war and a government enshrining a White Christian supremacy lie behind Eric Robert Rudolph's attack on the Atlanta Olympic park, other bombings of gay bars and abortion clinics, the killing of a Denver radio talk-show host, an assault on a Jewish day care center in Los Angeles, and many other incidents – including Ruby Ridge – perpetrated by Christian militia in recent years. The Christian Cosmotheism espoused by William Pierce and embraced by Timothy McVeigh was the ideological justification for McVeigh's bombing of the Oklahoma City Federal Building. In fact, there have been more attacks – far more, in fact – by Christian terrorist groups on American soil in the last fifteen years than Muslim ones. Aside from September 11 and the 1993 attempt to destroy the World Trade Center, almost all of the other terrorist acts are Christian.

Yet somehow, despite evidence to the contrary, the American public labels Islam as a terrorist religion rather than Christianity. The arguments that agree – or disagree – with this position often get mired in the tedious task of dredging up scriptural or historical examples to show the political and militant side of Islam (or, contrarily, of other religions like Christianity, Judaism, or Hinduism). Then opponents will challenge the utility of those examples, and the debate goes on. The arguments would not be necessary, however, if one did not assume that religion is responsible for acts of public violence in the first place.

THE ARGUMENT THAT RELIGION DOES *NOT* CAUSE TERRORISM

This position – that religion is *not* the problem – is taken by observers on the other side of the public discussion over religion after September 11. In some cases, they see religion as an innocent victim; in other cases, they see it as simply irrelevant. In *Dying to Win*, Robert Pape argues that religion is not the motive in most acts of suicide bombing.[3] Looking at a broad swath of cases of suicide activists in recent years, Pape concludes that they are not motivated by a blind religious fervor as much as a calculated political attempt. The primary motive is to defend territory. Pape accurately points out that until 2003, the most suicide bombings were conducted not by a religious group, but by a secular ethnic movement: the Tamil Tigers in Sri Lanka.

Pape bases his conclusions on an analysis of the database maintained by the Chicago Project of Suicide Terrorism. He provides a demographic profile of over 460 men and women – though they are mostly men. They are not, he argues, "mainly poor, uneducated, immature religious zealots or social losers,"[4] as they have sometimes been portrayed. What they have in common is the sense that their territory or culture has been invaded by an alien power that cannot easily be overthrown. In this desperate situation of social survival, they turn to the simplest and most direct form of militant engagement: using their own bodies as bombs. Contrary to the perception of many, suicide bombers are not religious loners, but are usually part of large militant organizations with well-honed strategies aimed at ousting foreign control from what they consider their own territory. The concessions made to such organizations in the past by the governments who have been opposed to them have given the organizations behind suicide bombings the confidence that their strategies work and are worth repeating.

Little is said about religion in Pape's book. The implication is that religious motives are, basically, beside the point. For this reason, there is no attempt to explain the extraordinarily ubiquitous role of religion in violent movements around the world, from Sikh activists in India to Christian militia in Idaho, and Muslim jihadis from Morocco to Bali. Nor is there any attempt to explain what difference religion makes when it enters into a conflict and religionizes the struggle, as both Muslim and Jewish extremists did in the Israel-Palestine dispute – a conflict that, prior to the 1990s, was largely a secular struggle over territorial control. One is left with the impression that, although Pape's study is useful in reminding us that acts of violence are about real things such as the defense of culture and territory, it still does not explain why religion has become such a forceful and difficult vehicle for framing these concerns in recent years.

Nonetheless, appreciation for Pape's position has been widespread, in part because it appears to contradict the U.S. administration's position that Islamic militants are opposed to freedom. Pape argues that, to the contrary, freedom is precisely what they are fighting for. Moreover, his arguments buttress the position of two other quite different camps: religious defenders who are eager to distance religion from the violent acts with which religion has recently been associated, and secular analysts who have always thought that secular factors – particularly economic and political concerns – are the main ingredients of social conflict.

This secular perspective is the one that lies behind the phrase "the use of religion for political purposes." When this phrase is employed, religion is dismissed of any culpability in creating an atmosphere of violence. A U.S. State Department official once told me that religion was being "used" throughout the Middle East, masking problems that were essentially economic in nature. He assured me that if jobs were to be had by unemployed Egyptians and Palestinians, the problem of religious politics in these impoverished societies would quickly vanish. From his point of view, it was unthinkable that religious activists would actually be motivated by religion, or at least by ideological views of the world that were framed in religious language. Similarly, Michael Sells' study of the role of Christian symbolism in resurgent Serbian nationalism, *The Bridge Betrayed*, was ridiculed by a reviewer for *The Economist* who saw the conflict as purely a matter of secular nationalism in which religion played no role.[5] The assumption of the reviewer, like that of the State Department official with whom I spoke, was that religion was the dependent variable: a rhetorical gloss over the real issues that were invariably economic or political.

From the perspectives of Pape and the State Department economist, religion is essentially irrelevant to the motivations of terrorism. Religious defenders agree, and take this point of view a step further. They state that religion is not just neutral about violence, it is opposed to it – and thus it is an innocent victim of political activists. In some cases, these religious defenders do not deny that there may be religious elements in the motives of violent activists, but they claim that these extreme religious groups do not represent the normative traditions. Most Buddhist leaders in Japan, for instance, distanced themselves from what they regarded as the pseudo-Buddhism of the Aum Shinrikyo sect that was implicated in the nerve-gas attack on the Tokyo subways. Most Muslims refused to believe that fellow members of their faith could have been responsible for anything as atrocious as the September 11 attacks – and hence the popular conspiracy theory in the Muslim world that somehow the Israeli secret police had plotted the terrible deed. Most Christians in America saw the religiosity of Timothy McVeigh as anti-Christian, even anti-religious, and refused to describe him as a Christian terrorist, despite the strong Christian subtext of the novel, *The Turner Diaries*, which McVeigh regarded as his Bible.[6]

Some scholars have come to the defense of religion in a similar way, by characterizing the religion of activists groups as deviant from the religious norm and therefore uncharacteristic of true religion. This is essentially the stance that Bruce Lawrence takes in defending Islam in

Shattering the Myth.[7] The term "fundamentalism" – applied not just to Christianity but to a whole host of religious traditions – is another way of excusing "normal" religion and isolating religion's problems to a deviant form of the species. It is used sometimes to suggest an almost viral spread of an odd and dangerous mutation of religion that, if left on its own, naturally leads to violence, autocracy, and other extremes. Fortunately, so this line of thinking goes, normal religion is exempt. Recently, however, "Islam" and "fundamentalism" have been tied together so frequently in public conversation that the term has become a way of condemning all of Islam as a deviant branch of religion. But even in this case, the use of the term "fundamentalism" allows for the defenders of other religions to take comfort in the notion that their kind of nonfundamentalist religion is exempt from violence or other extreme forms of public behavior.

These various points of view present us with two, or perhaps three or four, different answers to the question: Is religion a cause of terrorism? Avalos says yes; religion, in general, is a cause of terrorism.[8] The Islamophobes say yes; Islam, in particular, is a problem. Pape says no; religion is irrelevant to the fight to defend territory.[9] Other religious defenders say no: ordinary religion is innocent of violence, but some odd forms of religion might contribute to it.

THE ARGUMENT THAT RELIGION IS NOT THE PROBLEM, BUT IT *IS* PROBLEMATIC

It seems to me that it is not necessary to have to make one choice among these options. As anyone who has ever taken a multiple-choice test knows, there is a dilemma when presented with such absolute differences. The most accurate responses are often to be found in the gray categories: c) none of the above, or d) all of the above. In the case of the question regarding the involvement of religion in contemporary public life, the answer is not simply a matter of peculiar religion gone bad or of good religion being used by bad people. We know that there are strata of religious imagination that deal with all sides and moods of human existence: the peace and the perversity, the tranquility, and the terror.

In my own studies of cases of religious violence, I have found that religious language and ideas play important roles, though not necessarily the initial ones. The conditions of conflict that lead to tension are usually economic and social in character; often, as Pape discusses, a defense of territory or culture that is perceived to be under control by an outside power.[10] At some point in the conflict, however, usually at a time of frustration and desperation, the political contest becomes religionized. Then what was primarily a secular struggle takes on the aura of sacred conflict. This creates a whole new set of problems.

Since the 1980s, I have studied a variety of cases of contemporary religious activism. I started with the situation involving the Sikhs in the Punjab, a region in which I have lived for some years and know fairly well. I have also observed the rise of Hindu political violence and the Muslim separatist movement in Kashmir, the Buddhist anti-government protests in Sri Lanka, the Aum Shinrikyo movement in Japan, the Islamic revolution in Iran, and militant Messianic Jewish movements in Israel, as well as the Christian militia in the United States, Catholic and Protestant militants in Northern Ireland; and Sunni jihadi movements in Egypt, Palestine, and elsewhere in the Middle East.

I found in all of these cases an interesting replication of a central thesis. Though each group was responding to its own set of local social, economic, and political factors, there was a common ideological component: the perception that the modern idea of secular nationalism was insufficient in moral, political, and social terms. In many examples, the effects of globalization were in the background, as global economic and communications systems undercut the distinctiveness of nation-state identities. In some cases, the hatred of the global system was overt, as in the American Christian militia's hatred of the "new world order" and the Al-Qaeda network's targeting of the World Trade Center. Thus the motivating "cause" – if such a term can be used – was the sense of a loss of identity and control in the modern world.

This sense of social malaise is not necessarily a religious problem, but it is one for which ideologies, both secular-nationalist and religious-transnational, provide ready responses. Hence, in each of the cases I examined, religion became the ideology of protest. Particular religious images and themes were marshaled to resist what were imagined to be the enemies of traditional culture and identities: the global secular systems and their secular nation-state supporters.

There were other similarities among these cases. In each example, those who embraced radical anti-state religious ideologies felt personally upset with what they regarded as the oppression of the secular state. They experienced this oppression as an assault on their pride and identity, and felt humiliated as a result. The failures of the state, though economic, political, and cultural, were often experienced in personal ways as humiliation and alienation, as a loss of selfhood.

It is understandable, then, that the men (and they were usually men) who experienced this loss of pride and identity would lash out in violence – the way that men often do when they are frustrated. Such expressions of power are meant to, at least symbolically, regain their sense of manhood. In each case, however, the activists challenged these feelings of violence through images of collective violence borrowed from their religious traditions: the idea of cosmic war.

The idea of cosmic war was a remarkably consistent feature of all of these cases. Those people whom we might think of as terrorists regarded themselves as soldiers in what they imagined to be sacred battles. I call such notions of warfare "cosmic" because they are larger than life. They evoke great battles of the legendary past, and they relate to metaphysical conflicts between good and evil. Notions of cosmic war are intimately personal but can also be translated to the social plane. Ultimately, though, they transcend human experience. Often, activists employ images of sacred warfare that are found in every religious tradition – such as the battles in the Hebrew Bible (Old Testament), the epics of Hinduism and Buddhism, and the Islamic idea of *jihad*. What makes religious violence particularly savage and relentless is that its perpetrators have placed such religious images of divine struggle – cosmic war – in the service of worldly political battles. For this reason, acts of religious terror serve not only as tactics in a political strategy, but also as evocations of a much larger spiritual confrontation.

This brings us back to the question of whether religion is the problem. In looking at the variety of cases, from the Palestinian Hamas movement to al-Qaeda and the Christian militia, it was clear to me that, in most cases, there were real grievances – economic and social tensions that were experienced by large numbers of people. These grievances were not religious; they were not aimed at religious differences or issues of doctrine and belief. They were issues of social identity and meaningful participation in public life that, in other contexts, were expressed through Marxist and nationalist ideologies. But in this present moment of late modernity, these secular concerns have been expressed through rebellious religious ideologies. The grievances – the sense of alienation, marginalization, and social frustration – are often articulated in religious terms and seen through religious images, and the protest against them is organized by religious leaders through the medium of religious institutions. Thus, religion is not the initial problem; but the fact that religion is the medium through which these issues are expressed is *problematic*.

WHAT RELIGION BRINGS TO A VIOLENT CONFLICT

What is problematic about the religious expression of antimodernism, anti-Americanism and antiglobalization is that it brings new aspects to conflicts that were not a part of them. For one thing, religion personalizes the conflict. It provides *personal rewards* – religious merit, redemption, the promise of heavenly luxuries – to those who struggle in conflicts that, otherwise, have only social benefits. It also provides *vehicles of social mobilization* that embrace vast numbers of supporters who, otherwise, would not be mobilized around social or political issues. In many cases, it provides an *organizational network* of local churches, mosques, temples, and religious associations into which patterns of leadership and support may be tapped. It gives the legitimacy of *moral justification* to political encounters. Even more importantly, it provides *justification for violence* that challenges the state's monopoly on morally sanctioned killing. Using Max Weber's dictum that the state's authority is always rooted in the social approval of the state to enforce its power through the use of bloodshed – in police authority, punishment, and armed defense – religion is the only other entity that can give moral sanction for violence and is therefore inherently potentially revolutionary (at least).[11]

Religion also provides the image of *cosmic war*, which adds further complications to a conflict that has become baptized with religious authority. The notion of cosmic war gives an *all-encompassing world-view* to those who embrace it. Supporters of Christian militia movements, for instance, have described their "aha" experience, when they discovered the world-view of the Christian Identity totalizing ideology that helped them make sense of the modern world, their increasingly peripheral role in it, and the dramatic actions they can take to set the world right. It gives them roles as *religious soldiers* who can literally fight back against the forces of evil.

The image of cosmic war is a potent force. When the template of spiritual battle is implanted on to a worldly opposition, it dramatically changes the perception of the conflict by those engaged in it, and it vastly alters the way that the struggle is waged. It *absolutizes the conflict* into extreme opposing positions and *demonizes opponents* by imagining them to be satanic powers. This absolutism makes compromise difficult to fathom, and holds out the promise of *total victory* through divine intervention. A sacred war that is waged in a godly span of time need not be won immediately, however. The *time line of sacred struggle is vast;* perhaps even eternal.

I once had the occasion to point out the futility (in secular military terms) of the Islamic struggle in Palestine to Dr. Abdul Aziz Rantisi, the late leader of the political wing of the Hamas movement. It seemed to me that Israel's military force was such that a Palestinian military effort could never succeed. Dr. Rantisi assured me that "Palestine was occupied before, for two hundred years." He explained that he and his Palestinian comrades "can wait again – at least that long."[12] In his calculations, the struggles of God can endure for eons. Ultimately, however, they know they will succeed.

So, religion can be a problematic aspect of contemporary social conflict, even if it is not *the* problem, in the sense of the root cause of discontent. Much of the violence in contemporary life around the world that is perceived as terrorism is directly related to the absolutism of conflict. The demonization of enemies allows those who regard themselves as soldiers for God to kill with no moral impunity. Quite the opposite – they feel that their acts will give them spiritual rewards.

Curiously, the same kind of thinking has crept into some of the responses to terrorism. The "war on terrorism" that was launched by the U.S. Government after September 11 is a case in point. To the degree that the war references are metaphorical and meant to imply an all-out effort in the manner of previous administrations' "war on drugs" and "war on poverty," it is an understandable and appropriate response. The September 11 attacks were, after all, hideous acts that deeply scarred the American consciousness, and one could certainly understand that a responsible government would want to wage an all-out effort to hunt down those culpable and bring them to justice.

But among some who espouse a "war on terrorism," the militant language is more than metaphor. God's blessing is imagined to be bestowed on a view of confrontation that is, like cosmic war, all-encompassing, absolutizing, and demonizing. What is problematic about this view is that it brings impatience with moderate solutions that require the slow procedures of systems of justice. It demands instead the quick and violent responses of war that lend simplicity to the confrontation and a sense of divine certainty to its resolution. Alas, such a position can fuel the fires of retaliation, leading to more acts of terrorism, instead of fewer.

The role of religion in this literal "war on terrorism" is, in a curious way, similar to religion's role in the cosmic war imagined by those perpetrating terrorism. In both cases, religion is a problematic partner of political confrontation. Religion brings more to conflict than simply a repository of symbols and the aura of divine support. It problematizes a conflict through its abiding absolutism, its justification for violence, and its ultimate images of warfare, which demonize opponents and cast conflict in transhistorical terms.

Endnotes

Based on a paper originally delivered at the "National Policy Forum on Terrorism, Security and America's Purpose," Washington DC, September 6–7, 2005.

1   Robert A. Pape, *Dying to Win: The Strategic Logic of Suicide Terrorism* (New York: Random House, 2005); Hector Avalos, *Fighting Words: The Origins of Religious Violence* (New York: Prometheus Books, 2005).
2   Bernard, Lewis, *The Crisis of Islam: Holy War and Unholy Terror* (New York: Random House, 2003).
3   Pape, *Dying to Win*.
4   Ibid., p. 216.
5   Michael A. Sells, *The Bridge Betrayed: Religion and Genocide in Bosnia* (Berkeley: University of California Press, 1996).
6   Andrew Macdonald (pseudonym for William Pierce), *The Turner Diaries* (Hillsboro, WV: National Vanguard Books, 1978; reprinted by the National Alliance, Arlington, VA, in 1985, and by Barricade Books, New York, 1996.)
7   Bruce Lawrence, *Shattering the Myth: Islam Beyond Violence* (Princeton, NJ: Princeton University Press, 2000).
8   Avalos, *Fighting Words*.
9   Pape, *Dying to Win*.
10   Ibid.
11   Max Weber, "Politics as a Vocation," in Hans H. Gerth and C. Wright Mills, eds, *From Max Weber: Essays in Sociology* (New York: Oxford University Press, 1946).
12   Abdul Aziz Rantisi, co-founder and political leader of Hamas. Interview with the author, Khan Yunis, Gaza, March 1, 1998.

2 Religion, Violence, Nonsense, and Power

WILLIAM T. CAVANAUGH

The recent frequency of Islamist militant attacks in the name of God has added fuel to a long-standing Western notion that religion has a dangerous tendency to promote violence. The subject in this common notion is not just certain forms of Islamism or Islam in general but "religion," a category that is commonly held to include Christianity, Hinduism, and other major world faiths. The common Western notion is meant to be neutral with regard to particular religions; it does not discriminate against Muslims, for example, but sees religion as such as potentially dangerous. Any time disagreements are ratcheted up to a cosmic level, there is the danger of blood being spilled. For that reason, the Western liberal ideal has insisted on the domestic separation of church, synagogue, mosque, etc. from state, and the privatization of religion. And it has generally insisted that foreign policy promote this ideal in non-Western countries whenever possible.

The notion that people kill in the name of God is undeniable. Arguments that try to pin all violence on other factors – economic deprivation or political marginalization – are easily refuted by the terrorists' own words; they also assume a clear distinction between religious and political and economic factors that is impossible, even in theory, to pull off, as I argue later in the chapter. Nor does it work, despite frequent attempts, to claim that the Crusaders were not really Christians or Islamic terrorists are not really Muslims. Normatively, it is important for Christians and Muslims to claim that Crusaders and terrorists have gotten the message of Christianity and Islam all wrong. Descriptively, however, it is disingenuous for Christians and Muslims to absolve their own group from wrongdoing by disowning their bad coreligionists. We must do penance collectively for our collective sins.

People can and do commit violence in the name of God. But obviously people kill for all sorts of other things too. Behind the common tale of religion and violence, therefore, there must be a stronger claim: religion has a *greater* propensity to promote violence than what is not religion. What is not religion is called "secular." The idea that religion promotes violence depends entirely on this distinction between the religious and the secular.

UNSTABLE CATEGORIES

Imagine a table with two columns, religious and secular, and a line separating the two. In the "religious" column are generally included Christianity, Islam, Buddhism, Judaism, Hinduism, Confucianism, and a few other "world religions." Under "secular" we find nonreligious categories of human life such as politics and economics, as well as ideologies and practices like nationalism, atheism, Marxism, capitalism, and liberalism that might fall under such nonreligious categories. The common notion that religion is peculiarly prone to violence depends on the idea that these secular matters have less of a tendency to promote violence; it is commonly assumed that this is so because they have to do with purely mundane affairs. Religion, on the other hand, is seen as peculiarly incendiary because it raises the stakes to another level, where reason is trumped by passion. In examining academic arguments that religion foments violence, I have found that such arguments can be grouped into three types: religion is absolutist, religion is divisive, and religion is nonrational.[1]

Such arguments seem undeniable, to most of us living in liberal Western social orders, anyway. Terrorism, mostly of the Islamist kind, comes immediately to mind as confirmation. If we cast a glance over the extraordinarily bloody last hundred years or so, however, complicating evidence presses itself upon us. World War I, to which nationalism is generally assigned as primary cause, resulted in 38 million military and civilian casualties. Deaths under Marxist regimes are estimated in figures that range as high as 110 million. The death toll under the three regimes alone of Stalin, Mao, and the Khmer Rouge ranges from a low of 21 million to a high of 70 million; all were militantly atheist. The last hundred years have seen frequent war waged for oil, land, flags, free markets, democracy, ethnicity, and a host of other "secular" causes. What becomes of the idea that religion has a peculiar tendency to promote violence in the face of this evidence?

For some religion-and-violence theorists, the answer to this problem is simple: move the offending ideologies over the line to the other side of the table. Atheist Christopher Hitchens takes this approach in his best-selling book *God is Not Great: How Religion Poisons Everything*. Totalitarianism, he says, is essentially religious. According to

Hitchens, "the object of perfecting the species – which is the very root and source of the totalitarian impulse – is in essence a religious one."[2] Even when they try to extirpate religion, totalitarian regimes show themselves to be religious. "All that the totalitarians have demonstrated is that the religious impulse – the need to worship – can take even more monstrous forms if it is repressed."[3] Thus do atheists like Stalin and Kim Jong-il find themselves – undoubtedly to their great surprise – on the side of religion. Hitchens is not alone in this move. Political scientist Rudolph Rummel – relentless chronicler of communist tyranny and promoter of the theory that democratic regimes are essentially peaceful – counts Marxism as the bloodiest of all religions.[4] Religion is violent because it is *defined* as violent. Religion poisons everything because everything poisonous is labeled "religious."

For other religion-and-violence theorists, secular ideologies are not moved as a whole to the religious side of the table, but whatever is violent about them is attributed to religion. Take, for example, political scientist David Rapoport's comments on nationalism and religion. One element in its disposition toward violence

> is the capacity of religion to inspire total loyalties or commitments,
> and in this respect, it is difficult to imagine anything which
> surpasses the religious community. Religion has often had
> formidable rivals; in the modern world the nation sometimes has
> surpassed religion as a focus of loyalties, though significantly there
> is increasing propensity for academics to speak of 'civic religion'
> when discussing national symbols and rites. In any case, the
> ascendancy of the nation has occupied but a brief moment in history
> so far, and in a limited portion of the world – all of which only more
> underscores the durability and special significance of religion.[5]

Here nationalism is not a religion, but it acts like a religion and is sometimes called a religion, and the violence of nationalism counts as evidence of the violence of religion. Another reason that religion is peculiarly linked to violence, according to Rapoport, is that it uses violent language. He illustrates this point by giving examples of explicitly secular movements that have appropriated religious language in the service of violence. He quotes the secularist Abraham Stern:

> Like my father who taught me to read in Torah
> I will teach my pupils; stand to arms, kneel and shoot
> Because there is a religion of redemption – a religion of the war of
>   liberation
> Whoever accepts it – be blessed; whoever denies it – be cursed.[6]

Instead of concluding that "secular" liberation movements can inspire just as much passion and commitment and violence as "religious" movements can – or that the Stern Gang was, as Stern himself acknowledged, dedicated to a kind of "religion," which throws the whole religious/secular distinction into question – Rapoport offers Stern's poem as evidence that *religion* has a disposition toward violence. As with nationalism, here secular terrorism acts like a religion and is called a religion, but is not religious, even though it counts as evidence of religion's violent tendencies.

The argument that religion has a peculiar disposition toward violence depends upon a sharp dividing line between the religious and the secular, but religion-and-violence arguments engage in frequent smuggling across that border. Political theorist Bhikhu Parekh issues a blistering indictment of religion: "It arouses powerful and sometimes irrational impulses and can easily destabilize society, cause political havoc, and create a veritable hell on earth."[7] Parekh confesses, however, that "several secular ideologies, such as some varieties of Marxism, conservatism, and even liberalism have a quasi-religious orientation and form, and conversely formally religious languages sometimes have a secular content, so that the dividing line between a secular and a religious language is sometimes difficult to draw."[8] Violent and irrational impulses are popping up everywhere, even in liberalism, which inspires the creation of the category "quasi-religious" to try to corral them all back onto religion's side. Sociologist Mark Juergensmeyer has made a career out of exploring the peculiar tendency of religion to contribute to violence, but the whole project seems to fall into confusion when he states flatly that "secular nationalism is 'a religion'"[9] and even that "the secular is a sort of advanced form of religion."[10] What becomes of the dividing line between "secular" and "religious" – upon which the whole argument depends – if the secular is a form of religion?

Some religion-and-violence theorists deal with the problem here by openly and consistently expanding the category of "religion." Richard Wentz's book *Why People Do Bad Things in the Name of Religion* includes not only Islam, Christianity, Buddhism, and the like, but also consumerism, secular humanism, football fanaticism, faith in technology, and a host of other ideologies and practices under the rubric "religion." He concludes, "Perhaps all of us do bad things in the name of (or as a representative of) religion."[11] Wentz has intuited correctly that people do violence for all sorts of reasons. Where he goes wrong is in thinking that he can obliterate the line between religious and secular and still end up blaming violence on religion. Instead of an argument for why religion has a greater tendency than the secular to promote violence, Wentz has simply taken everything for which people do violence and labeled it "religion."

Religion-and-violence arguments are rife with this kind of nonsense because they depend upon a stable dividing line between religious and secular that does not exist. The distinction between religious and secular is always in flux. It is a modern and Western distinction, a line socially constructed in different ways for different purposes, and not simply a feature of the way things are. Religion-and-violence theorists construct the distinction for their own purposes, to condemn certain things and ignore others. A brief history of the distinction shows that this has always been the case.

HISTORY OF THE DISTINCTION

Once there was no religious/secular distinction. Wilfred Cantwell Smith went looking for an equivalent concept to "religion" in ancient Greece, Egypt, India, China, and Japan, and found none.[12] The Romans had the term *religio*, but as Augustine writes in *The City of God*, the "normal meaning" of the term was "an attitude of respect in relations between a man and his neighbor."[13] This attitude is something we would consider to be "secular." In Roman society, obligations and devotion to civic duties, gods, friends, family, and civil authorities were all bound in a web of relations. There was no religion/politics distinction; how could there be when Caesar was a god? When the religious/secular distinction is introduced to Western society in the medieval period, it is primarily used to denote a distinction between two types of priests, those who are part of an order and those "secular" priests who belong to a diocese. There was no realm of purely secular and mundane affairs to which Christianity was indifferent or peripheral, and though there was a distinction between ecclesiastical and civil authorities, the religion/politics distinction would have to await the modern era.

Timothy Fitzgerald finds no evidence in English of a religious/secular distinction in the way we use it now until the late seventeenth century. The religion/politics distinction is even later.[14] These distinctions first appear in the writings of figures like John Locke and William Penn. To make a long and complex story brief and simple,[15] the distinction is the result of the struggle between ecclesiastical and civil authorities for power in early modern Europe. The new territorial states arose in the sixteenth and seventeenth centuries in part by appropriating powers formerly in the hands of the church; ecclesiastical courts were abolished, and the rights to nominate bishops and abbots, control over church revenues, monopoly on the means of violence, and the primary allegiance of the people were transferred to the nascent state. The first use of the term "secularization" was to indicate the transfer of property from ecclesiastical to civil control. Under these circumstances, the religion/secular and religion/politics divides were invented to exclude ecclesiastical authority from certain types of public power. Religion, as it became in Locke's writings, was invented as a universal and essentially interior impulse, completely distinct from the mundane business of politics and economics. The church would henceforth be confined to the ambit of religion.

Once the religious/secular distinction was created in the West, it was subsequently exported to the rest of the world in the process of colonization. In their first encounters with the natives, Western explorers reported back home with remarkable consistency that the natives had no religion at all.[16] Once they colonized the natives, however, the religious/secular distinction was found quite useful. Western scholars began to fit the locals' cultural systems – even those without gods, like Theravada Buddhism and Confucianism – into taxonomies of "world religions," despite resistance from native elites. Chinese elites in the late nineteenth century, for example, rejected the idea that Confucianism was a religion, because religion was seen to be otherworldly and individualistic.[17] Hindu nationalists today "refuse to call Hinduism a religion precisely because they want to emphasize that Hinduism is more than mere internalized beliefs. It is social, political, economic, and familial in nature. Only thus can India the secular state become interchangeable with India the Hindu homeland."[18] The religious/secular distinction, nevertheless, was imposed on colonized peoples in large part because it facilitated the quarantining of the local culture to the private sphere of "religion." In the case of India, to make Hinduism a religion was to take everything it meant to be Indian and confine it to a nonpublic sphere; to be public meant to be British.

THE DISTINCTION AS AN ACT OF POWER

The point of this very brief history is to show that the religious/secular distinction upon which the common notion that religion promotes violence depends is an invented, contingent, and ever-shifting distinction, not simply a part of the way things are. Where the line gets drawn between religious and secular is, furthermore, dependent on what kinds of power one wants to authorize and what kinds one wants to exclude. This becomes especially apparent if we examine how the myth of religious violence is used today.

In domestic matters, the myth of religious violence is used to exclude certain kinds of practices from the public sphere. Until 1940 the Supreme Court invoked "religion" as a unifying force in American society. Since 1940, however, the Supreme Court has repeatedly raised the specter of religious violence in banning school prayer, banning optional religious education from public school buildings, banning public aid to religious schools, and so on. When the Supreme Court invoked the danger of religious conflict in *Aguilar* v. *Felton* (1985) to ban nonsectarian remedial education for low-income kids from taking place in parochial schools, Justices O'Connor and Rehnquist dissented, writing, "There is little record support for the proposition that New York City's admirable Title I program has ignited any controversy other than this litigation."[19] This dissent highlights the fact that these Supreme Court decisions are not based on any evidence of actual religious violence in American life. The period after 1940 saw interdenominational strife in the United States at historical lows; the use of the myth of religious violence has not been a response to empirical fact as much as it has been a useful narrative that has been produced by and has helped produce consent to the increasing secularization of the American social order.

In foreign policy, the myth of religious violence has been used to justify attitudes and actions toward nonsecular social orders, especially Muslim ones. We assume that the reason for turmoil in the Middle East is religion. Muslims have not learned to separate mosque from state, religion from politics, and so the passions of religion continue to wreak havoc in the public sphere. Our foreign policy is geared toward moving them – by force, if necessary – toward liberal, Western-style democracy, which is the key to peace. The Iraq War was meant to bring the blessings of liberalism to the Middle East. And so the myth of religious violence becomes a justification for war on behalf of secularism. There are many subtle versions of this secularist argument for military intervention; here is a blunt version by bestselling New Atheist author Sam Harris:

> Some propositions are so dangerous that it may even be ethical to kill people for believing them. This may seem an extraordinary claim, but it merely enunciates an ordinary fact about the world in which we live. Certain beliefs place their adherents beyond the reach of every peaceful means of persuasion, while inspiring them

to commit acts of extraordinary violence against others. There is, in fact, no talking to some people. If they cannot be captured, and they often cannot, otherwise tolerant people may be justified in killing them in self-defense. This is what the United States attempted in Afghanistan, and it is what we and other Western powers are bound to attempt, at an even greater cost to ourselves and innocents abroad, elsewhere in the Muslim world. We will continue to spill blood in what is, at bottom, a war of ideas.[20]

CONCLUSION

As this quote from Harris makes clear, people kill for all sorts of things. People are just as capable of killing for atheism or secularism as they are of killing for gods. The attempt to come to general conclusions about violent behavior is not illuminated but confused and obscured by trying to divide "religious" from "secular" ideologies and practices. Devotion to so-called secular ideologies and practices can be just as absolutist, divisive, and irrational as devotion to so-called religions. The idea that "religion" is peculiarly prone to violence is not based in empirical fact, but is an ideological justification for the dominance of secular social orders, orders that can and do inspire violence. The myth of religious violence causes us to turn a blind eye to the causes of non-Western grievances against the Western world. We reduce the cause of Muslim anger at the West to their "religion," thus casting a convenient fog of amnesia over Western aggressions on behalf of Western interests: the 1953 overthrow of a democratic government in Iran, support for corrupt and tyrannical governments in the Muslim world, the plundering of Arab countries' oil riches, the Iraq War, support for Israeli occupation of Palestinian land, Abu Ghraib, "extraordinary rendition," and the rest of it. Doing away with the myth of religious violence helps level the playing field: let's examine the violence fomented by ideologies of all kinds, including those we tend to regard as "secular" and therefore benign. Instead of dividing the world *a priori* into reasonable people (us) and irrational people (them), we can perhaps promote peace by doing away with such binaries.

Endnotes

1   I examine nine such arguments in the first chapter of my book *The Myth of Religious Violence: Secular Ideology and the Roots of Modern Conflict* (New York: Oxford University Press, 2009).

2 Christopher Hitchens, *God Is Not Great: How Religion Poisons Everything* (New York: Twelve, 2007), p. 232.

3 Ibid., p. 247.

4 Rudolph J. Rummel, "The Killing Machine That Is Marxism," *World Net Daily*, December 15, 2004, www.wnd.com/2004/12/28036/

5 David C. Rapoport, "Some General Observations on Religion and Violence" in *Violence and the Sacred in the Modern World*, ed. Mark Juergensmeyer (London: Frank Cass, 1992), p. 120.

6 Ibid., 121.

7 Bhikhu Parekh, "The Voice of Religion in Political Discourse" in *Religion, Politics, and Peace*, ed. Leroy Rouner (Notre Dame, IN: University of Notre Dame Press, 1999), p. 72.

8 Ibid., p. 74.

9 Mark Juergensmeyer, *The New Cold War?: Religious Nationalism Confronts the Secular State* (Berkeley: University of California Press, 1993), p. 15.

10 Mark Juergensmeyer, *Global Rebellion: Religious Challenges to the Secular State, from Christian Militias to al Qaeda* (Berkeley: University of California Press, 2008), p. 23.

11 Richard E. Wentz, *Why People do Bad Things in the Name of Religion* (Macon, GA: Mercer University Press, 1993), p. 37.

12 Wilfred Cantwell Smith, *The Meaning and End of Religion* (New York: Macmillan, 1962), pp. 54–55.

13 Augustine, *City of God*, trans. Henry Bettenson (Harmondsworth: Penguin Books, 1972), X.1 [373].

14 Timothy Fitzgerald, *Discourse on Civility and Barbarity: A Critical History of Religion and Related Categories* (New York: Oxford University Press, 2007).

15 I tell the story in much greater detail in chapter 2 of *The Myth of Religious Violence*.

16 See David Chidester, "Colonialism" in *Guide to the Study of Religion*, ed. Willi Braun and Russell T. McCutcheon (London and New York: Cassell, 2000), pp. 427–28.

17 Peter Beyer, "Defining Religion in Cross-National Perspective: Identity and Difference in Official Conceptions" in *Defining Religion: Investigating the Boundaries between the Sacred and the Secular*, ed. Arthur L. Greil and David G. Bromley (Oxford: JAI, 2003), pp. 174–80.

18 Richard S. Cohen, "Why Study Indian Buddhism?," in *The Invention of Religion: Rethinking Belief in Politics and History*, ed. Derek R. Peterson and Darren R. Walhof (New Brunswick, NJ: Rutgers University Press, 2002), p. 27.

19 Sandra Day O'Connor and William Rehnquist in *Aguilar* v. *Felton*, 473 U.S. 402 (1985), p. 429.

20 Sam Harris, *The End of Faith: Religion, Terror, and the Future of Reason* (New York: W. W. Norton & Company, 2004), pp. 52–53.

3 Discounting Religion in the Explanation of Homegrown Terrorism: A Critique

LORNE L. DAWSON

INTRODUCTION

Politicians, public officials, and scholars have been scrupulous, for the most part, in denying any direct causal relationship between Islam and terrorism, and more generally between being religious per se and being a terrorist. They are justifiably concerned about the negative implications of such an association for the peaceful Islamic populations of their countries. But the connection persists because so many terrorists continue to provide religious justifications for their actions, especially in the context of one of the most perplexing and challenging forms of terrorism – suicide bombings. We are confronted with hundreds, if not thousands, of videotaped testimonials by bombers offering justifications of their actions that are saturated with religious rhetoric. The ambiguities of this broader situation are reflected in the scholarly debate about the significance of religious beliefs as a primary motivator for terrorist.[1] As a sociologist of religion who is now engaged in terrorism studies,[2] I have noted a marked reticence to treat religion as an independent variable in assessments of the causality of terrorism. The scientific study of social phenomenon must take into consideration the systematic and differential analysis of the reciprocal effects of multiple variables. Yet the study of jihadi terrorism, and especially the so-called homegrown variety, usually fails to do so. More often than not the causal role of religion is acknowledged, or at least implied, and then explicitly or implicitly discounted. There is a pervasive and unquestioned inclination to minimize the significance of the religious pronouncements of homegrown jihadists, by either categorizing them as nothing more than propaganda, treating them as merely the surface manifestation of deeper irrational impulses, or explaining them away in favor of other social, economic, and political grievances that are thought to be more plausible. But this interpretive prejudice will not stand up to scrutiny and it is counterproductive to understanding and reducing the threat posed by al Qaeda and Islamic State inspired terrorism.

THREE ILLUSTRATIONS OF THE PROBLEM

The work dealing with religious terrorism is vast and variable and I cannot survey it here. Nor, in the space available, can I definitively demonstrate the pervasiveness of this prejudice in terrorism studies. Rather I will sample the ways in which religion is treated as a causal variable in three studies by some of the most prolific, astute, and influential scholars of terrorism: Marc Sageman, Andrew Silke, and Clark McCauley. They all happen to be psychiatrists or psychologists by training, but the argument applies to the work of others as well. My comments are not meant to disparage their research or the other merits of the studies I am criticizing. I continue to be inspired by the example these researchers set, and it is their stature in the field that recommends using samples of their work to illustrate the problem. My focal concern, it must be stressed, is the treatment of religion in the case of Western homegrown terrorism and not all forms of jihadism internationally.

Marc Sageman

The treatment of religion in Sageman's seminal book *Understanding Terror Networks*[3] is relatively confused, and it is curious that no one seems to have noticed. Many cross-cutting lines of inquiry are squeezed into a deceptively brief and seemingly coherent few pages on "faith"[4] as a factor in the radicalization process of jihadi terrorists. Sageman begins by noting the relatively strong role that religion seems to play in the lives of his overall sample of international mujahideen. Most came from fairly religious families and many are reported to have been particularly devout as children (49%). But, as he observes, his sub-sample of European jihadists is anomalous, since most come from fairly secular backgrounds. This exception would imply, as the rest of his book indicates, that religion is not necessarily a primary cause of jihadi terrorism. But in all cases, he further acknowledges, there was a marked upsurge in religiosity just prior to joining the jihad. This upsurge is particularly noteworthy for the Europeans, whose commitment to Islam went from 8% to 100%.[5] Sageman downplays the significance of this finding, saying:

We should be careful not to ascribe a causal relationship to this increased devotion on the part of future mujahedin. This shift in faith may very well be a reflection of a more general process of engagement in the jihad. In this case, it would be more indicative of an effect rather than a cause of this process. At this point, the evidence is still descriptive and does not yet justify conclusions about the contribution of this increased faith to the process of joining the global jihad.[6]

In the general scheme of things, this is certainly sage advice. But it is rather disingenuous in this instance. Almost nothing we know about the possible motivations of terrorists escapes this methodological dictum, given our lack of reliable primary data from a sufficiently large or varied sample. Just a few paragraphs earlier, moreover, Sageman stated that we should not be surprised that joining the jihad is usually preceded by a shift in degree of devotion "given the fact that the global Salafi jihad is a Muslim revivalist organization."[7] In fact the single most consistent and pronounced indicator of jihadi radicalization, as his own work suggests and no one has refuted, is the adoption of a more religious lifestyle, and more particularly extreme beliefs and practices. But clearly, for whatever reason, Sageman is uncomfortable with this finding and he tries to explain away the anomaly set by the European jihadists by characterizing them as simply lonely people looking for companionship.

> In an expatriate community, especially in an unwelcoming non-Muslim Western country, the most available source of companionship with people of similar background is the mosque. Disillusioned with the society that excluded them and the empty promises of the Left ... second-generation or expatriate Maghreb Arabs went to the mosque and met new friends. Islam was a way to restore their dignity, gain a sense of spiritual calling, and promote their values.[8]

The real issue, by implication, is a sense of belonging and dignity, and not religion per se. Yet he cannot avoid interjecting the phrase "a sense of spiritual calling" into his description, which connotes that we are not talking about any form of companionship. There is something more involved than the companionship provided by sports, for example, and the difference matters, especially in the face of the statements made by the terrorists themselves and the life and death realities of terrorism.

As I argue elsewhere,[9] this attempt to reduce a religious phenomenon to a social one, and one which is somehow more primordial, will not stand up to scrutiny. How do we know that the terrorists were feeling lonely and turned to the mosque for social support? Where is the actual evidence? This speculation is plausible for foreign students and new immigrants, but how much sense does it make for those born in Europe? They are not far from their family, friends, and all that is familiar. So how "can we say that both groups were driven by loneliness and alienation? ... Loneliness may help explain why some individuals initially convert to Islam and maybe even a more cohesive form of Islamic fundamentalism, but is it relevant in explaining the further radicalization of some? Of the many who turn to radical religion for solace, why do so few become radicalized to violence?"[10] The linkage between loneliness and being a terrorist, as mediated by religion, is hypothetical and unspecific at best. But I suspect it seems eminently plausible to most readers because it is in alignment with their preconceptions about why people participate in religious groups, and even more why marginal individuals supposedly gravitate to extreme types of religious commitments. The primary function of religion is thought to be compensatory. This simplistic preconception could be popular and unquestioned in nature or it might be more reflective and Durkheimian in nature[11]; either way it is unsubstantiated and counterproductive, since it diverts us from giving more due regard to the terrorists' own definition of their situation.

Andrew Silke

In 2008 Silke published an excellent summary analysis of radicalization research in the article "Holy Warriors: Exploring the Psychological Processes of Jihadi Radicalization."[12] I was attracted to this article by the very graphic emphasis given to the notion of religion in its title. But the reference to "holy warriors" is quite misleading. In twenty pages of text (excluding references), less than a page is dedicated to "The Role of Religion."[13] In this article Silke demonstrates that there is no significant correlation between psychopathology and terrorism, though there is a potential link to the youthful, male tendency to deviancy. He also notes the counterintuitive correlation with education, occupation, and marriage. Terrorists are not disproportionately drawn from the marginalized segments of society, quite the contrary. Poverty is not predictive of membership in extremist groups. Alternatively, he argues, the emphasis should fall on issues of social identity and group loyalties, and the catalytic impact of perceived injustices and the psychology of vengeance. In discussing the contribution of each factor the role of religion would appear to be crucial, since we are talking about the identity, loyalties, and perceptions of Muslims in Europe. But Silke only mentions religion in passing and implies that more generic social factors and processes are more important than any type of extremist ideology in mobilizing the turn to violence.

In addressing the need to investigate issues of social identity Silke states: "The key aspects of social identity in the context of jihadism are: (1) the role of religion and (2) group loyalties."[14] Four short paragraphs are dedicated to explaining the role of religion.

The first brief paragraph cursorily describes the global aspirations of the Salafi–jihadist ideology. The second paragraph summarizes some of Sageman's findings on the religious background of Islamist extremists, laying the emphasis on the fact that only "18 percent ... had an Islamic religious primary or secondary education." The third and longest paragraph, serves to further undermine the significance of religion as a factor in radicalization by stressing that "the majority" of jihadists "were not described as being religious as youth," and "8 percent were raised as Christians."[15] Silke does note the shift of 99 percent to being very religious prior to joining the jihad, but he reiterates Sagemen's loneliness and companionship argument to explain away the significance of this surge. The paragraph ends by reassuring readers that it is the group bonds formed by these individuals that matter, which happen to form in the setting provided by the mosques, and that the resultant radicalization "does not typically result from the teachings of the official hierarchy within the mosque." Following through on this theme, in the fourth and final paragraph he stresses "that not all Salafist Muslims support the global jihad." In fact most do not. "Thus, in order to understand the mind-set of Islamist terrorism, one needs to move beyond the limits of religious doctrine and explore other driving factors."[16]

As with Sageman, there are many cross-cutting themes raised by this brief statement of the role of religion in radicalization. Once again we are presented with the contradictory tendencies to strongly identify the extremism in question with a specific religious ideology while refusing to attribute any special significance to the religious component or character of that ideology. The investigation of the relevant aspects of the religiosity is truncated, it seems, by a fear of casting reprobation on Islam per se. The analysis gravitates to more comfortable ground, issues of identity, perceived injustice, and vengeance that just happen to be encoded religiously in this case. Whatever the merits of Silke's intuitions about the real causes of radicalization in the case of jihadists, the nature of the religious commitments warrants more attention. On the one hand, while many terrorists have been inspired by other kinds of ideologies, there appears to be something special or different about religious terrorism.[17] On the other hand, there appears to be something religious-like about the more fanatical secular ideologies that have driven terrorism, and the nature of the commitments and satisfactions they provide.[18] Minimally we need to do more work on distinguishing between religious and secular forms of terrorism.[19] But this will require researchers being less squeamish about exploring the religiosity of some terrorists.

In his conclusion, Silke advances an argument that is new and very important. "It is difficult," he states, "to see beyond the common myths and assumptions that are often offered as explanations for terrorist violence. Partly this is because the process of involvement is, in many respects at odds with our understanding of the development and course of other types of offending." He goes on to quickly summarize the well-known risk factors for early onset offending and concludes "most of these factors are absent in the lives of jihadis, and indeed many terrorists appear to come from backgrounds that would normally protect against the onset of offending." Terrorists are not typical criminals. They "are a distinct group, and in many ways the origins of their unconventional behaviour are exceptional." Criminologists, then, "will have to work hard to develop theories and models that can comfortably account for the distinctive patterns seen in the lives of terrorists."[20] Given the pronounced surge in religiosity before joining, surely religion should be considered one of the distinctive factors warranting further careful study? Little sustained attention has been given, however, to the age-old linkage of religion, morality, and personal and social identities.[21] If the standard criminogenic factors do not apply to jihadis, then even if the process of joining a youth gang is analogous, there is also a significant difference. Perhaps the individuals seeking to resolve their identity issues by joining the jihad, and not a gang, are driven by a moral imperative? Jihadis spend a great deal of time talking about doing the right thing and striving to be virtuous. Perhaps we should listen more carefully? I suspect it is this aspect of their nature, whether rooted in socialization or character, which explains the pull of an ideology that promises absolute moral clarity and transcendent purpose. Joining the jihad, at least in the West, may be more like being drawn to a new religious movement than a criminal gang.[22]

Clark McCauley

In their book *Friction: How Radicalization Happens to Them and Us*,[23] Clark McCauley and Sophia Moskalenko provide us with the best, and long overdue, application of the findings of experimental social psychology to the process of radicalization. The linkages are numerous and the analysis is comprehensive. They apply the insights gleaned into human motivations, cognitive processes, and small group dynamics to an ongoing case study of Russian anarchist terrorists of the late nineteenth and early twentieth centuries. But they also seek, more limitedly, to mine the implications for understanding contemporary jihadist terrorists. Less than two pages in the concluding chapter, however, are dedicated to an analysis of the role of "ideology in political radicalization."[24] In this brief discussion McCauley and Moskalenko run through many of the standard arguments for minimizing the significance of beliefs and ideology in fomenting radicalization to violence, and more specifically for side-stepping giving any serious attention to religion.

First they reference the "long history of research in social psychology that shows that beliefs alone are a weak predictor of action," emphasizing that the "separation of belief and action is particularly notable in the realm of politics."[25] Second, they note, in line with their own research, "that there are many paths to radicalization that do not involve ideology. Some may join a radical group for thrill and status, some for love, some for connection and camaraderie. Personal and group grievance can move individuals toward violence, with ideology serving to rationalize the violence."[26] This latter claim, that ideology comes into play as a post-hoc "justification for violence" is their third argument. Ideology provides, they acknowledge, "a framing and interpretation that makes violence not only acceptable but necessary." But they assert, with the jihadists in mind, this "frame is only loosely related to traditional interpretations of the Koran's strictures against attacking civilians."[27] Fourth and finally, they argue, "There is a growing realization that radicalization and terrorism cannot be reduced to the prevalence of bad ideas, that the 'center of gravity' of the jihadist threat is not a radical form of Islam ... [and even] most Wahabbist or *Salafi* Muslims do not support terrorism."[28]

The brief analysis utilizes aspects of the arguments advanced by Sageman and Silke, and it appears to be driven by a similar desire to push the public beyond a naïve and singular fixation on Islamism or "bad ideas." This is understandable, up to a point, and McCauley and Moskalenko have helped to improve our grasp of the complex motivations driving terrorism. But in this case they have overshot the mark, leaving us with an obverse oversimplification. No credible scholar asserts that "beliefs alone" are the "prime mover in radicalization,"[29] but McCauley and Moskalenko have pitched their argument about ideology with such a straw dog in mind. Many factors are involved, and as I have argued in numerous presentations to the Integrated National Security Enforcement Teams in Canada, at the Basillie School of International Affairs, the Canadian Forces College, on Parliament Hill, and elsewhere, we are moving toward a complex ecological model of the social structural, group dynamic, and personal variables involved in radicalization, which recognizes the role of both shared trans-contextual and more idiosyncratic variables. In that mix many of us would argue that the impact of specific ideologies is pivotal.[30] No two individuals radicalize in exactly the same way or for the same reasons, but there is a clear pattern to the process and a significant commonality of constituent elements.[31] What I have in mind is too complex to explicate here, but the process of framing and interpreting events and experiences, the task of ideology, does not happen in some after-the-fact and separate moment. It is an integral part of the process by which potential terrorists enter into the alternate worldview that scholars acknowledge is a necessary precursor to engaging in jihadi terrorism.[32] It is this process that distinguishes the situation as an instance of terrorism and not just criminality. This framing process begins well before the process of conversion to an extremist standpoint is complete, and it is the first and most conspicuous indicator that such a conversion is underway. It is most certainly part of the surge in religiosity that precedes becoming a jihadi. What possible explanatory dividend can be obtained from minimizing this fact? This, of course, is true no matter what the content of the ideology happens to be. But when the ideology portrays a stark clash of forces of absolute evil and good, as in the case of the jihadi narrative, and declares that all true believers have a funda-mental moral obligation to use violence to advance a transcendently justified end, the ancillary role assigned to beliefs by McCauley and Moskalenko seems implausible and irresponsible. Much more is involved than assenting to beliefs and acting on them, but that moment of assent is crucial in shaping the intent to act, as well as the identity of the terrorist.

In noting the lack of correspondence between the jihadist recom-mendation of violence and traditional Islamic dictates condemning attacks on civilians, McCauley and Moskalenko are inadvertently rely-ing on the very premise they are explicitly rejecting, namely that beliefs matter. Otherwise there is no point in invoking what is theologically normative. But in any event, the seeming contradiction in beliefs is almost irrelevant given the enormous range and plasticity of religious teachings, in general, and most particularly in the case of a decentralized religion like Islam. The flood of *fatwas* supporting the activities of the jihadi terrorists[33] demonstrate the overwhelming futility of using references to what is supposedly normative to cast aspersions on the primacy of religion as an instigator of violence. Faulty theology is not a reliable indicator of degree of religiosity or the primacy of religion in someone's motivations, as social psychologists should know. But many analysts fall prey to this illogical inference, arguing that the discrepancies between how jihadists, on the one hand, and how mainstream Muslims and scholars of Islam on the other hand, interpret the basic elements of the al-Qaeda ideology somehow refutes the sincerity of the religious commitments of the jihadists.[34]

In the midst of their discussion McCauley and Moskalenko make another erroneous, and regrettably very common assertion, one that touches on several issues often raised in dismissing the significance of religion as a motivator of terrorism. "Osama bin Laden's speeches offer another clue," they state:

> He emphasizes Muslim grievances against the United States – support for authoritarian Muslim leaders, support for Israel, U.S. troops in Muslim countries – but spends little time selling the global caliphate that he asserts is the answer to these grievances. . . . [so] ideology for jihadist groups may be more a product of contention that a cause of contention.[35]

Intentionally or otherwise this statement is misleading. Bin Laden's public statements were political and deal with specific grievances. But this does not mean they were not also, or even more fundamentally, religious. These are not exclusive categories, unless one accepts certain Western liberal ideologies, and Islamist modes of thought very self-consciously reject the modern Western tradition of separating "church and state." There is no differentiation between political and religious goals and ideals in their purposefully pre-modern and anti-Western agenda. More specifically, referencing the lack of attention given to the caliphate is disingenuous, since it is only a nominal expression of Bin Laden's religiosity. The role played by the caliphate in the jihadist ideology is no more important than that played by the ideal of a communist society in the writings of Marx. Marx's relative inattention to delineating the nature of the new communist social order hardly warrants casting doubt on the authenticity of his commitment to this ideal in making his trenchant critique of capitalism. Bin Laden's statements are framed extensively in religious language, and the positions adopted are anchored in abundant references to the Qur'an and other religious sources, and not to other political sources of authority. Each of the grievances with the United States, for example, are premised on the affront posed to Allah and to Muslims, rather than such things as the sovereignty of Arab states or other straightforwardly political concerns.

In this regard Bruce Lawrence offers an instructive comment in the introduction to his compilation of Bin Laden's statements:

> Objectively speaking, bin Laden is waging a war against what many – admirers as well as critics – now call the American empire. But it is crucial to note that he himself never uses this vocabulary ... He defines the enemy differently. For him, jihad is aimed not at imperium, but at "global unbelief." Again and again, his texts return to this fundamental dichotomy. The war is a religious war. It subsumes a political war, which he can wage with terms appropriate to it, as he demonstrates in his addresses to the peoples of Europe or of America. Yet the battle in the end is one of faith.[36]

In the more recent and perhaps more perilous case of the terrorism inspired by the ideology of the Islamic State in Syria and Iraq the prominence of religious language is even more conspicuous and significant.[37] But the bottom line is we are dealing with groups that have pitted themselves against the rest of the world on the basis of a religious identity, and their propaganda is based on that fundamental distinction.

CONCLUSION

I have no way of knowing for sure what is motivating the tendency to discount the role of religion in explaining the motivations of contemporary terrorists in much of the work done by leading scholars. I can only infer possible reasons from what is said, what is not said, and how the arguments are formulated. In my work as a sociologist of new religious movements I have found that most contemporary North Americans and Europeans find strong, and hence often intolerant, religious convictions baffling, if not repugnant. This is even more so for most social scientists. Perhaps this prejudice is interfering with their capacity to fairly assess the origins and nature of homegrown jihadi terrorism and the wave of individuals leaving to fight for the Islamic State in Syria and Iraq. But whatever the reason, the force of my argument lies in the delineation of the weaknesses in the cases made for dismissing religion as a significant variable in accounting for terrorism. In other words, my focus is on how this happens and whether it is adequate, rather than definitively arguing why it is happening. An answer to the latter question remains too speculative.

It is significant, however, that these leading researchers made these arguments without anticipating any problems or objections. It is also important that the reviewers of their work seemingly did not raise any serious concerns, and I have yet to encounter any direct criticisms on this tendency from readers of these and similar works. This indicates, I suspect, an implicit consensus about the nature of religion and its relationship with politics, namely that it is a private matter, and as such it is inappropriate for religious values to exert a significant influence on public policy and affairs. But this is a conception of religion derived from the unique history of modern Europe and the differentiation of spheres of action stemming from the wars of religion and campaigns of violent persecution fomented by the Protestant Reformation. In the premodern European world, in most of the rest of the world prior to European imperialism, and definitely in the heritage of Islam, no such clear division of powers is recognized or desired. The things we deem religious are part and parcel of all aspects of life, and in the quest to live in a world full of meaning, the distinction between the private and public spheres is minimized and the separation of religion and politics is categorically rejected.[38] Operating from conflicting base assumptions about the nature and role of religion in societies, the interlocutors in this case, scholars and jihadi terrorists, are talking past each other and it is hard to see how this misunderstanding can foster a better grasp of the process of radicalization leading to violence.

So far every effort to delineate the macro social, political, and economic "root causes" of terrorism, as well as the more micro psychological and social-psychological factors influencing terrorist radicalization, has come up short. There is a persistent "explanatory gap"[39] since it is clear that far more people are affected by the "causes" in question than ever become terrorists. In other words, the factors may be necessary for explaining who becomes a terrorist, but they are not sufficient, on their own or in combination.[40] This explanatory gap is not unique to terrorism studies, but its manifestation is particularly egregious in this case. In the end, I would argue, the tendency to discount religion as an important and independent factor in the motivation of terrorism needlessly aggravates this explanatory gap problem, since much of the primary data available about the motivations of jihadi terrorists is *prima facie* religious, while the support for most of the psychological and social motivations favored by researchers is still often speculative at best. I am not postulating that religion is the cause of terrorism, but simply that we need to acknowledge that many terrorists think it is primary, so in effect it is, and if we wish to be effective in countering this kind of terrorism then this self-understanding must be taken into account. This may appear to be obvious, but some of the best scholarship on the topic keeps missing or dismissing the point.

Endnotes

1 Nasra Hassan, "An Arsenal of Believers: Talking to the 'Human Bombs,'" *The New Yorker*, November 19 (2001); M. Bloom, *Dying to Kill: The Allure of Suicide Terror* (New York: Columbia University Press, 2005); R. Pape, *Dying to Win: The Strategic Logic of Suicide Terrorism* (New York: Random House, 2005); M.M. Hafez, *Manufacturing Human Bombs: The Making of Palestinian Suicide Bombers* (Washington D.C.: United States Institute of Peace Press, 2006); Scott, Atran, "The Moral Logic and Growth of Suicide Terrorism," *The Washington Quarterly* 29 (2006), 127–147 and *Talking to the Enemy: Religion, Brotherhood, and the (un)making of Terrorists* (New York: HarperCollins, 2010); Assaf, Moghadam, "Suicide Terrorism, Occupation, and the Globalization of Martyrdom: A Critique of *Dying to Win*," *Studies in Conflict and Terrorism* 29 (2006), 707–729; Robert, Brym, "Religion, Politics, and Suicide Bombing: An Interpretive Essay," *Canadian Journal of Sociology* 33 (2008), 89–108.

2 Lorne L. Dawson, "The Study of New Religious Movements and the Radicalization of Home-grown Terrorists: Opening a Dialogue," *Terrorism and Political Violence* 21 (2010), 1–21; P. Bramadat and L.L. Dawson (eds.), *Religious Radicalization and Securitization in Canada and Beyond* (Toronto: University of Toronto Press, 2014); David C. Hofmann and Lorne L. Dawson, "The Neglected Role of Charismatic Authority in the Study of Terrorist Groups and Radicalization," *Studies in Conflict and Terrorism* 37 (2014), 348–368.

3 M. Sageman, *Understanding Terror Networks* (Philadelphia: University of Pennsylvania Press, 2004).

4 Sageman, *Understanding*, pp. 93–94.

5 Sageman, *Understanding*, pp. 93–94; E. Bakker, *Jihadi Terrorists in Europe: Their Characteristics and the Circumstances in which They Joined the Jihad* (The Hague: Netherlands Institute of International Relations, Clingendael, 2006).

6 Sageman, *Understanding*, p. 93.

7 Sageman, *Understanding*, p. 93.

8 Sageman, *Understanding*, p. 93.

9 Lorne Dawson, "Trying to Make Sense of Homegrown Terrorist Radicalization: The Case of the Toronto 18," in Paul Bramadat and Lorne

Dawson (eds.) *Religious Radicalization and Securitization in Canada and Beyond*, pp. 64–91 (Toronto: University of Toronto Press, 2014), pp. 82–83.

10   Dawson, "Trying to Make Sense," 83.

11   E. Durkheim, *The Elementary Forms of Religious Life*. Translated by J.W. Swain (New York: Free Press, 1965 [1912]).

12   Andrew Silke, "Holy Warriors: Exploring the Psychological Processes of Jihadi Radicalization," *European Journal of Criminology*, 5 (2008), 99–123.

13   Silke, "Holy Warriors," 110–111.

14   Silke, "Holy Warriors," 110.

15   Silke, "Holy Warriors," 110.

16   Silke, "Holy Warriors," 111.

17   M. Juergensmeyer, *Terror in the Mind of God: The Global Rise of Religious Violence* (Berkeley CA: University of California Press, 2000); Jeffry M. Bales, "Denying the Link between Islamist Ideology and Jihadist Terrorism: "Political Correctness" and the Undermining of Counterterrorism," *Perspectives on Terrorism* 7 (2013), 5–46; Heather S. Gregg, "Three Theories of Religious Activism and Violence: Social Movements, Fundamentalists, and Apocalyptic Warriors," *Terrorism and Political Violence* 25 (2014), 338–360.

18   A. Orisin, *Anatomy of the Red Brigades: The Religious Mindset of Modern Terrorists* (Ithaca, New York: Cornell University Press, 2011).

19   Jonathan, Fine, "Contrasting Secular and Religious Terrorism," *The Middle East Quarterly* (Winter 2008), 59–69; Heather S. Gregg, "Defining and Distinguishing Secular and Religious Terrorism," *Perspectives on Terrorism* 8 (2014), 36–51.

20   Silke, "Holy Warriors," 119.

21   H.J. Mol, *Identity and the Sacred* (New York: Free Press, 1976); Renate, Ysseldyk, Kimberly Matheson, and Hymie Anisman, "Religiosity as Identity: Toward an Understanding of Religion from a Social Identity Perspective," *Personality and Social Psychology Review* 14 (2010), 60–71.

22   Lorne L. Dawson, "Who Joins New Religious Movements and Why: Twenty Years of Research and What Have We Learned?" *Studies in Religion/Sciences Religieuses* 25 (1996), 141–161; Marat Shterin and Akhmet Yarlykapov, "Reconsidering Radicalisation and Terrorism: The New Muslims Movement in Kabardino-Balkaria and Its Path to Violence," *Religion, State, and Society* 39 (2011), 303–325.

23   C. McCauley and S. Moskalenko, *Friction: How Radicalization Happens to Them and Us* (New York: Oxford University Press, 2011).

24   McCauley and Moskalenko, *Friction*, 219–221.

25   McCauley and Moskalenko, *Friction*, 119–220.

26   McCauley and Moskalenko, *Friction*, 220.

27   McCauley and Moskalenko, *Friction*, 220.

28   McCauley and Moskalenko, *Friction*, 221.

29   McCauley and Moskalenko, *Friction*, 220 and 221.

30   Jonathan Leader Maynard, "Rethinking the Role of Ideology in Mass Atrocities," *Terrorism and Political Violence* 26 (2014), 821–841.

31 Donatella della Porta, "On Individual Motivations in Underground Political Organizations," in Bert Klandersmans, Hanspeter Kriesi, and Sidney Tarrow (eds.) Social Movements and Violence: Participation in Underground Organizations, *International Social Movement Research* 4, 3–28, (Greenwich, CT: JAI Press, 1992); Max Taylor and John Horgan, "A Conceptual Framework for Addressing Psychological Process in the Development of the Terrorist," *Terrorism and Political Violence* 18 (2006), 585–601; Darcy M.E., Noricks, "The Root Causes of Terrorism," in Paul K. Davis and Kim Cragin (eds.) *Social Science for Counterterrorism: Putting the Pieces Together*, 11–70, (Arlington, VA: National Defence Institute, RAND corp., 2009); Anja, Dalgaard-Nielsen, "Violent Radicalization in Europe: What we Know and What we do not Know," *Studies in Conflict and Terrorism* 33 (2010), 797–814.

32 Donatella della Porta, "Recruitment Process in Clandestine Political Organizations: Italian Left-Wing Terrorism," in Bert Klandersmans, Hanspeter Kriesi, and Sidney Tarrow (eds.) *International Social Movement Research* 1, 155–169, (Greenwich, CT: JAI Press, 1988); Martha Crenshaw, "The Subjective Reality of the Terrorist: Ideological and Psychological Factors in Terrorism," in Robert O. Slater and Michael Stohl (eds.) *Current Perspectives on International Terrorism*, 12–46, (London: MacMillan Press, 1988); Quintan, Wiktorowicz, *Radical Islam Rising: Muslim Extremism in the West* (Lanham, MD: Rowman and Littlefield, 2005); John Horgan, *Walking Away from Terrorism: Accounts of Disengagement from Radical and Extremist Movements* (New York: Routledge, 2009).

33 Shmuel Bar, *Warrant for Terror: Fatwas of Radical Islam and the Duty of Jihad* (Lanham, MD: Rowman and Littlefield, 2006).

34 For example, Tom Quiggin, "Understanding al-Qaeda`s Ideology for Counter-Narrative Work," *Perspectives on Terrorism* 3 (2009), 18–24.

35 McCauley and Moskalenko, *Friction*, 220.

36 Bruce Lawrence, (ed.) *Messages to the World: The Statements of Osama Bin Laden* (London: Verso, 2005), xx.

37 Graeme Wood, "What ISIS Really Wants," *The Atlantic* (March 2015), 78–94; Alex P. Schmind, "Challenging the Narrative of the 'Islamic State,'" International Centre for Counter-Terrorism Research Paper. The Netherlands: The Hague (2015).

38 Jonathan Z. Smith, "Religion, Religions, Religious," in Mark C. Taylor (ed.) *Critical Terms for Religious Studies* (Chicago: University of Chicago Press, 1998); D. Dubuisson, *The Western Construction of Religion: Myths, Knowledge, and Ideology*. Trans. W. Sayers. (Baltimore, MD: Johns Hopkins University Press, 2003 [1998]).

39 Dawson, "Trying to Make Sense," 66–67; Marc Sageman, "The Stagnation of Terrorism Research," *Terrorism and Political Violence* 26 (2014), 565–580.

40 J. Horgan, *The Psychology of Terrorism* (New York: Routledge, 2005); Kim R Cragin, "Resisting Violent Extremism: A Conceptual Model for Non-radicalization," *Terrorism and Political Violence* 26 (2014), 337–353.

4 Religion, Radicalization and the Causes of Terrorism

TOM MILLS AND DAVID MILLER

What causes terrorism and how can it be prevented? This is one of the great political questions of our time and over the last decade and a half, considerable resources have been allocated not only to state counter-terrorism programmes, but also to research which might shed some light on this question and inform counter-terrorism policies and practices. Terrorism experts have explored a host of possible causes. Low levels of education, economic and financial crisis, globalisation, inequality, occupation, political repression, poverty, psychopathy and state failure; these are just some of the factors examined in the literature, which tends to emphasise the multiplicity of causes and the complexity of the issue.[1] But whilst terrorism experts seem collectively unable to reach any firm conclusions as to the most significant causes of their object of study, the policy agenda, to which they largely orientate themselves, has focused increasingly on Muslims; and, with the usual disclaimers, the experts have followed.

ISLAM AND TERRORISM

Though political elites rarely refer to Islam *per se* as a principle cause of terrorism – a claim which though not uncommon is largely restricted to fringe movements – it is nevertheless widely assumed in policy circles that some extreme version of Islam has been a major driving force behind contemporary terrorism. Islamism, Political Islam, Wahhabism and Salafism are a few of the usual suspects appearing in policy pronouncements and the terrorism studies literature, along with more vague references to Islamic extremism, fundamentalism, radicalism and so on. So whilst Islam is routinely lauded as a religion of peace, and ordinary or moderate Muslims are usually invoked in distinction to the terrorists, radicals and extremists, contemporary political violence is still overwhelmingly seen as basically a Muslim problem, and it is largely Muslims who are targeted by counter-terrorism policies and practices.

This may seems defensible, even sensible at a surface level. After all, evidence can be produced that suggests that Muslim groups are responsible for the majority of contemporary global non-state political violence. Consider, for example, the figures in the 2014 Global Terrorism Index, published by the Institute for Economics and Peace. They suggest that two-thirds of the deaths resulting from terrorist attacks in 2013 were attributable to just four groups, all of which exhibit 'religious ideologies based on extreme interpretations of Wahhabi Islam', namely the Islamic State, Boko Haram, the Taliban and al-Qaeda and its affiliates.[2] The report, moreover, places this violence in the broader context of a significant rise in religiously motivated (Muslim) terrorism since 2000. Religion, it is suggested, has since that year overtaken both nationalists/separatists and political causes to become the main 'driving ideology for terrorism'.[3]

If religion, and some variant of Islam in particular, is now *the* major driving force behind terrorism, it would seem to make sense to make it the focus of research. But approaches which do so are, at best, rooted in an erroneous set of assumptions, leading to a highly limited understanding of contemporary political violence. First, by focusing in on a particular set of actors – the violent non-state organisations or movements we label 'terrorists' – a whole set of relevant actors and factors are either pushed into the background, or ignored altogether. The role of states, for example, is obscured, as are the broader geopolitical contexts within which acts of political violence and particular conflicts take place. Second, the causal primacy that then tends to be afforded to the ideology of 'terrorists' only serves to further narrow and depoliticise analysis. Conflicts within such a framework come to be understood as driven largely by the ideas professed and propagated by a particular subset of belligerents, without adequate attention to how those set of ideas relate to the real circumstances in which they are formed and mobilised (including the ideas and practices of adversaries). This problem is even more marked in the case of religiously motivated terrorism, which can be much more readily dismissed as irrational and implacable.

All this had led to some highly unsatisfactory understanding of contemporary conflicts and the role of religion within them. But the problem here is not merely one of inadequate reasoning. This chapter argues that the overwhelming focus on Islam and Muslims in terrorism policies and terrorism research reflects the interests of Western states which are themselves major driving forces behind the contemporary conflicts of which 'terrorists' are part. Such states, principally the United States and its close allies in Europe and the Middle East, have recklessly pursued policies known to fuel 'terrorism', whilst at the same time fostering forms of knowledge and expertise which are geared towards the management of political violence, rather than developing an understanding of its underlying causes. In this sense, the problem is not so much depoliticised analysis as politically compromised expertise.

In this chapter we draw attention, in particular, to experts who have mobilised ideas about terrorism and influenced how state interests are construed, and to the policies and practices that are then put in place. It should be stressed from the outset that 'terrorism experts' have produced some important work on political violence, and that the networks of which they are part are by no means homogenous, politically or intellectually. Nevertheless, we do consider their field to be seriously limited by its axiomatic assumptions, and by the related set of interests around which it has cohered.

THE RISE OF TERRORISM EXPERTISE

Terrorism studies first emerged as a field in the 1970s when a core group of researchers, referring to themselves as the 'terrorism mafia', sought to develop 'terrorism' as a legitimate object of study: 'Institutional entrepreneurs organized projects, organizations, and activities that both facilitated the growth of experts' relations between themselves and communicated expert knowledge to other audiences.'[4] Notable pioneers in this inchoate field included Yonah Alexander, an international studies professor affiliated with the Center for Strategic and International Studies (CSIS), a Washington-based 'strategic' think tank, based at Georgetown University until 1986; Martha Crenshaw, an American political scientist; Brian Crozier, a British counter-subversion writer and conservative activist; Brian Jenkins, a US Special Forces veteran based at the RAND Corporation; Walter Laqueur, a Zionist historian also affiliated with CSIS; and Paul Wilkinson, a British politics lecturer and former RAF officer. These early experts formed an 'invisible college'[5] which 'communicated informally, convened periodic terrorism meetings, developed terrorism incident databases ... shared ideas, and secured funding'.[6] Relatively marginal in academia, the experts, in Stampnitzky's terms, occupied 'an interstitial space between academia, the state, and the media',[7] with the state acting as 'the key instigator' in the development of their field.[8]

Whilst the US state was crucial, terrorism studies was also fostered by private political networks already operating in this 'interstitial space', of which a good number of the 'terrorism mafia' were already part. Crozier and Laqueur had both been deeply involved in covert intelligence and propaganda operations, and Wilkinson later joined the former's Institute for the Study of Conflict, which emerged from a London-based CIA propaganda front. The CSIS, with which both Alexander and Laqueur were affiliated, was well known for having been close to the CIA, and was at that time directed by Ray Cline, a former CIA analyst and another seminal 'terrorism expert'. The RAND Corporation, where Jenkins was based, is well known as an exemplar of the 'military-industrial-academic complex'.[9] The same Cold War political networks, closely connected to Western military and intelligence apparatuses, had previously played an important role in the development of expertise in counterinsurgency – that is the theory and practice of defeating independence movements in the former colonial world – and terrorism experts drew heavily on that body of knowledge.[10]

Stampnitzky argues that an important change took place with the shift from counter-insurgency to counter-terrorism.[11] The former, she argues, mostly analysed the non-state military adversaries of the United States in morally neutral terms and regarded them as rational actors, whilst the latter regarded them as 'evil, pathological, irrational'.[12] This characterisation of counter-insurgency theory is questionable, but terrorism experts certainly tended to portray 'terrorists' in such terms. At best, the notion that 'terrorists' might be rational political actors was 'contested' within terrorism studies.[13]

THE SOVIET TERROR NETWORK AFFAIR

Some 'terrorism studies' literature, though, did address what were thought to be the underlying causes of political violence. From the early 1980s, especially, it was claimed that 'terrorism' was organised and supported by the Soviet Union as part of its strategy to undermine the 'free world'.[14] This idea was popularised by the journalist Claire Sterling in her book, *The Terror Network* (1981), which argued that the Soviet Union was providing 'the terrorist network with the goods and services necessary to undermine the industrialized democracies of the West'.[15]

Sterling's work influenced some key members of the Reagan administration, notably Alexander Haig at the State Department and William Casey at the CIA. But it was not regarded as credible by many US intelligence analysts. Part of the reason for this is that Sterling's account drew on disinformation disseminated by the CIA, members of which then briefed against her account.

Another key source of disinformation in Sterling's book was a Jerusalem-based organisation called the Jonathan Institute, which had publicised misquotes from CIA reports. These were then quoted verbatim by Sterling.[16] The Jonathan Institute, named after Jonathan Netanyahu, the brother of the right-wing Israeli politician, Benjamin Netanyahu, was formed in 1976. Amongst its stated goals were to 'determine the roots of the terrorism which engulfs the world', and to 'advance the idea ... that if the West wishes to maintain its position in the most pivotal area in the world, the Middle East, it must back Israel, the very heart of that area and its foremost bearer of Western ideals'. The Jonathan Institute held high profile conferences on terrorism in 1979 in Jerusalem and 1984 in Washington, DC, which portrayed terrorism as 'a moral evil' largely attributable to Soviet largesse. These conferences, in which Benjamin Netanyahu played a central role, brought together politicians and policy experts from the United States and Israel, and a few from the United Kingdom. Many of the participants had roots in the aforementioned Cold War propaganda networks and were agitating against the less belligerent foreign policy and more egalitarian domestic policies pursued by the US Government. The neoconservatives, as this loose network of Zionists and Cold War ideologues became known, were part of a broader conservative backlash that was then underway, and were representative of a close alliance that had formed between elites in the United States and Israel.

Stampnitzky argues that the Soviet terror network theory was part of a politicisation of terrorism expertise during the 1980s, which undermined the efforts of the 'terrorism mafia' to 'develop "terrorism studies" as a new field of research'. She distinguishes the seminal terrorism experts from a 'new group of individuals, tightly networked and affiliated with a small number of more politically oriented think tanks and organizations'. This interpretation, however, overlooks how far members of the 'terrorism mafia', and their arguments, overlapped with those of the neoconservatives. Brian Jenkins, of RAND, as Stampnitzky notes, publicly expressed scepticism about Sterling's thesis. But he was amongst the more 'realist' of the terrorism mafiosi. A good number had been connected to the same anti-communist political networks that disseminated the material Sterling popularised in *The Terror Network*. Yonah Alexander and Walter Laqueur, for example, were both based at the CSIS, which was central to its propagation.[17] Paul Wilkinson, who was one of the key players involved in the development of terrorism studies, and is counted amongst the more sober of the terrorism experts by Stampnitzky, was in fact a supporter of the Soviet terror network theory. After *The Times* reported that the CIA's national intelligence survey contradicted claims made by the Reagan White House about the Soviet Union's role in 'international terrorism',[18] Wilkinson wrote a letter to the paper accusing the CIA of 'misinforming the United States Government and public', and claiming that 'processes of Soviet involvement in terrorism have been carefully analysed by Western specialists since the early seventies'.[19]

As Wilkinson's remarks illustrate, the line between the neocon think tankers and the more realist terrorism studies scholars is not at all clear cut. Certainly some were sceptical of overtly conspiracist accounts of Soviet involvement in 'international terrorism'. But they shared with proponents of the Soviet terror network theory an implicit understanding of who is and is not a terrorist – albeit without sharing any clear definition of terrorism – and offered no alternative causal explanation in place of the master conspirators in Moscow. As Stampnitzky notes, most speakers at a 1976 US State Department conference on terrorism – who included Crenshaw, Jenkins and Wilkinson – 'doubted that the direct causes of terrorism could be discovered in political or socioeconomic conditions' and 'were skeptical of the argument that the way to stop terrorism was to "remove its causes"'.[20]

NEW WORLD ORDER, NEW TERRORISM

In March 1990, with America's Cold War adversary on the brink of collapse, President George H. W. Bush – who had attended the 1979 Jerusalem conference with Ray Cline – stated in his National Security Strategy that the threats to US 'interests' in the Middle East 'could not be laid at the Kremlin's door':

> Instability ... will continue, whether or not exploited by the Soviets. Religious fanaticism may continue to endanger American lives, or countries friendly to us in the Middle East, on whose energy resources the free world continues to depend. The scourge of terrorism, and of states who sponsor it, likewise remains a threat.[21]

This was, in part, a pitch to Congress for the maintenance of enormous levels of military expenditure, despite the rapprochement between the superpowers. The public refutation of the Soviet terror network theory ironically now served the same interests as its earlier propagation. Even without the Soviet Union, it was now claimed, terrorism would continue and, if anything, would increase.[22] There would still be threats to 'the security of Israel and moderate Arab states as well as the free flow of oil', and the United States would still have to defend these 'interests' militarily.

Despite the novel candid approach, this still represented something of an inversion of reality. The reason 'instability' would continue was precisely *because* the United States would continue to provide military and diplomatic support for Israel and the autocratic Arab states. What had changed, however, was the basis on which such policies could be justified. This presented something of a challenge. 'How do we maintain the cohesion among allies and friends,' the National Security Strategy mused, 'as the perceived threat of a common danger weakens?'[23]

THE NOTION OF A CLASH OF CIVILISATIONS

Foreign policy intellectuals quickly discovered new threats. More conservative commentators alluded to a 'clash of civilisations'. The phrase was made famous by the political scientist, Samuel P. Huntington. His work was funded by key conservative foundations including the John M. Olin Foundation, the Bradley Foundation and the Smith Richardson Foundation. Huntington's pessimistic vision – a riposte to the liberal triumphalism of Francis Fukuyama's equally famous declaration of the 'End of History' – was set out in an article and subsequent book, both based on a 1992 lecture he gave at the neoconservative American Enterprise Institute. Huntington's argument was not merely that the West would clash with Islamic civilisation, but more broadly that cultural and religious differences between people in different regions of the world would inevitably lead to conflict. On the specific question of 'conflict between Islam and the West', Huntington wrote of 'a [quasi] war of terrorism versus air power', which had been waged in previous decades and which he claimed was representative of a 'clash' between the two cultures.[24] Another influential proponent of this idea of civilisational conflict, and conflict between Islam and the West in particular, was the British-born Orientalist Bernard Lewis, who had used the phrase 'clash of civilisation' in an earlier influential essay, cited by Huntington,[25] entitled 'The Roots of Muslim Rage'.[26] Lewis claimed that hostility towards the United States in the Muslim world was not primarily attributable to US policies, but an 'irrational but surely historic reaction of an ancient rival against our Judeo-Christian heritage';[27] a 'formless resentment and anger of the Muslim masses', channelled by the Islamic fundamentalists' struggle against secularism and modernity.[28]

The notion of a 'clash of civilisation', which attributed 'terrorism' in the Middle East to Islamic culture, would influence conservative movements during the 'War on Terror', particularly right-wing Christians, Zionists and more fringe analysts. Most 'terrorism experts', though, initially at least, resisted this 'culturalist' reading, as Kundnani characterises it.[29] Instead they echoed the consensus amongst much of the Western foreign policy establishment that the post–Cold War era would be bedevilled by religious and nationalist fervour, rogue states and the spread of WMDs. These themes featured prominently in the writings of terrorism experts during the 1990s, a number of whom began to point to the ascendance of a 'new terrorism', more lethal and implacable than that which had predominated during the Cold War. One of the original members of the 'terrorism mafia', Walter Laqueur, was one such expert. He wrote of a coincidence of 'religious-sectarian-nationalist convictions', 'with the development of weapons of mass destruction', claiming it represented 'a threat unprecedented in the history of mankind.'[30]

Nevertheless, the 'new terrorism' literature placed a particular emphasis on religious terrorists, who were seen as a greater threat, more violent and irrational, than their secular counterparts. Reference was often made to the Japanese cult Aum Shinrikyo, which was responsible for a nerve gas attack on the Tokyo underground; to the Oklahoma bomber Timothy McVeigh; as well as to ultra-conservative religious movements in the United States and Israel. The analytical focus, however, was largely on Muslims. In his discussion of 'Islamic radicalism', Laqueur expressed doubt about the peaceful nature of Islam. He noted the prevalence of 'anti-Western' sentiment amongst Muslim populations and the 'compelling coincidence' that most violent conflicts take place in 'Muslim counties or those with active Muslim minorities'; though he considered that this may be down to 'social and cultural factors rather than religious'.[31] 'Islam in modern history has not engaged in acts of mass violence on a Hitlerian or the Pol Pot scale', Laqueur conceded. But he thought the parallels between Nazism and 'political Islam' were in some ways 'striking', and claimed that: 'Radical Muslims exhibit hostility toward all those who are different, a free-floating rage, and a tradition of violence that favors the appearance of terrorism.'[32]

Another leading exponent of the 'new terrorism' thesis was the RAND analyst, Bruce Hoffman, who founded the influential Centre for the Study of Terrorism and Political Violence (CSTPV) at St. Andrew's University with Paul Wilkinson. In a 1993 RAND paper,

Hoffman, like Laqueur, warned of the possibility of 'terrorists' stealing and then using a nuclear weapon, or some other weapon of mass destruction.[33] His focus was on the rise of 'holy terror', which, he claimed, exhibited a 'radically different value systems, [and] mechanisms of legitimization and justification' than its secular counterpart. The 'holy terrorists', he claimed, are 'unconstrained by the political, moral or practical constraints that seem to affect other terrorists',[34] and 'view violence as an end in itself'.[35] A major source for Hoffman's account of 'holy terror' in the Muslim world was a book of that name by Amir Taheri,[36] an Iranian born conservative commentator and author. Taheri, whose work has been criticised for inaccurate claims about Islam and Iran, now chairs the European Board of the Islamophobic Gatestone Institute. Hoffman later contributed a chapter to a 1999 RAND collection on the 'new terrorism' introduced by Brian Jenkins, in which it was argued that 'much previous analysis of terrorism based on established groups [has been rendered] obsolete'.[37] Hoffman's 1993 RAND paper, meanwhile, was reproduced in an amended form as a chapter on religion in his 1998 book, *Inside Terrorism*. That book was updated after September 11th and according to Google Scholar is now the most highly cited single book on terrorism. In it, Hoffman argues that 'the religious imperative for terrorism is the most important defining characteristic of terrorist activity today',[38] and though he does not himself use the term 'new terrorism', he offers a clear statement of the basic precepts of the 'new terrorism' thesis. The 'new generation of terrorists', he writes,

> is not only characterized by more salient theological influences, but in some cases has embraced millenarian, if not apocalyptic aims. They are themselves also less cohesive organizational entities, with a deliberately more diffuse structure and membership with distinctly more opaque command and control relationships. Accordingly, they represent a different and potentially more lethal threat than ... 'traditional' terrorist adversaries.[39]

Incredibly, Hoffman's book contains no discussion of the causes of 'terrorism', old or new. Other exponents of the 'new terrorism' thesis, however, have attempted to explain the underlying causes of this new threat. Cronin, for example, suggests that rather than seeing contemporary terrorism as motivated by religion, it is 'more accurate to see it as part of a larger phenomenon of antiglobalization'.[40] For Cronin – who acknowledges her 'huge debt' to 'terrorism mafia' member Martha Crenshaw[41] – 'globalization and terrorism are intricately intertwined forces',[42] with international integration and new information technologies impacting on 'terrorists' just as they do states and other non-state actors.[43] She argues that globalisation is an underlying cause of terrorism since it leads 'frustrated populations and international movements ... to lash out', particularly at the United States, with acts of 'expressive violence'.[44] A similar argument has been advanced by Peter Neumann, the director of the International Centre for the Study of Radicalisation and Political Violence (ISCR) at King's College London. A late proponent of the 'new terrorism' thesis, Neumann draws extensively on the terrorism studies literature, and on Hoffman in particular, but declares his 'frustration' at treatment of 'terrorism as something that can be studied in isolation from broader socio-political trends and developments'.[45] Neumann's central thesis is that 'the rise of the new terrorism' has been facilitated by the social changes associated with 'late modernity and globalization',[46] concepts he borrows from sociologists Bauman and Giddens, the latter of whom is also an exponent of the 'new terrorism' thesis.[47] Like Cronin, Neumann argues that global integration and new communicative and information technologies have made terrorism more international. He also argues that these processes can help explain the rise of 'mass-casualty terrorism', suggesting that a proliferation of media messages, and an increasingly desensitised global media audience has meant that 'more spectacular and brutal attacks' are necessary in order for terrorists to have an impact.[48] Like Hoffman and others, Neumann argues that religious extremism has facilitated more lethal forms of violence, since it more readily dehumanises potential victims than the 'universalist' ideologies of the 'old terrorism'.[49] Essentially the 'new terrorism', in Neumann's account, is understood as a ferocious form of identity politics arising as a kind of pathology of the universalising liberal global order.

In addition to Hoffman, a key influence on Neumann, and on other 'new terrorism' theorists, is Mark Juergensmeyer, an American sociologist and religious studies scholar 'intellectually aligned with core members' of the 'terrorism mafia'.[50] Juergensmeyer's arguments about religion and terrorism are laid out in his 2000 book *Terror in the Mind of God*, which became 'a core text for advocates of the new terrorism hypothesis'.[51] For Juergensmeyer, as for Neumann, religion is not a cause of terrorism, but as a medium for grievances it is 'problematic' since it exacerbates 'conflict through its abiding absolutism, its justification for violence, and its ultimate images of warfare that demonize opponents and cast the conflict in transhistorical terms.'[52]

BRINGING RIGOUR TO THE STUDY OF THE 'NEW' TERRORISM?

Attempts by Juergensmeyer, Neumann and others to introduce some sociological rigour to the 'new terrorism' thesis are at least an advance on its more outlandish and moralistic formulations. But they still fall short. Neumann in particular gives little sense of what might cause such extreme discontent amongst the 'new terrorists' and the broader political movements of which they are part beyond a general *anomie* arising out of the conditions of global capitalism and its 'aggressive promotion of universal values'.[53] This is a basic problem with 'terrorism studies' more generally. Without any grasp of the violence and injustices of the US-dominated global order, an analytical void arises which was once occupied by the spectre of the Soviet Union, but more recently filled with erroneous assumptions about Islam or Islamic culture, or vague allusions to crises of identity and 'grievances' mobilised by 'extremist' ideologies and movements, usually qualified with disclaimers about the great complexity of the problem and the multiplicity of the causes and solutions. In either case, what is lost is a rational analysis of the forms of political violence conventionally labelled 'terrorism', and their underlying causes.

It is not that the accounts typically advanced by terrorism experts offer no insights into particular groups and movements. The problem is that in focusing on particular actors, and the cultures of violence they propagate, they simply describe in detail precisely what needs to be explained. What makes these inadequate theories effective, meanwhile, is that despite their intellectual shortcomings they are readily able to neutralise plainly relevant factors by incorporating them into a framework which gives foundational primacy to other aspects – typically 'culture' in general or particular 'extremist' ideologies and movements – and even claim to thereby offer a broader or more penetrating analysis than, for example, a perfunctory focus on Western foreign policy. Thus Lewis readily concedes that the 'policies and actions, pursued and taken by individual Western governments ... have aroused the passionate anger of Middle Eastern and other Islamic peoples'. US support for Israel, he writes, is 'certainly a factor of importance', and he considers that the argument that 'American support for hated regimes' is behind 'Anti-Americanism' has 'some plausibility'.[54] Nevertheless, he insists that 'something deeper is involved than these specific grievances'.[55] In a similar way, the proponents of 'reformist' arguments which appeal to a violent or extremist subset of Muslims, rather than Islam itself, are readily able to admit that Western foreign policy plays an important role, whilst still focusing on how such 'grievances' are mobilised by 'extremists' and the ideas they propagate.

WHAT CAUSES TERRORISM?

Peter Neumann has noted that in the early period of the 'War on Terror', it was 'very difficult to talk about the "roots of terrorism," which some commentators claimed was an effort to excuse and justify the killing of innocent civilians', and has urged 'experts and officials' to examine 'the political, economic, social and psychological forces that underpin terrorism and political violence'.[56] Yet seven years later, he concedes that the search for 'root causes' has so far been in vain:

> There are many explanations, theories and models for why people join militant groups. The pathways are said to be complex, the reasons multi-faceted. An entire field of academic study has emerged out of the search for the causes of violent extremism. Yet no political scientist, sociologist, economist, historian or psychologist has discovered a universal formula. Nor is there a scholarly consensus on what factors – or combinations of factors – are important. The places in which political violence happens are too different, the individual circumstances too varied.[57]

Can we say with more certainty than these experts what causes 'terrorism'? Part of the problem with this question is that there is no clear understanding of to what the term 'terrorism' refers. Essentially 'terrorism' is a pejorative term used to describe political violence of which the user disapproves. Central to Stampnitzky's account is the failure of terrorism experts to 'discipline' the politicised concept of 'terrorism' into a rational object of scholarly inquiry; which is a rather obscure way of expressing the fact that 'terrorism' is a term of political rhetoric rather than a scholarly concept.[58]

In Western policy circles, and in the 'terrorism studies' literature oriented towards it, the term 'terrorism' has tended to mean the violence of non-state opponents of the United States and its allies. The question: 'What causes terrorism?' , then, can be restated more concisely as: 'What causes non-state groups and movements to violently oppose the US and its allies?' To this, we can now perhaps add a further racial element, and pose the question: 'What causes specific Muslim groups to violently oppose the US and its allies?'

Putting aside the question of violence for the moment, the question of why so many Muslims find themselves politically opposed to 'the West', is a fairly straightforward one. As the US Defense Science Board noted in a report for the US Department of Defense in 2004:

> Muslims do not 'hate our freedom,' but rather, they hate our policies. The overwhelming majority voice their objections to what they see as one-sided support in favor of Israel and against Palestinian rights, and the longstanding, even increasing support for what Muslims collectively see as tyrannies, most notably Egypt, Saudi Arabia, Jordan, Pakistan, and the Gulf states.[59]

As to why such opposition has assumed an especially violent character, the allusions by Juergensmeyer and others to religious ideology may be superficially convincing to liberals who regard all religion as irrational and reactionary, or to conservatives who consider Islam as exhibiting a particular propensity to violence. But the more straightforward explanation is that the violence exhibited by certain groups and movements in the Middle East is a product of the violent context from which they emerge. Huntington is at least fairly candid about US violence towards the Middle East, noting that between 1980 and 1995, the key period for the emergence of the 'new terrorism', 'the United States engaged in seventeen military operations in the Middle East, all of them directed against Muslims. No comparable pattern of U.S. military operations occurred against the people of any other civilization.'[60] In the two decades since then, Western policies have remained broadly consistent and Western state violence has only increased. In terms of how this impacts on 'terrorism', the findings reported in the Institute for Economics and Peace's 2015 Global Terrorism Index are revealing. The researchers found no correlation between 'terrorism' and religious prevalence. Neither was any significant correlation found between 'terrorism' and the percentage of Muslims in a population. They did, however, find strong correlations with ongoing armed conflict, state terrorism ('political terror'), political instability, religious violence and hostility between religious groups.[61] What this suggests, then, is that insofar as 'terrorism' can be meaningfully said to have an underlying cause, it is likely to be found in war and political repression, especially in societies where violence and oppression assume a sectarian character. If we apply these statistical findings to the recent history of the Muslim world, a fairly clear picture emerges. Violent groups, many exhibiting ultra-conservative and sectarian religious ideologies, such as the Taliban, al-Qaeda and Islamic State, have emerged from highly repressive polities, and from violent occupations and civil wars which have often assumed a sectarian character or had such a character fostered by invading or occupying forces. In the case of contemporary Middle Eastern 'terrorism', it is clear that the occupations of Afghanistan and Iraq, and the subsequent civil war in Syria are central factors.

Indeed, Neumann now concedes that the only clear cause of 'terrorism' is 'instability, ethnic and religious division, violence and repression.'[62] Yet, despite this, he has been part of a push in Western policy-making circles towards highly authoritarian counter-terrorism policies which focus not on reducing violent conflict and political repression around the world, but rather on monitoring and managing the political ideas and 'values' of citizens, and Muslims in particular. This apparent contradiction was already evident in Neumann's 'new terrorism' book, in which he affords relatively little attention to what leads groups or movements to 'turn to violence'. In his brief discussion of this question, Neumann notes that traumatic events such as violent state repression, or a foreign invasion can act as 'triggers' pushing radical movements towards violence.[63] But this is an insight that remains marginal in his overall account of political violence. When it later comes to making policy recommendations, rather than advocating approaches likely to reduce war and political repression, Neumann suggests policy makers combat extremist ideas with the use of 'public relations and public diplomacy professionals' and the development of online 'counter-narratives'.[64] He then goes on to advocate a more proactive approach able to anticipate the next 'wave' of terrorism by 'looking at the evolution of political movements which exist at the fringes of the mainstream ... their ideas, narratives and internal dynamics, as well as their changing attitudes towards political participation'.[65]

IDEAS AND INTERESTS

Such apparent contradictions make more sense if experts like Neumann are understood not as 'free floating' intellectuals, but as constituents of organisational and financial networks which create incentives for certain problems to be addressed and certain ideas to be produced – giving rise to a particular sort of intellectual culture. Since long before September 11th, the 'field' of terrorism expertise has been hindered not (only) by the intellectual shortcomings of its adherents, but by the set of interests, which have constituted it as a field. Terrorism studies has been shaped by and around certain influential figures and key journals, funding sources and organisational 'hubs' – such as university departments, research centres and private think tanks – all of which have influenced the nature of knowledge and expertise produced and, we believe, militated against a social scientific understanding of political violence and its underlying causes.

To illustrate the point, let us take the example of Peter Neumann and his proximate network. He is a Professor of Security Studies at King's College London's Department of War Studies. That department was set up in 1964 by Michael Howard, a protégée of the influential journalist and military strategist B. H. Liddell Hart, who earlier helped Howard set up the Atlanticist strategic think tank, now known as the International Institute for Strategic Studies with financial backing from the Ford Foundation.[66] King's College is close to the British military – its Defence Studies Department provides academic training to the armed forces and advice to the Ministry of Defence – and Neumann studied for his PhD under Michael Rainsborough, a former official at the Ministry of Defence. Rainsborough is another proponent of the 'new terrorism' thesis and has offered a revision of the Soviet terror network theory, arguing that the end of the Cold War and globalisation 'sped the pace of terror networking'.[67] A Visiting Professor at their department is David Omand, the United Kingdom's former Security and Intelligence Co-ordinator and reputedly the main architect of the United Kingdom's counter-terrorism policy. Omand, who provided a blurb for Neumann's 'new terrorism' book, has likened what he calls 'international terrorist ideology' to a parasite or virus and argues that Western states must develop 'a counter-narrative that will help groups exposed to the terrorist message make sense of what they are seeing around them'.[68]

Whilst at the Department of War Studies, Neumann was appointed the 'academic director' for the 2005 International Summit on Democracy, Terrorism and Security, a gathering of leading international terrorism experts convened by the Club de Madrid, an elite policy forum made up of former Prime Ministers and Presidents. The religion working group of that conference was headed by Mark Juergensmeyer, who in an academic output from the conference anticipated Neumann's arguments about the 'new terrorism'. In the 'present moment of late modernity' , Juergensmeyer writes, violent religious movements have arisen in reaction to 'the global system', expressing grievances over 'social identity and meaningful participation in public life that in other contexts were expressed through Marxist and nationalist ideologies'.[69]

Neumann subsequently co-founded the ISCR. Based at King's, the think tank is a partnership between the University of Pennsylvania in the United States, the Interdisciplinary Center Herzliya in Israel and the Regional Center on Conflict Prevention in Jordan. A key player in its establishment was the London based American businessman Henry Sweetbaum, who hoped to set up a research centre to challenge the academic boycott of Israel.[70] His efforts eventually gave rise to the establishment of ICSR in 2007, which was launched in January 2008 at a conference at which the then Home Secretary announced the UK Government's new counter-terrorism initiative. Amongst the other keynotes at that conference were the Club de Madrid's Mary Robinson, the Vice-President of Colombia, Francisco Santos Calderon and the Secretary-General, Council of Europe, Terry Davis, both of whom had attended the aforementioned Madrid Summit.

The ICSR is now one of the most prominent research centres in the world of terrorism expertise and has enjoyed particular prominence for its research on foreign fighters in the Syrian civil war. On its website, it is praised by one of its Patrons for its 'independence and neutrality'. It is standard for think tanks to assert their independence in this way, but in reality such organisations typically draw on private funding, political connections and academic affiliations for finance, prestige and publicity, and Neumann's outfit is no exception. Whilst it does not disclose its funding, our research has identified over £700,000 of donations to ICSR and King's since 2007 from the Atkin family, Conservative Party donors who have also funded the Henry Jackson Society, the United Kingdom's foremost neoconservative think tank as well as funding the controversial Jerusalem Foundation which is reported to be engaged in developments in settlements in occupied East Jerusalem.[71]

Neumann's ICSR co-founder, John Bew, was at one stage a Vice President of the Henry Jackson Society, which began as a coalition of neoconservatives and liberal interventionists, but has since assumed a more hardline right-wing agenda.[72] Along with the Centre for Social Cohesion – a think tank it subsumed in 2011 – and Policy Exchange, the think tank closest to the United Kingdom's current Conservative Government, the Henry Jackson Society has been central to the dissemination of neoconservative ideas on 'terrorism' and 'extremism'.[73] The arguments advanced by these think tanks have been part of a push towards treating 'terrorism' as a symptom of liberal policies on immigration and cultural diversity. In essence, the argument advanced by the conservative movements especially, has been that multiculturalism and a broader loss of confidence in Western or Enlightenment values has allowed violent extremist ideas to flourish amongst ethnic minorities. The somewhat more liberal sounding formulation of the same argument, advanced by Neumann and ISCR colleague, is that 'terrorism' and 'extremism' are at root problems of identity.[74]

The think tanks involved in propagating these arguments have shared ideas, donors and personnel with the ICSR. ICSR's Alexander Meleagrou-Hitchens, for example (the son of the 'New Atheist' activist Christopher Hitchens), previously worked at both Policy Exchange and the Centre for Social Cohesion. At the latter think tank he was involved in drafting an October 2008 private briefing that relied on evidence from the Society of Americans for National Existence, an organisation that sought to make Islam illegal.[75] He has also written for the aforementioned Gatestone Institute, which appears to be almost entirely funded by the Abstraction Fund, a conservative foundation responsible for bankrolling a number of Islamophobic outfits, which provided funds to the Henry Jackson Society in 2011. Another ICSR analyst is Shiraz Maher, who has also written for Gatestone. Maher also previously worked at Policy Exchange where he attacked the Labour Government for its engagement with non-violent, but allegedly still 'extremist', Muslim groups and advocated a counter-subversion strategy explicitly modelled on Cold War anti-communism.[76] Maher's work at Policy Exchange was praised by Michael Gove, the United Kingdom's foremost neoconservative politician and first chairman of the think tank. Gove hosted the Parliamentary launch of the Henry Jackson Society.

Before becoming a terrorism expert, Shiraz Maher was involved in the non-violent Pan-Islamic group, Hizb ut-Tahrir, a background he shares with a number of other British counter-extremist experts, notably Maajid Nawaz and Ed Husain, co-founders of the Quilliam Foundation. These ex-extremists have lent credibility to the erroneous ideas about Islam and 'terrorism' propagated by outfits like the Henry Jackson Society and have an inescapable interest in propagating the assumption that 'terrorism' is rooted in 'extremist' political ideas, since their claims to expertise are based in this assumption.

Quilliam was set up and launched at around the same time as ICSR, and between 2008/9 and 2011/12 received over £2.9 million in funding from the British Government.[77] This Government support, which was channelled through the Department for Communities and Local Government, the Foreign Office and the Home Office, ended in 2011/2, and that same year Quilliam established a US fundraising arm. A director of that outfit was Chad Sweet, a former investment banker and Directorate of Operations at the CIA. Under the second Bush administration, Sweet was Chief of Staff at the Department of Homeland Security, which at that time was headed by Henry Jackson Society Patron

Michael Chertoff, and which contracted Quilliam to deliver training for its Radicalization Awareness Program (RAP). The Quilliam Foundation was at one stage close to the Centre for Social Cohesion, but there was a breakdown in the relationship in 2009 when a former CSC member of staff who moved to Quilliam attacked CSC director Douglas Murray as a 'preacher of hate'. Murray responded that Quilliam 'represent[s] the toxic juncture at which intense personal ambition and government propaganda meet'.

Quilliam is still headed by its co-founder Maajid Nawaz, whilst Ed Husain, whose book *The Islamist* was reportedly written in consultation with British officials,[78] has since joined the Council of Foreign Relations in the United States. A third founder, Rashad Ali, moved to the Henry Jackson Society before becoming a Fellow at the Institute for Strategic Dialogue where another former Quilliam expert, Erin Marie Saltman, is also based. The Institute for Strategic Dialogue have collaborated with ICSR on research on radicalisation, and the two organisations share a research fellow on extremism, Melanie Smith. The Institute for Strategic Dialogue was set up by the late Lord Weidenfeld, a veteran British Zionist whose company Weidenfeld & Nicolson published Walter Laqueur, Bernard Lewis, Claire Sterling's *The Terror Network*, Benjamin Netanyahu's *Terrorism: How the West Can Win* – the output from the second Jonathan Institute terrorism conference – and more recently Michael Gove's neoconservative polemic, *Celsius 7/7*.

NETWORKS, POWER AND ISLAMOPHOBIA

The above account, which focuses in on the UK based 'radicalisation' experts, is just a snapshot of much more extensive and complex network of political entrepreneurs, philanthropists, financiers and foundations, think tankers, journalists, authors, academics and more fringe political protagonists and propagandists who make up the world of terrorism expertise. This network, or these networks, are constantly in flux and do not share uniform ideas or interests. But the field of terrorism expertise is no more a shapeless morass of actors delivering an authentically pluralistic set of ideas than it is a well delineated field offering disinterested scientific expertise. Rather it is a field constituted by, and oriented towards, the interests of the US state and its close allies, and shaped by certain political networks that penetrate and envelop such states. They include neoconservative, Zionist and other conservative movements, as well as more liberal and technocratic factions of the foreign policy establishment.

Whilst sections of the terrorism studies field are explicitly 'critical' in orientation, rejecting the axiomatic assumptions of the field, and the interests those assumptions reflect, the 'critical' movement is largely confined to academia and has not disrupted the broader field. Indeed, though 'terrorism studies' has been subject to significant criticism on intellectual and political grounds it has nevertheless grown exponentially in the last decade and half, and whilst scarcely any more cogent, has proved at least resilient, perhaps even innovative – developing new conceptual vocabulary in partnership with state actors as the policy agenda has evolved.

The latest phase in this development has had serious consequences for how Islam is understood and how Muslims are treated. Counterterrorism policies in Europe, North America and elsewhere disproportionately target Muslims, and are increasingly focused on political ideas and values, rather than on potential security threats. Such policies give rise to an atmosphere of suspicion and hostility towards Muslims, increasing the likelihood of widespread discrimination and racist violence. But such policies also constitute a direct and unwarranted threat to the human rights and civil liberties of Muslims, who as a result of targeted counter-terrorism policies are more likely to suffer state violence, unlawful detention, miscarriages of justice and so on, just as in an earlier period in the United Kingdom, citizens of Irish descent were more vulnerable to such threats.[79] The current threat we face, moreover, is not merely to Muslim citizens. The dominant policy response to 'terrorism' has always been to expand executive powers and to reduce liberal safeguards, usually in the name of defending democracy. But the current phase of counter-terrorism has not only augmented investigative powers, it has led to an unprecedented level of monitoring and surveillance of citizenry; to overt and covert encroachments into civil society and the public sector explicitly intended to monitor and manage political opinion. This threatens the religious freedoms, civil liberties and human rights of Muslims first and foremost. But it is no exaggeration to characterise such measures as a severe threat to democracy.

Endnotes

1   e.g. Tore Bjørgo, "Introduction." In Tore Bjørgo (ed.), *Root Causes of Terrorism: Myths, Reality and Ways Forward* (Abingdon and New York: Routledge, 2006), pp. 1–15. Louise Richardson, "The Roots of Terrorism: An Overview." In Louise Richardson (ed.), *The Roots of Terrorism* (Abingdon and New York: Routledge, 2006), pp. 1–16. Peter R. Neumann and Brooke Rogers, *Recruitment and Mobilisation for the*

Islamist Militant Movement in Europe. A study carried out by King's College London for the European Commission (Directorate General Justice, Freedom and Security, 2007).

2   *Global Terrorism Index: Measuring and Understanding the Impact of Terrorism* (Institute for Economics and Peace, 2014), p. 2.

3   Ibid., p. 31.

4   Lisa Stampnitzky, *Disciplining Terror: How Experts Invented 'Terrorism'* (Cambridge: Cambridge University Press, 2013), p. 42.

5   Alex P. Schmid, Albert J. Jongman and Michael Stohl, *Political Terrorism: A New Guide to Actors, Authors, Concepts, Databases, Theories, & Literature* (New Brunswick, NJ: Transaction Publishers 2005). Edna O. F. Reid, , "Analysis of terrorism literature: a bibliometric and content analysis study." Dissertation, USC School of Library and Information Management, University of Southern California, Los Angeles, CA, 1983. Edna O. F. Reid, "Terrorism research and the diffusion of ideas." *Knowledge, Technology and Policy*, Vol. 6, No. 1, (1993), pp. 17–37. Edna O. F. Reid, and H. Chen, "Mapping the contemporary terrorism research domains." *International Journal of Human–Computer Studies*, Vol. 65, (2007), pp. 42–56.

6   Reid and Chen, "Mapping the contemporary terrorism research domains," p. 43.

7   Stampnitzky, *Disciplining* Terror, p. 47.

8   Ibid., p. 66.

9   Henry A. Giroux, *University in Chains: Confronting the Military-Industrial-Academic Complex* (New York: Routledge, 2015).

10   Charles Maechling Jr., "Counterinsurgency: The First Ordeal by Fire." In Michael T. Klare and Peter Kornbluh (eds.), *Low-Intensity Warfare: Counter-insurgency, Proinsurgency and Antiterrorism in the Eighties* (New York: Pantheon Books, 1988), pp. 21–46. Philip Schlesinger, "On the Shape and Scope of Counter Insurgency Thought." In Gary Littlejohn (ed.), *Power and the State* (London: Croom Helm, 1978), p. 98–127. Michael T. Klare, "The Interventionist Impulse: US Military Doctrine for Low-Intensity Warfare." In Michael T. Klare and Peter Kornbluh (eds.), *Low-Intensity Warfare: Counter-insurgency, Proinsurgency and Antiterrorism in the Eighties* (New York: Pantheon Books, 1988), pp. 49–79. Stampnitzky, *Disciplining Terror*, pp. 60–1.

11   Stampnitzky, *Disciplining Terror*, p. 50.

12   Ibid.

13   Ibid., p. 79.

14   Edward S. Herman, *The Real Terror Network: Terrorism in Fact and Propaganda* (Cambridge, MA: South End Press, 1982), pp. 47–82.

15   Claire Sterling, *The Terror Network: The Secret War of International Terrorism* (New York: Holt, Rinehart and Winston, 1980), p.54.

16   Phillip Paull, International terrorism: the propaganda war. MA Thesis, San Francisco State University, 1982, p. 4.

17   This is noted by Stampnitzky, but she takes it as evidence that Alexander had 'split from most of' the terrorism mafia by 'becoming an advocate of the terror network theory' (Stampnitzky, *Disciplining Terror*, p. 124).

18   "CIA finds no proof of Soviet terror link," *The Times*, 30 March 1981, p. 5.
19   Paul Wilkinson, "USSR aid to terrorists," *The Times*, 4 April 1981, p. 13.
20   Stampnitzky, *Disciplining Terror*, pp. 41, 49
21   George H. W. Bush, *National Security Strategy of the United States* (Washington, D.C: The White House, 1990), pp. 13, 6.
22   Ibid., p. 6
23   Ibid., p. 8
24   Samuel P. Huntington, *The Clash of Civilizations and the Remaking of World Order* (London: Penguin, 1997), p. 217.
25   Huntington, *The Clash of Civilizations*, p. 213.
26   Bernard Lewis, "The roots of Muslim rage," *The Atlantic Monthly*, September 1990, pp. 47–60.
27   Ibid., p. 60.
28   Ibid., p. 59.
29   Arun Kundnani, *The Muslims are Coming!: Islamophobia, Extremism, and the Domestic War on Terror* (London: Verso Books, 2014), pp. 56–65.
30   Walter Laqueur, *The New Terrorism: Fanaticism and the Arms of Mass Destruction* (New York: Oxford University Press, 1999), pp. 4, 79.
31   Ibid., pp. 127–128
32   Ibid., p.129
33   Bruce Hoffman, *"Holy Terror": The Implications of Terrorism Motivated by a Religious Imperative* (Santa Monica, CA: RAND Corporation, 1993), p. 11. This paper was later published in the key 'terrorism studies' journal, *Studies in Conflict & Terrorism*. (Bruce Hoffman, "'Holy terror': the implications of terrorism motivated by a religious imperative." *Studies in Conflict & Terrorism*, Vol. 18, No.4, (1995), pp. 271–284.
34   Hoffman, *"Holy Terror"*, p. 2.
35   Ibid., p. 3
36   Amir Taheri, *Holy Terror: The Inside Story of Islamic Terrorism* (London: Sphere Books, 1987).
37   Ian O. Lesser, et al., *Countering the New Terrorism.* (Santa Monica, CA: The Rand Corporation, 1999), p. 2.
38   Bruce Hoffman, *Inside Terrorism.* Revised Edition (New York: Columbia University Press, 2006), p. 82.
39   Ibid., p. 271.
40   Audrey Kurth Cronin, "Behind the curve: globalization and international terrorism," *International Security*, Vol. 27, No. 3, (2002–3), p. 35.
41   Ibid., p. 30.
42   Ibid., p. 52.
43   Ibid., pp. 46–51.
44   Ibid., p. 51.
45   Peter R. Neumann, *Old and New Terrorism: Late Modernity, Globalization and the Transformation of Political Violence* (Cambridge: Polity, 2009), p. 150.

46 Ibid., p. 11.
47 Anthony Giddens, The Future of World Society: The New Terrorism. Lecture at the LSE, 10 November 2004.
48 Neumann, *Old and New Terrorism*, p. 118.
49 Ibid., pp. 118–121.
50 Stampnitzky, *Disciplining Terror*, p. 155.
51 Ibid., pp. 155, 154.
52 Mark Juergensmeyer, "Religion as a Cause of Terrorism." In Louise Richardson (ed.), *The Roots of Terrorism* (Abingdon and New York: Routledge, 2006), p. 143.
53 Neumann, *Old and New Terrorism*, p. 159
54 Lewis, "The roots of Muslim rage," p. 52.
55 Ibid., p. 53.
56 Peter Neumann, *Perspectives on Radicalisation and Political Violence. Papers from the First International Conference on Radicalisation and Political Violence, London 17–18 January 2008* (London: International Centre for the Study of Radicalisation and Political Violence), p. 4.
57 Vaira Vike-Freiberga and Peter R. Neumann, ICSR insight – violence and its causes, 26 October 2015. http://icsr.info/2015/10/icsr-insight-violence-causes/.
58 Stampnitzky, *Disciplining Terror*.
59 *Report of the Defense Science Board Task Force on Strategic Communication* (Washington, D.C: Office of the Under Secretary of Defense For Acquisition, Technology, and Logistics, 2004), p. 40.
60 Huntington, *The Clash of Civilizations*, p. 217.
61 *Global Terrorism Index: Measuring and Understanding the Impact of Terrorism* (Institute for Economics and Peace, 2015), pp. 100–104.
62 Vike-Freiberga and Neumann, ICSR insight.
63 Neumann, *Old and New Terrorism*, p. 101.
64 Ibid., p. 158.
65 Ibid., p. 162.
66 Brian Holden Reid, "Michael Howard and the evolution of modern war studies." *The Journal of Military History*, Vol. 73, No. 3, (2009), p. 880. "Strategic Studies Institute formed. Mr. Alastair Buchan first Director," *The Times*, 28 November, p. 6.
67 Jones David Martin and Mike Smith, "Contemporary Political Violence – New Terror in the Global Village." In David Martin Jones (ed.), *Globalisation and the New Terror: The Asia Pacific Dimension* (Cheltenham, UK and Northampton, MA, USA: Edward Elgar, 2004), pp. 4, 6.
68 David Omand, "Countering international terrorism: the use of strategy." *Survival*, Vol. 47, No. 4, (2006), p. 109.
69 Juergensmeyer, "Religion as a Cause of Terrorism," pp. 140–141
70 "Henry Sweetbaum," Powerbase, 15 July 2015. http://powerbase.info/index.php/Henry_Sweetbaum.
71 David Miller and Tom Mills, "The media and 'experts' in terrorism," *Discover Society*, 1 March 2015. www.discoversociety.org/2015/03/01/the-media-and-experts-in-terrorism/.

72   Tom Griffin et al, *The Henry Jackson Society and the Degeneration of British Neoconservatism: Liberal interventionism, Islamophobia and the 'War on Terror.'* (Glasgow: Public Interest Investigations, 2015).

73   Mills, Tom, Griffin, Tom and Miller, David, 2011. *The Cold War on British Muslims: An Examination of Policy Exchange and the Centre for Social Cohesion.* Glasgow: Public Interest Investigations. Griffin et al., *The Henry Jackson Society and the Degeneration of British Neoconservatism.*

74   Peter R. Neumann, "A crisis of identity and the appeal of jihad," *New York Times*, 5 July 2007. www.nytimes.com/2007/07/05/opinion/ 05iht-edneuman.1.6509818.html. Shiraz Maher, "The roots of radicalisation? It's identity, stupid," *Guardian*, 17 June 2015. www.theguardian.com/commentisfree/2015/jun/17/roots-radicalisation-identity-bradford-jihadist-causes.

75   Mills, Griffin and Miller, *The Cold War on British Muslims*, pp.43–44

76   Ibid.

77   Department for Communities and Local Government, Freedom of Information response, 7 May 2015. Purpose: counter-radicalisation training. Hansard, 15 March 2011, column 22WH www.publications .parliament.uk/pa/cm201011/cmhansrd/cm110315/halltext/ 110315h0001.htm.

78   Nafeez Ahmed, "UK's flawed counter-terrorism strategy," *Le Monde Diplomatique*, December 2013.

79   Paddy Hillyard, *Suspect Community: People's Experience of the Prevention of Terrorism Acts in Britain* (London: Pluto Press, 1993).

5 The Role of the Devoted Actor in War, Revolution, and Terrorism

SCOTT ATRAN

INTRODUCTION: THE DEVOTED ACTOR

"The Devoted Actor" is a theoretical framework developed by a group of scholars and policymakers at ARTIS International[1] – a nonprofit group that uses social science research to help resolve seemingly intractable political and cultural conflicts – to better understand the social and psychological mechanisms underlying people's willingness to make costly sacrifices for a group and a cause.[2] Our research indicates that when people act as "Devoted Actors," they are deontic (i.e., duty-based) agents who mobilize for collective action to protect cherished values in ways that are dissociated from likely risks or rewards. Devoted actors represent a dimension of thought and behavior distinct from instrumental rationality in resisting material compromises over such values.[3]

There is an evolutionary rationale to willingness to make costly sacrifices for the group, even fighting to the death and against all odds. Especially when a perceived outside threat to one's primary reference group is very high, and survival prospects very low, then only if sufficiently many members of a group are endowed with such a willingness to extreme sacrifice can the group hope to parry stronger but less devoted enemies who are less committed to disregarding the costs of action. From an evolutionary perspective, collective actions such as hunting and fighting are vulnerable to defectors, hence difficult to initiate. But if some highly motivated individuals are willing to initiate activity, this may reduce the costs for others to join; and such an "advancement in the standard of morality and an increase in the number of well-endowed men ... always ready to give aid to each other and to sacrifice themselves for the common good, would be victorious over other tribes."[4]

The Devoted Actor Framework integrates two hitherto independent research programs in cognitive theory, "sacred values" and "identity fusion," while drawing on key insights from sociological[5]and anthropological[6] analyses of religion and community.[7] Sacred values (SVs) are nonnegotiable preferences whose defense compels actions beyond evident reason; that is, regardless of calculable costs and consequences.[8] Identity fusion occurs when personal and group identities collapse into a unique identity to generate a collective sense of invincibility and special destiny.[9] These two programs account for different aspects of intractable intergroup conflicts; however, here I argue that SVs and identity fusion interact to produce willingness to make costly sacrifices for a primary reference group, even unto death, and the sacrifice of the totality of self-interests.

ASPECTS OF SACRED VALUES

Humans often make their greatest exertions and sacrifices, including killing or dying for ill or good, not just to preserve their own lives or kin and kith, but for an idea — the abstract conception they form of themselves, of "who I am" and "who we are." This is the "the privilege of absurdity; to which no living creature is subject, but man only" of which Hobbes wrote in *Leviathan*.[10] At least since the rise of chiefdoms and state-level societies, religion has been the locus of this privilege and power of absurdity.[11] For countless religious and nonreligious thinkers, from Augustine to Kierkegaard and Galileo to A.J. Ayer, what Hobbes deemed the "incomprehensible" nature of core religious beliefs, such as a sentient but bodiless deity, renders them immune to empirical or logical scrutiny.[12]

Religious consensus over values does not primarily involve fact checking or reasoned argument, but ensues from ritual communion and emotional bonding.[13] Costly commitment to idiosyncratic and apparently absurd beliefs and associated values can deepen trust by reliably identifying cooperators, while galvanizing group solidarity for common defense (whatever selection processes are involved[14]). Although all religions have a "marked idiosyncrasy" and bias in their moral message;[15] the more belligerent a group's environment, the more proprietary the group's SVs and rituals, increasing in-group reliance but also disbelief, distrust, and potential conflict with other groups.[16] By contrast, fully reasoned social contracts that regulate individual interests to share costs and benefits of cooperation can be less distancing between groups but also more liable to collapse: awareness that more advantageous distributions of risks and rewards may be available in the future makes defection more likely.[17] Even ostensibly secular nations and transnational movements usually contain important quasi-religious rituals and beliefs.[18] Even the most successful human rights movements, including liberal democracy as well as the civil rights movement to correct the "original sin" of its tolerance of slavery,[19] were inspired by beliefs "sacred and inalienable" (as Thomas Jefferson put it in his original draft of the Declaration of Independence).

Thus, while the term SVs intuitively denotes religious belief, in what follows SVs refer to any preferences regarding objects, beliefs, or practices that people treat as both incompatible or nonfungible with profane issues or economic goods, as when land or law becomes holy or hallowed, and as inseparable from people's conception of "self" and of "who we are." This includes the "secularized sacred" as exemplified, for example, in political notions of "human rights"[20] or in the transcendent ideological –*isms* that have dominated political life ever since the Enlightenment's secularization of the universal religious mission to redeem and save "humanity" through political revolution (colonialism, liberalism, socialism, anarchism, communism, fascism, etc.).[21]

Our prior research indicates that when people act in defense of SVs, they act in ways that cannot be reliably predicted by assessing material risks and rewards, costs, and consequences. This feature holds even when taking into consideration modifications and constraints on instrumental rationality, such as: cognitive limitations on gathering and processing information,[22] desire to avoid cognitive dissonance[23] or conform to group thinking,[24] lack of cultural awareness,[25] intrinsic indivisibility of resources,[26] or other psychological biases and ecological constraints.[27] Of course, instrumental and deontic (i.e., rules and obligations) matters interact in the real world to motivate the actions of individuals and groups, and any explanatory or descriptively adequate account must be able to model and predict this interaction.

Nevertheless, acts by devoted actors are not chiefly motivated by instrumental concerns. Instead, they are motivated by SVs that drive actions independent from, or all out-of-proportion to, likely outcomes. Devotion to some core values may represent universal responses to long-term evolutionary strategies that go beyond short-term individual calculations of self-interest but that advance individual interests in the aggregate and long run.[28] This may include devotion to children, to community, or even to a sense of fairness.[29] Other such values are clearly specific to particular societies and historical contingencies, such as the sacred status of cows in Hindu culture or the sacred status of the Sabbath or Jerusalem in Judaism, Christianity, and Islam. Sometimes, as with India's sacred cows[30] or sacred forests,[31] what is seen as inherently sacred in the present may have a more materialistic origin, representing the accumulated material wisdom of generations who resisted individual urges to gain an immediate advantage of meat or firewood for the long-term benefits of renewable sources of energy and sustenance. Yet, despite the longstanding material advantages associated with these values, unconditional devotion to such SVs in a rapidly changing world can also be materially disadvantageous: for example, when a hitherto closed commons suddenly becomes an open commons, then continued cultural commitment to values for protection of the commons may be highly maladaptive by facilitating extinction of native conservationists in areas now open to exploitation by foreign extractors.[32]

Our empirical studies in multiple cultures and distressed zones across the world indicate that sincere attachment to SVs entails: 1) commitment to a rule-bound logic of moral appropriateness to do what is morally right no matter the likely risks or rewards, rather than following a utilitarian calculus of costs and consequences;[33] 2) immunity to material tradeoffs, coupled with a "backfire effect," where offers of incentives or disincentives to give up SVs heighten refusal to compromise or negotiate;[34] 3) resistance to social influence and exit strategies,[35] which leads to unyielding social solidarity, and binds genetic strangers to voluntarily sacrifice for one another; 4) insensitivity to spatial and temporal discounting, where considerations of distant places and people, and even far past and future events, associated with SVs significantly outweigh concerns with here and now;[36] 5) brain-imaging patterns consistent with processing obligatory rules rather than weighing costs and benefits, and with processing perceived violations of such rules as emotionally agitating and resistant to social influence.[37] Commitment to SVs can mobilize parochial altruists, such as suicide bombers, to give their lives for the group.[38] And it can be key to success or failure of insurgent or revolutionary movements with far fewer material means than the armies or police arrayed against them (which tend to operate more on the basis of typical "rational" reward structures, such as calculated prospects of increased pay or promotion[39]). Ever since the nineteenth-century anarchists, science education in engineering and medical studies has been a frequent criterion of leadership for these movements because such a course of study demonstrates hands-on capability and potential for personal and costly sacrifice through long-term commitment to a course of study that requires delayed gratification. Al-Qaeda, like other revolutionary groups, was initially formed and led by fairly well-off and well-educated individuals, the plurality of whom studied engineering and medicine.[40]

DEVOTED ACTORS ARE DEONTIC ACTORS

Most theories and models related to violent intergroup conflict assume that civilians and leaders make rational calculations. [41] If the total cost of the war is less than the cost of the alternatives, they will support war. But in another set of studies,[42] we found that when people are confronted with violent situations, they ignore quantifiable costs and benefits consistently, relying instead on SVs. We asked a representative sample of 650 Israeli settlers in the West Bank about the dismantlement of their settlements as part of a peace agreement with Palestinians. Some subjects were asked about their willingness to engage in nonviolent protests, whereas others were asked about violence. Besides willingness to violently resist eviction, subjects rated how effective they thought the action would be and how morally right the decision was. When it came to nonviolent options such as picketing and blocking streets, rational behavior models predicted settlers' decisions. In deciding whether to engage in violence, the settlers reacted differently. Rather than how effective they thought violence would be in saving their homes, settlers' willingness to engage in violent protest depended only on how morally correct they considered it to be.

Our research with political leaders and general populations shows that SVs – not political games or economics – underscore seemingly intractable conflicts, like those between the Israelis and the Palestinians or Iran and the Western allies, which defy the rational give-and-take of business-like negotiation.[43] Consider the Israeli–Palestinian conflict, where rational cost–benefit analysis says the Palestinians ought to agree to forgo sovereignty over Jerusalem or the claim of refugees to return to homes in Israel in exchange for an autonomous state encompassing their other pre-1967 lands because they would gain more sovereignty and more land than they would renounce. They should support such an agreement even more if the United States and Europe sweeten the deal by giving every Palestinian family substantial, long-term economic assistance. Instead, we find that the financial sweetener makes Palestinians more opposed to the deal and more likely to support violence to oppose it, including suicide bombings. Israeli settlers also have rejected a two-state solution that required Israel to give up Judea and Samaria or to "recognize the legitimacy of the right of Palestinian refugees to return" (in an agreement not actually requiring Israel to absorb the refugees). But the Israelis, too, were even more opposed if the deal included additional long-term financial aid or a guarantee of living in peace and prosperity.[44]

In another series of studies, we found that a relatively small but politically significant portion of the Iranian population believes that acquiring nuclear energy (but not necessarily nuclear weapons) has become an SV in the sense that proposed economic incentives and disincentives backfire by leading to increased and more emotionally entrenched support.[45] Here, it appears that SVs can emerge for issues with relatively little historical background and significance when they become bound up with conflicts over collective identity: the sense of "who we are." For a minority of Iranians (13 percent in these experiments), the issue had become a sacred subject through association with religious rhetoric and ritual (e.g., Iranian women marching and chanting in favor of "nuclear rights" while waving the Koran). This group, which tends to be close to the regime, now believes a nuclear program is bound up with national identity and with Islam itself, so that offering material rewards or punishments to abandon the program only increases anger and support for it.

SVs do not make people opposed to any sort of compromise. Instead, they appear to invoke specific taboos, protecting these values against material tradeoffs. Offering people materially irrelevant symbolic gestures can work where material incentives do not. For example, Palestinians were more willing to consider recognizing the right of Israel to exist if the Israelis offered an official apology for Palestinian suffering in the 1948 war. Similarly, Israeli settlers were less disapproving of compromising sacred land for peace if Hamas and the other major Palestinian groups symbolically recognized Israel.[46]

Our survey results were mirrored by our discussions with political leaders.[47] Mousa Abu Marzook (the deputy chairman of Hamas) said "No" when we proposed a trade-off for peace without granting a right of return. He became angry when we added in the idea of substantial American aid for rebuilding: "No, we do not sell ourselves for any amount." But when we mentioned a potential Israeli apology for 1948, he said: "Yes, an apology is important, as a beginning. It's not enough because our houses and land were taken away from us and something has to be done about that." His response suggested that progress on SVs might open the way for negotiations on material issues, rather than the reverse. We obtained a similar reaction from Israeli leader Benjamin Netanyahu. We asked him whether he would seriously consider accepting a two-state solution following the 1967 borders if all major Palestinian factions, including Hamas, were to recognize the right of the Jewish people to an independent state in the region. He answered, "O.K., but the Palestinians would have to show that they sincerely mean it, change their anti-Semitic textbooks." Making these sorts of wholly intangible symbolic but sincere gestures, like recognition of a right to exist or an apology, simply does not compute in any utilitarian calculus. And yet the science suggests that these gestures may be the best way to cut through the knot.

More systematic understanding of what kinds of symbolic gestures involving SVs are likely to be effective in conflict prevention and resolution, including signatures of emotional sincerity, could provide novel possibilities for breakthroughs to avoid or lessen conflict. More recently, in a meeting of senior Iranians, Saudis, Israelis, Americans, and British arranged by members of our team and Lord John Alderdice (Convenor, UK House of Lords) at Oxford on the nuclear issue in early September 2013, we informally monitored expressions of devotion to values, including emotional attachment, and suggested opening negotiations via a symbolic gesture evoking SVs rather than political positions. In response, we received a message that Iran's President Rouhani would publicly acknowledge the Holocaust in New York (which U.S. and Israeli officials told us would be a positive development for negotiations).

These and other studies suggest that social groups have "sacred rules" for which their people would fight and risk serious loss/death rather than compromise. In another study with a representative sample of over 700 adults in the West Bank and Gaza, we asked:

> If a person wanted to carry out a bombing (which some … call suicide attacks) against the enemies of Palestine but his father becomes ill, and his family begs the chosen martyr to take care of his father, would it be acceptable to delay the attack indefinitely?
>
> If a person wanted to carry out a bombing (which some … call suicide attacks) against the enemies of Palestine but his family begs him to delay martyrdom indefinitely because there was a significantly high chance the chosen martyr's family would be killed in retaliation, would it be acceptable to delay the attack indefinitely?

Palestinians tended to reason about political violence in a noninstrumental manner by showing more disapproval over a delay of a martyrdom attack to rescue an entire family than over a delay of a martyrdom attack to take care of an ill father. These results indicate that when people are reasoning between duty to war or to family, they are not making instrumental decisions but decisions based on perceptions of moral obligations that can change as a result of instrumentally irrelevant alterations in context.[48] If people perceive that a sacred rule was violated, they may feel morally obliged to retaliate against the wrongdoers — even if the retaliation does more harm than good.

THE IMPORTANCE OF GROUP DYNAMICS AND IDENTITY FUSION

Our fieldwork with captured and would-be suicide terrorists, and political and militant leaders and supporters in violent conflict situations, suggests that some behaviors that punctuate the history of human intergroup conflict do indeed go beyond instrumental concerns.[49] Historical examples include the self-sacrifice of Spartans at Thermopylae, the Jewish Zealots in revolt against Rome, defenders of the Alamo, the Waffen SS "volunteer death squads" during the Soviet siege of Budapest, some cohorts of Japanese Kamikaze, and the jihadi pilot bombers of 9/11.[50] Such events exemplify that humans fight and kill in the name of abstract, often ineffable values – like God, national destiny, or salvation.[51]

Although SVs may operate as necessary moral imperatives to action, they are not sufficient. It is important to understand that group morality does not operate simply from ideological canon or decontextualized principles that drive decisions and actions, but it is almost always embedded and distributed in social groups; most effectively in intimate networks of "imagined kin": brotherhoods, motherlands, fatherlands, homelands, and the like.[52] Knowledge of the moral imperatives that drive people to great exertions toward one political goal or another, as well the group dynamics that bind individuals to sacrifice for one another in the name of those values, appear indispensable to extreme actions where prospects of defeat and death are very high, as with terrorism and revolution.

Thus, our working hypothesis is that parochially altruistic action occurs, or devoted acts are created, when self identity becomes fused with a unique collective identity, and when identity itself is fused with SVs. Important values may influence extreme behavior particularly to the extent that they become embedded or fused with identity and internalized. When internalized, important moral values lessen societal costs of policing morality through self-monitoring, and blind members to exit strategies.[53]

There is more to group dynamics than just collections of people, their behavior, and ideas. There is the web of relationships that make the group more than the sum of its individual members.[54] It is this networking among members that distributes thoughts and tasks that no one part may completely control or even understand.[55] Case studies of suicide terrorism and related forms of violent extremism suggest that "people almost never kill and die [just] for the Cause, but for each other: for their group, whose cause makes their imagined family of genetic strangers – their brotherhood, fatherland, motherland, homeland."[56]

In this vein, the theory of "identity fusion" holds that when people's collective identities become fused with their personal self-concept, they subsequently display increased willingness to engage in extreme progroup behavior when the group is threatened.[57] As such, fusion can help us understand part of the complexity of group dynamics that leads to action when privileged values are threatened. Fusion theory differs from various social identity theories in emphasizing group cohesion through social networking and emotional bonding of people and values, rather than through processes of categorization and association, thus empowering individuals and their groups with sentiments of exceptional destiny and invincibility.

In recent cross-cultural experiments, Swann et al.[58] begin from observations made by Atran[59] for militant and terrorist groups and find that when fused people perceive that group members share core physical attributes and values, they are more likely to project familial ties common in smaller groups onto the extended group. This enhances willingness to fight and die for a larger group that is strongly identified with those values, such as a religious "brotherhood." Considerations of commitment to comrades and cause bear directly on some of the world's most pressing concerns. Indeed, in recent remarks,[60] President Obama endorsed the judgment of his U.S. National Intelligence Director: "We underestimated the Viet Cong... we underestimated ISIL [the Islamic State] and overestimated the fighting capability of the Iraqi army ... It boils down to predicting the will to fight, which is an imponderable."[61] Yet, if the methods and results suggested by our research ultimately prove reliable, then predicting who is willing to fight and who isn't, and why, could be ponderable indeed, and important to the evaluation and execution of political strategy.

In this regard, Whitehouse et al.[62] provide evidence that fusion with a family-like group of comrades in arms, which can be felt as even stronger than genetic family ties, may have underpinned the willingness of recent revolutionary combatants in Libya to fight on, even in the face of death and defeat. But apart from this single study of fighters in the field, fusion studies have concerned mostly student populations in hypothetical scenarios rather than populations in actual conflict zones, and have neglected the role of SVs in generating devoted actions. Accordingly, in another set of studies, we provided historical analyses from recent wars and presented empirical evidence from North Africa and Europe in support of the Devoted Actor Hypothesis:[63]

> Devoted Actor Hypothesis: People will become willing to protect morally important or sacred values through costly sacrifice and extreme actions, even being willing to kill and die, particularly when such values are embedded in or fused with group identity, becoming intrinsic to "Who I am" and "Who We are."[64]

In these studies, people expressed "parochial altruism" the most when they were fused with a kin-like group of like-minded friends, and felt that a cherished value they considered sacred was under threat. Specifically, Moroccans interviewed and tested in two neighborhoods associated with terrorist actions, where we had previously carried out anthropological fieldwork,[65] expressed willingness to make costly sacrifices for the implementation of strict Sharia, when they were fused with a kin-like group of friend and considered Sharia law as sacred. They were also most supportive of militant Jihad. Complementing this experimental study in the field, an online study showed that Spaniards who were fused with a kin-like group of friends and considered democracy as sacred, were most willing to make costly sacrifices for democracy, after being reminded of jihadi terrorism.[66] They were also more likely to consider their own group more formidable and jihadis as weak, which may facilitate costly actions against the "enemy." These results corroborate previous findings among Americans and Palestinians that devoted actors are most likely to commit themselves to extreme actions of parochial altruism if they perceive themselves to be under existential threat from outside groups.[67]

KURDEITY VS. THE CALIPHATE: RECENT RESEARCH AT THE FRONT

Thus far, discussion of our studies has focused mainly on expressed willingness to make costly sacrifices for fused groups and sacred causes. Although the enduring and seemingly intractable nature of the conflicts from which we have drawn our subject populations suggest a strong relationship between expressed and actual willingness to make costly sacrifices, here we have no direct measures to confirm the relationship (although we do have outcome measures that involve lesser material sacrifices). In what follows, however, the subjects are militants and frontline combatants, whose expressed willingness to make costly sacrifices, including fighting and dying, is directly confirmed through participant observation of their actions.

In this regard, in March 2015, we completed the first round of study in Kirkuk, Iraq with captured fighters from the Islamic State, and with Kurds in the frontline areas between Mosul and Erbil. We found that the Kurds demonstrate a will to fight that matches the Islamic State's. When we asked the Islamic State prisoners "What is Islam?" they answered "my life." Yet it was clear that they knew little about the Quran, or Islamic history, other than what they'd heard from al-Qaeda and Islamic State propaganda. For them, the cause of religion is fused with the vision of a caliphate – a joining of political and religious rule – that kills or subjugates any nonbeliever. By contrast, the Kurds' commitment to Islam is surpassed by their commitment to national identity; theirs is a more open-minded version of Islam. They have defended Yazidis and Christians, as well as Arab Sunnis, who make up the bulk of the more than one million displaced persons in Iraqi Kurdistan. But perhaps what most reveals commitment by the Kurds is how they hold the line with so little material assistance.[68]

We interviewed and tested (on fusion, SVs, costly sacrifices) 28 Kurdish combatants and 10 noncombatants (e.g., suppliers, medics, etc.) in battle areas 1 to 3 kilometers from forces of the Islamic State, including respondents randomly chosen among special forces (Zerevani) from the front at Mosul Dam, Peshmerga fighters from the Kurdistan regional Government at (the now depopulated village of) Rwala on the Mahmour front, and Kurdish soldiers from a joint Kurd-Arab Sunni unit of the Iraqi Army at the Qeremerdi forward outpost.[69] Using our standard experimental procedures,[70] we found that 36 respondents are fused with "Kurds," 35 with "family," 23 with "close, family-like group" of comrades, and 14 with "Islam." But in rankings of relative importance of identity fusion, 21 respondents reported that fusion with "Kurds" trumps all other forms of identity fusion; 3 privileged Islam, while only 1 respondent considered fusion with "family" as foremost, and *no* respondent held that "close-family like group" as primary. There were also more than twice as many expressions of devotion to "Kurdistan" (N=23) than to democratic values of "electoral democracy" and "free speech" (N=10) as SVs for which respondents are willing to fight and die. Finally, all but one person who held "Kurdistan" as an SV were fully fused with "Kurds," indicating that defense of "Kurdeity" (as the Kurds themselves term their commitment to fellow Kurds, as well as to defense of "our Kurdistan homeland") is the most important obligation in life, deserving of costly sacrifice unto death if necessary (i.e., 22 respondents – several of whom had previously been wounded – would be willing to die and sacrifice their families in defense of Kurdeity, versus 3 who would be willing to sacrifice Kurdeity and family for Islam, and 1 who would be willing to sacrifice Kurdeity and Islam for family).

Indeed, we have frequently encountered devoted actors who clearly demonstrate emotional ties to family and concerns for self, yet show their willingness to sacrifice these important interests. For example, one Kurdish fighter told us that during an Islamic State offensive that took his village, he had a (tragic) choice: to go into the village before IS forces had established control and take his family out, or help stabilize the front to prevent IS from advancing. The choice, he said, haunts his every waking hour. In this short exchange, he demonstrated the pain of trading off his familial obligations for the sake of fighting for Kurdeity (and we found similar sentiments expressed, and acted upon, in our interviews with fighters from the Islamic State and al-Qaeda's Jabhat an-Nusra, but *not* in interviews with Iraqi army).

These preliminary findings with frontline participants in the struggle for survival against the Islamic State suggests that, at least in this case (and quite possibly others), larger groups that are sacralized (in terms of territory, cultural history, language, etc.) can be the primary locus of identity fusion, and of the interaction between identity fusion and SVs in producing costly sacrifices, including fighting and dying. If this is so, then the primary relationship between identity fusion and willingness to fight needn't always be at the level of a close, family-like group. In other words, the strongest and most powerful forms of sacrifice for group and cause do not always require a process of "upscaling" from a localized family-like cohort of comrades to an extended ideological community, but may inhere in a larger, sacralized community to begin with, especially in "tight societies" that have strong social norms and strict channels of socialization.[71] Such larger and tight societies include the geographically bounded but stateless cultural sphere of Kurdistan, as well as the global jihadi archipelago, where information from across the world and cyberspace narrows mightily to fit the imagined utopia of the Caliphate – a transcultural niche, for which the actors of Kurdistan are fighting unto death to defeat and the devoted actors of the Islamic State are fighting unto death to make real.

CONCLUSION: LIBERAL DEMOCRACY, THE ISLAMIC STATE, AND THE FUTURE OF OUR WORLD

For the future of democracy and human rights, the core existential issue may be: how is it that values of liberal and open democracy increasingly appear to be losing ground to those of narrow ethno-nationalisms and radical Islam, in a tacit alliance that is tearing the European middle class (the mainstay of European democracy) in ways similar to the undermining of republican values by fascists and communists in the 1920s and '30s? Consider this:

> "Mr. Hitler," wrote George Orwell in his review of *Mein Kampf*, "has grasped the falsity of the hedonistic attitude to life. Nearly all western thought ... certainly all 'progressive' thought, has assumed tacitly that human beings desire nothing beyond ease, security and avoidance of pain."[72] In such a view of life, there is no room for greatness and glory, which, as Darwin noted, motivates heroes and martyrs to motivate others to survive and even triumph against great material odds. "Hitler knows ... that human beings don't only want comfort, safety, short working-hours, hygiene, birth-control and, in general, common sense; they also, at least intermittently, want struggle and self-sacrifice."

In our preferred world of liberal democracy, tolerance of diversity and distributive justice, violence – especially extreme forms of mass bloodshed – are generally considered pathological or evil expressions of human nature gone awry, or collateral damage as the unintended consequence of righteous intentions. But across most human history and cultures, violence against other groups is universally claimed by the perpetrators to be a sublime matter of moral virtue; for without a claim to sublime virtue, it is difficult to endeavor to kill large numbers of people innocent of direct harm to others.

In this vein, to dismiss the Islamic State as just another form of "terrorism" or "violent extremism," to insist that it's brutality is simply "immoral," "nihilistic," or "apocalyptic" and therefore inevitably self-destructive; or to refuse to call it by the name it calls itself in the vain hope that doing so will somehow undermine it, is counterproductive and deluding. From an evolutionary and historical vantage, no developments are really deviant or extreme unless they quickly die, for those developments that continue to survive are the very stuff of historical change and evolution. From this perspective – and in light of our interviews and psychological experiments with IS and AQ (Nusra) fighters on the ground, and with volunteers from Europe and North Africa, as well as those who oppose and fight them – the rise of IS is, arguably, the most influential and politically novel countercultural force in the world today. Here, peer communities of imagined kin – bands of "brothers and sisters" drawn willy-nilly from across more than 80 countries and many more ethnic groups – commit ritual oaths and perform intensely violent actions in devotion to a new world order.[73]

Of all those opposed to IS, only the devoted actors of Kurdeity succeed, on their own turf, in resisting the devoted actors of the Islamic State. But, because this is a fight for the future and for the young people who will be that future, what can be done to mobilize yearning youth to a countervailing cause? What dreams may come from current government policies that offer little beyond promises of comfort and security?[74] People who are willing to sacrifice everything, including their lives – the totality of their self-interests – will not be lured away just by material incentives or disincentives. The science suggests that SVs are best opposed with other SVs that inspire devotion, or by sundering the fused social networks that embed those values.

Across cultures and through much of human history, religions – and, most formidably, variants of the Abrahamic religions – have been the surest and most sustained repositories of SVs and a privileged abode of devoted actors.[75] Social contracts and secular ideologies that are not based on transcendent beliefs that fuse individuals to communities and blind them to exit strategies, and which are largely immune to logical and empirical scrutiny from within, tend to be less enduring. So the big question is: if not religion, then what can best compete?

ACKNOWLEDGMENTS

The research was supported by the Minerva initiatives of the Air Force Office of Scientific Research (MINERVA FA9550-14-1-0030 DEF) and the Office of Naval Research (Grant N000141310054).

Endnotes

1   See http://artisresearch.com/.
2   Scott Atran, Robert Axelrod, and Richard Davis, "Sacred Barriers to Conflict Resolution," *Science* 317 (2007), pp. 1039–1040; Scott Atran, *Talking to the Enemy: Violent Extremism, Sacred Values, and What It Means to be Human* (London: Penguin, 2010); Scott Atran, Hammad Sheikh, and Ángel Gómez, "Devoted Actors Fight for Close Comrades and Sacred Cause," *Proceedings of the National Academy of Sciences,*

USA, 111 (2014), pp.17702–17703; Scott Atran and Jeremy Ginges, "Devoted Actors and the Moral Foundations of Intractable Inter-group Conflict," in Jean Decety, and Thalia Wheatley, eds, *The Moral Brain* (Cambridge, MA: MIT Press, 2015), 69–85; Hammad Sheikh, Jeremy Ginges, Alin Coman, and Scott Atran, "Religion, Group Threat, and Sacred Values," *Judgment and Decision Making* 7 (2012), pp. 110–118.

3   Scott Atran and Robert Axelrod, "Reframing Sacred Values," *Negotiation Journal* 24 (2008), pp. 221–246; Jeremy Ginges, Scott Atran, Sonya Sachdeva, and Douglas Medin, "Psychology Out of the Laboratory: The Challenge of Violent Extremism," *American Psychologist* 66 (2011), pp. 507–519; Morteza Dehghani, Scott Atran, Rumen Iliev, Sonya Sachdeva, Jeremy Ginges, and Douglas Medin, "Sacred Values and Conflict Over Iran's Nuclear Program," *Judgment and Decision Making* 5 (2010), pp. 540–546; Gregory Berns and Scott Atran, "The Biology of Cultural Conflict," *Philosophical Transactions of the Royal Society – B* 367 (2012), pp. 633–639.

4   Charles Darwin, *The Descent of Man, and Selection in Relation to Sex* (London, England: John Murray, 1871).

5   Émile Durkheim, *The Elementary Forms of Religious Life* (New York: The Free Press, [1912] 2012); Max Weber, *The Sociology of Religion* (Boston: Beacon Press, 1963).

6   Victor Turner, *The Ritual Process* (Chicago, Illinois: Aldine, 1969); Roy Rappaport, *Ritual and Religion in the Making of Humanity* (New York: Cambridge University Press, 1999).

7   Mircea Eliade, *The Sacred and the Profane* (New York: Harcourt Brace, 1959).

8   Jeremy Ginges, Scott Atran, Douglas Medin, and Khalil Shikaki, "Sacred Bounds on the Rational Resolution of Violent Political Conflict," *Proceedings of the National Academy of Sciences, USA* 104 (2007), pp. 7357–7360; Jonathan Baron and Mark Spranca, "Protected Values," *Organizational Behavior and Decision Processes* 70 (1997), pp. 1–16; Philip Tetlock, "Thinking the Unthinkable: Sacred Values and Taboo Cognitions," *Trends in Cognitive Science* 7 (2003) pp. 320–324; Jesse Graham and Jonathan Haidt, "Sacred Values and Evil Adversaries," in Phillip Shaver and Mario Mikulincer, *The Social Psychology of Morality* (New York: APA Books, 2013), pp. 11–31.

9   William Swann, Jolanda Jetten, Ángel Gómez, Harvey Whitehouse, and Brock Bastian, "When Group Membership Gets Personal: A Theory of Identity Fusion," *Psychological Review* 119 (2012), pp. 441–456.

10 Thomas Hobbes, *Leviathan* (New York: E.P. Dutton [1651] 1901), p. 29.

11 Ara Norenzayan, *Big Gods: How Religion Transformed Cooperation and Conflict* (Princeton: Princeton University Press, 2013); Scott Atran, "Moralizing Religions: Prosocial or a Privilege of Wealth?" *Behavioral and Brain Sciences* (in press).

12 Scott Atran, *In Gods We Trust: The Evolutionary Landscape of Religion* (New York: Oxford University Press, 2002). See also Alfred Jules Ayer, *Language, Truth, and Logic* (London: Penguin, [1936] 2001); Søren

Kierkegaard, *Kierkegaard's Concluding Unscientific Postscript* (Princeton: Princeton University Press, [1844] 1941); Hobbes, *Leviathan*.

13   Turner, *The Ritual Process*; Scott Atran and Ara Norenzayan, "Religion's Evolutionary Landscape: Counterintuition, Commitment, Compassion, Communion. *Behavioral and Brain Sciences* 27 (2004), pp. 713–730.

14   Scott Atran and Joseph Henrich, "The Evolution of Religion: How Cognitive By-products, Adaptive Learning Heuristics, Ritual Displays, and Group Competition Generate Deep Commitments to Prosocial Religions," *Biological Theory* 5 (2010), pp. 18–30; Ara Norenzayan and Azim Shariff, "The Origin and Evolution of Religious Prosociality," *Science* 322 (2008), pp. 58–62.

15   Clifford Geertz, "Religion as a Cultural System," in Clifford Geertz, ed., *The Interpretation of Cultures* (New York: Basic Books, 1973), p. 87.

16   Richard Sosis, Howard Kress, and James Boster, "Scars for War: Evaluating Alternative Signaling Explanations for Cross-cultural Variance in Ritual Costs," *Evolution and Human Behavior* 28 (2007), pp. 234–247; David Sloan Wilson, *Darwin's Cathedral* (Chicago: University of Chicago Press, 2002).

17   Atran and Axelrod, "Reframing Sacred Values."

18   Benedict Anderson, *Imagined Communities: Reflections on the Origin and Spread of Nationalism* (London, England: Verso, 1983).

19   Simon Schama, *The American Future: A History* (New York: Ecco, 2009), p. 182.

20   Christian Smith et al., "Roundtable on the Sociology of Religion," *Journal of the American Academy of Religion* 81 (2013), pp. 1–36.

21   John Gray, *Al Qaeda and What It Means to be Modern* (London: Faber and Faber, 2007). Marvin Harris, "Cultural Ecology of India's Sacred Cattle," *Current Anthropology* 7 (1966), pp. 261–276.

22   Herbert Simon, *Models of Bounded Rationality* (Cambridge, MA: MIT Press, 1997).

23   Leon Festinger, *A Theory of Cognitive Dissonance* (Stanford: Stanford University Press, 1962).

24   Solomon Asch, *Social Psychology* (New York: Oxford University Press, 1987).

25   Thomas Schelling, *The Strategy of Conflict* (Cambridge, MA: Harvard University Press, 1960).

26   James Fearon, "Rationalist Explanations for War," *International Organization* 49 (1995), pp. 379–414.

27   Daniel Kahneman, *Thinking Fast and Slow* (New York: Farrar, Straus and Giroux, 2011).

28   Scott Atran and Douglas Medin, *The Native Mind and the Cultural Construction of Nature* (Cambridge, MA: MIT Press, 2008).

29   Atran and Axelrod, "Reframing Sacred Values."

30   Harris, "Cultural Ecology of India's Sacred Cattle."

31   Krishna Upadhaya, Harendra Pandey, P.S. Law, and Radhey Tripathi, "Tree Diversity in Sacred Groves of the Jaintia Hills in Meghalaya, Northeast India." *Biodiversity and Conservation* 12 (2003) pp. 583–597.

32 Atran and Medin, *The Native Mind.*

33 Scott Atran, "Genesis of Suicide Terrorism," *Science* 299 (2003), pp. 1534–1539; Will Bennis, Douglas Medin, and Daniel Bartels, "The Costs and Benefits of Calculations and Moral Rules," *Perspectives on Psychological Science* 5 (2010), pp. 187–202; Jeremy Ginges and Scott Atran, "War As a Moral Imperative – Not Practical Politics by Other Means," *Proceedings of the Royal Society – B* 27 (2011), pp. 2930–2938.

34 Ginges, Atran, Medin, and Shikaki, "Sacred Bounds"; Dehghani, Atran, Iliev, Sachdeva, Ginges, and Medin, "Sacred Values and Conflict."

35 Atran and Henrich, "The Evolution of Religion"; Hammad Sheikh, Jeremy Ginges, and Scott Atran, "Sacred Values in Intergroup Conflict: Resistance to Social Influence, Temporal Discounting, and Exit Strategies," *Annals of the New York Academy of Sciences* 1299 (2013), pp. 11–24.

36 Atran, *Talking to the Enemy*; Sheikh, Ginges, and Atran, "Sacred Values in Intergroup Conflict."

37 Gregory Berns, Emily Bell, C. Monica Capra, Michael Prietula, Sara Moore, Brittany Anderson, Jeremy Ginges, and Scott Atran, "The Price of Your Soul: Neural Evidence for the Non-Utilitarian Representation of Sacred Values," *Philosophical Transactions of the Royal Society – B* 367 (2012), pp. 754–762; Melanie Pincus, Lisa La Viers, Michael Prietula, and Gregory Berns. "Conforming Brain and Deontological Resolve," *PlosOne* 9:8 (2014), doi: 10.1371/journal.pone.0106061.

38 Atran, "Genesis of Suicide Terrorism"; Jeremy Ginges, Ian Hansen, and Ara Norenzayan, "Religion and Popular Support for Suicide Attacks," *Psychological Science* 20 (2009), pp. 2–230.

39 Scott Atran and Jeremy Ginges, "Religious and Sacred Imperatives in Human Conflict." *Science* 336 (2012), pp. 855–857.

40 Peter Bergen and Michael Lind, "A Matter of Pride: Why We Can't Buy off Osama Bin Laden," *Democracy Journal*, winter (2007), available at www.democracyjournal.org/article.php?ID=6496; Diego Gambetta and Steffan Hertog, "Engineers of Jihad," *Sociology Working Papers*, no. 2007–10 (2007), available at www.nuff.ox.ac.uk/users/gambetta/Engineers%20of%20Jihad.pdf.

41 Fearon, "Rationalist Explanations for War"; Carl von Clausewitz, *On War* (New York: Barnes and Noble, [1832] 1956).

42 Ginges and Atran, "War as a Moral Imperative."

43 Atran, Axelrod, and Davis, "Sacred Barriers to Conflict Resolution"; Dehghani, Atran, Iliev, Sachdeva, Ginges, and Medin, "Sacred Values and Conflict"; Ginges, Atran, Medin, and Shikaki, "Sacred Bounds"; Ginges, Atran, Sachdeva, and Medin, "Psychology Out of the Laboratory."

44 Ginges, Atran, Medin, and Shikaki, "Sacred Bounds."

45 Dehghani, Atran, Iliev, Sachdeva, Ginges, and Medin, "Sacred Values and Conflict."

46 Ginges, Atran, Medin, and Shikaki, "Sacred Bounds"; Scott Atran and Jeremy Ginges, "How Words Could End a War," *New York Times*,

January 24, 2009, available at www.nytimes.com/2009/01/25/opinion/25atran.html?pagewanted=all&_r=0.

47   Atran, Axelrod, and Davis, "Sacred Barriers to Conflict Resolution."

48   Jeremy Ginges and Scott Atran, "Why Do People Participate in Violent Collective Action: Selective Incentives or Parochial Altruism?" *Annals of the New York Academy of Sciences* 1167 (2009), pp. 115–123.

49   Atran, *Talking to the Enemy*.

50   Atran, *Talking to the Enemy*; Ginges, Atran, Sachdeva, and Medin, "Psychology Out of the Laboratory."

51   Atran and Ginges, "Religious and Sacred Imperatives."

52   Atran *Talking to the Enemy*; Scott Atran, *US Government Efforts to Counter Violent Extremism*, US Senate Armed Services Committee, 2010–2011. Testimony, Response to Questions, 2011, available at www.jjay.cuny.edu/US_Senate_Hearing_on_Violent_Extremism.pdf.

53   Atran and Henrich, "The Evolution of Religion."

54   Robin Dunbar, Chris Knight, and Camilla Power, eds. *The Evolution of Culture* (Edinburgh: Edinburgh University Press, 1999).

55   Dan Sperber, "Anthropology and Psychology: Towards an Epidemiology of Representations," *Man*, N.S. 20 (1985), pp. 73–89; Atran, *In Gods We Trust*.

56   Atran, *Talking to the Enemy*, p. 33.

57   Swann, Jetten, Gómez, Whitehouse, and Bastian, "When Group Membership Gets Personal."

58   William Swann, Michael Buhrmester, Ángel Gómez, Jolanda Jetten, Brock Bastian, Alexandra Vázquez, and Airong Zhang, "What Makes a Group Worth Dying For? Identity Fusion Fosters Perception of Familial Ties, Promoting Self-sacrifice," *Journal of Personality and Social Psychology* 106 (2014), pp. 912–926.

59   Atran, *Talking to the Enemy*.

60   Sebastian Payne, "Obama: U.S. Misjudged the Rise of the Islamic State, Ability of Iraqi Army," *Washington Post*, September 28, 2014, available at www.washingtonpost.com/world/national-security/obama-us-under estimated-the-rise-of-the-islamic-state-ability-of-iraqi-army/2014/09/28/9417ab26-4737-11e4-891d-713f052086a0_story.html.

61   David Ignatius, "James Clapper: We Underestimated the Islamic State's 'Will to Fight'," *Washington Post*, September 18, 2014, available at: www.washingtonpost.com/opinions/david-ignatius-we-underesti mated-the-islamic-state-james-clapper-says/2014/09/18/f0f17072-3f6f-11e4-9587-5dafd96295f0_story.html.

62   Harvey Whitehouse, Brian McQuinn, Michael Buhrmester, and William Swann, "Brothers in Arms: Libyan Revolutionaries Bond Like Families," *Proceedings of the National Academy of Sciences, USA* 111 (2014), pp. 17783–17785.

63   Atran, Sheikh, and Gómez, 2014; Hammad Sheikh, Ángel Gómez, and Scott Atran, "Empirical Evidence for the Devoted Actor Model," *Current Anthropology* (in press).

64   Atran and Ginges, "Devoted Actors and the Moral Foundations."

65   Atran, *Talking to the Enemy*.

66 The term "jihadi" is commonly used to refer to self-declared *mujahedin* (holy warriors) of the global movement for the worldwide defense, spread and conquest of the world by Islam: ruled in accordance with a strict, literalist version of Islamic law, ethics and administration, or *sharia*, that requires absolute obedience and denies that interpretation is possible (Sayyid Qutb, *Milestones (Ma'alim fil Tariq)* (1964), available at www.izharudeen.com/uploads/4/1/2/2/4122615/milestones_www.iz harudeen.com.pdfpdf). Any nominal Muslim who denies this truth, or works against it, is subject to excommunication (*takfir*) and may be killed as an apostate (*murtad*). Thus, "jihadis" are also commonly referred to as "tafkiris." In jihadi-takfiri canon, the contrast between "greater jihad" as an inner struggle to submit to God, and the "lesser jihad" of physical holy war, is spurious. Upon the Prophet Mohammed's death, his companions (*al-salaf al-salahin*), especially the early Caliphs Omar and Othman, considered jihad only as offensive war to expand the frontiers of the House of Islam (*Dar al-Islam*) against infidels (*kuffar* and *taghut*; see Abu Bakr Naji, "The Management of Savagery [Idaraat at-Tawahoush]" [2004], available at https://azelin.files.wordpress.com/2010/08/abu-bakr-naji-the-management-of-savagery-the-most-critical-stage-through-which-the-umma-will-pass.pdf) and their House of War (*Dar al-Harb*). The idea of "greater jihad" as inner struggle appears to be a Sufi introduction from the Abbasid period (Tamim Ansary, *Destiny Disrupted: A History of the World through Islamic Eyes* [New York: Public Affairs, 2009]). Jihadis reject Sufism as sinful (*haram*) and subject to takfir.

67 Sheikh, Ginges, Coman, and Atran, "Religion, Group Threat, and Sacred Values."

68 Scott Atran and Douglas Stone, "The Kurds' Heroic Stand Against ISIS," *New York Times*, March 16, 2015, available at www.nytimes.com/2015/03/16/opinion/the-kurds-heroic-stand-against-isis.html.

69 *Ibid.*

70 Sheikh, Gómez, and Atran, "Empirical Evidence for the Devoted Actor Model," in press.

71 Michele Gelfand et al., "Differences between Tight and Loose Cultures: A 33-nation Study," *Science* 332 (2011), pp. 1100–1104.

72 George Orwell, "Review of *Mein Kampf*," in Sonia Orwell and Ian Angus, eds, *The Collected Essays, Journalism, and Letters of George Orwell*, vol. 2 [New York: Harcourt, Brace Jovanovich, (1940) 1968].

73 Scott Atran, Lydia Wilson, Richard Davis, and Hammad Sheikh, "Devoted Actors, Sacred Values, and Willingness to Fight: Preliminary Studies with ISIL Volunteers and Kurdish Frontline Fighters." Presented in conjunction with the U.S. Dept. of Defense Minerva Initiative to the Strategic Multilayer Assessment of ISIL in support of SOCCNET, November 2014, Washington DC, available at http://artisresearch.com/wp-content/uploads/2014/11/Atran_Soccnet_MINERVA_ISIS.pdf.

74 Scott Atran, "The Role of Youth in Countering Violent Extremism and Promoting Peace," address to the United Nations Security Council,

New York, April 23, 2015, available at http://blogs.plos.org/neuroan thropology/2015/04/25/scott-atran-on-youth-violent-extremism-and-promoting-peace/.

75   But the popular notion of a "clash of civilizations" (Samuel Hunting-ton, *The Clash of Civilizations and the Remaking of the World Order* [New York: Simon & Schuster, 1996]) between Islam and the West is woefully misleading. Violent extremism represents not the resurgence of traditional cultures, but their collapse, as young people unmoored from millennial traditions flail about in search of a social identity that gives personal significance and glory. This is the dark side of global-ization (Atran, "The Role of Youth"). They radicalize to find a firm identity in a flattened world where vertical lines of communication between the generations are replaced by horizontal peer-to-peer attachments that can span the globe. For example, young people whose grandparents were Stone-Age animists in Sulawesi, far removed from the history of the Arab and Muslim world, earnestly told me they dream of fighting in Iraq or Palestine in defense of Islam (Atran, *Talking to the Enemy*).

6 Girard on Apocalypse and Terrorism

ESPEN DAHL

Although highly disputed, the French-American philosophical anthropologist René Girard's theory of violence and archaic religion has had a major impact on the current theoretical discussion. From the 1960s and onward, Girard has put forward and continually developed his thought in different phases: first, he established the theory of mimetic desire, second, he elaborated its consequences for archaic religion and sacrifice, and third, Girard elaborated his Judeo-Christian deconstruction of sacrificial myths. Soon after the attack on the Twin Towers, on September 11, 2001, Girard expressed the opinion that "What is happening today is mimetic rivalry on a global scale."[1] Taking his cue from this, Girard has gradually developed what might be regarded as a fourth phase of his thought, in which he links religious terrorism and Biblical apocalypse in order to shed light on the structure of violence in the contemporary world.[2] "I see it [9/11] as a seminal event, and it is fundamentally wrong to minimize it," says Girard in an interview. He continues: "I personally think that it represents a new dimension, a new world dimension."[3] According to this view, though limited in scope, terrorism nevertheless announces a new historical state – one that, however, has long been underway.

In an attempt to spell out in more detail the implications of Girard's view of apocalypse and terrorism, their internal logic and historical dimensions, it is first necessary to prepare the ground with a sketch of Girard's general conception of religion and violence.

RELIGION, VIOLENCE, AND REVELATION

Violent conflicts develop from the specific way in which humans are brought into relationships. Girard first presupposes that humans are fundamentally directed by their desires –ideals, values, and goals – but these desires are not in any way fixed as biological drives. Desires must be shaped, and this shaping presupposes another specifically human feature, namely that we are mimetic animals: we acquire our specific desires through imitation of others. If one look at the development of children or the acquisition of specific skills, everyone starts out as a disciple who imitates a model. More fundamentally then, the particular skills in each case, what is mediated through such imitation, is the model's own desired objects, values, and ideals. Girard's mimetic theory is hence triangular: we have the disciple, the model, and the desired object; the disciple orients his or her desire by integrating the model's desire.[4] When the disciple's imitation is perfect, the disciple will gradually transform from the status of a novice into the status of a rival to the model, insofar as they become more or less equally fit to obtain the desired object. It is this conflictual situation from which human violence originally occurs.

Mimetic rivalry is contagious; it has a tendency to spread from individual to collective parties that are dragged into the conflict. The mutual opposition will both continue to spread throughout society as well as increase the urge for the desired object, escalating like a growing snowball. As the conflict rises to higher levels, attention will be deflected from the original desired object to the opponent who is fought. To the same degree that opponents will see one another as strict opposites, they will, from an outsider's perspective, appear more and more alike. This follows from the mimetic structure of conflicts' reciprocity: attacks are replied to in kind by counter-attacks according to the chain reaction of vengeance.[5] In the course of this process, initial distinctions, orders, and hierarchies that structure society will decompose, drawing nearer and nearer a state of what Girard calls undifferentiation. The chaotic situation means that one is less and less capable of distinguishing friends from foes. In such a mimetic crisis, the community is at the brink of a destructive fight of the all against the all.

According to Girard, the state of crisis seems universally to lead to a particular kind of resolution:

> But suddenly the opposition of everyone against everyone else is
> replaced by the opposition of all against one. Where previously there
> had been chaotic ensemble of particular conflicts, there is now the
> simplicity of a single conflict: the entire community on the one
> side, and on the other, the victim.[6]

In the state of crisis, everyone will be on the lookout for someone to blame, that is, a scapegoat. The scapegoat will be picked out from the margins of the community, both sufficiently different to awaken attention, and sufficiently integrated into the community to represent the conflict – and, above all, not powerful enough to strike back. It does not matter that the victim is not the true cause of the mimetic crisis, as long as the mob is convinced of its blame. Having thus convinced themselves, all of the potential violence can be drained away from the internal conflict and channeled into the execution or expulsion of the victim. Giving violence an outlet has the astonishing effect of immediately putting an end to rivalry, and returning the community to its previous peace and order. The surrogate-victim mechanism thus has the power to restore peace – notably through violent means.

This resolution to the internal, violent tendency of communities is at the heart of religious myths and rituals. By projecting a sacred power onto the scapegoat, its blame as well as its superhuman power to restore peace, myths cloud both aspects. Its essential function is to blind the community to the fact that the victim is arbitrarily chosen and thus to provide legitimation of their violence against it. In sacrificial rituals the entire mimetic cycle, from its mimetic crisis to its resolution, is re-enacted: "I contend that the objective of the ritual is the proper reenactment of the surrogate-victim mechanism; its function is to perpetuate or renew the effect of this mechanism; that is, to keep violence *outside* the community."[7] Significantly, as a stylized imitation of the mimetic cycle, most rituals will employ a double substitution: the original victim is a substitute for the community, while in the ritual the substitute is a surrogate-victim, typically a sacrificial animal. The ritual execution will than take on the power of the original scapegoat, and provide a permanent outlet for accumulating violence.

Rituals and taboos work together to found culture and to prevent violence from again reaching the stage of a mimetic crisis:

> Prohibitions attempt to avert the crisis by prohibiting those behaviours that provoke it, and if the crisis recurs nonetheless, or threatens to do so, ritual then attempts to channel it in a direction that would lead to resolution, which means a reconciliation of the community at the expense of what one must suppose to be an arbitrary victim. In fact no individual victim can ever be responsible for the mimetic crisis.[8]

The last sentence betrays an insight that cannot be produced from within archaic religion itself. Its myth will invariably disguise the truth. Strangely enough, it is central to Girard's conviction that the insight into the innocence of the victim nevertheless stems from a particular religious legacy, namely the Judeo–Christian legacy. Admittedly, the Bible is full of narratives that fit neatly into Girard's understanding of the myth: it recounts states of crisis, the all against one, and the ensuing restoration of order, governed by prohibitions and rituals. We find it repeated in the expulsion from the Garden of Eden, the flood, in the rivalry between Cain and Abel, Joseph and his brothers, and so forth. There is, however, one decisive difference in the Biblical versions: Neither Cain's, not the Joseph brothers' acts are confirmed by God; God takes the side of the innocent victim. Even though this is not a univocal tendency in the Hebrew Bible, the theme of divine care for victims points steadfastly forward to what, to Girard's mind, is its culmination in the Gospels.

In the Gospel account of the passion of Christ, the pattern of myth and the mimetic cycle are once more confirmed: it takes place in an occupied society in a mimetic crisis, the crowd certainly turns their aggression from one another to one scapegoat that stands out, and, once put to death, the society regains stability, whereupon the victim rises from the dead. Far from being a play of irony, Girard thinks that this mythical structure inherently belongs to the revelation pertaining to the Cross. The Passion incarnates the myth in order to unmask its illusions: there is no sacred justification of the victim mechanism – the victim is the very Son of God.[9] This does not only hold for Christ; as an exemplar of all myths, its works back into them all. The scapegoating can only work as long as one is ignorant of the victim's innocence; if one so much as doubt its legitimacy, it becomes impossible to channel all violence through it. The resurrection of Christ is therefore the triumph over the sacred violence camouflaged in myths:

> The resurrection of Christ crowns and finishes both the subversion and the unmasking of mythology, of archaic ritual, of everything that insures the foundation and perpetuation of human cultures. The Gospels reveal everything that human beings need to understand their moral responsibility with regard to the whole spectrum of violence in human history and to all the false religions.[10]

Christ's death and resurrection subverts myths from the inside, and, in so doing, it exposes the lies of sacrificial violence and renders them ineffective. After the Cross, humans must learn to live without sacrificial myths, rituals, and scapegoats.

REVELATION AND APOCALYPSE

One might assume a rather optimistic view of history as a consequence of Girard's understanding of the Biblical revelation, leading to the decline of violence and the protection of victims. Girard does think that the demystification of religion is good in itself, also that it has had an historical impact that is hard to exaggerate. Surprisingly perhaps, Girard nevertheless thinks that the revelation has also paved the way for the apocalypse: "Demystification, which is good in the absolute, has proven bad in the relative, for we were not prepared to shoulder its consequences."[11]

Even though these prospects come to the fore in the most recent, fourth phase of his theory, they have long been foreshadowed. As early as 1978, in *Things Hidden since the Foundation of the World*, he counters any Christian optimism with regard to universal history, understood as progress toward a final goal: "In modern times, when people have talked about a Christian vision of history they have not really been talking about a radically Christian appropriation of history, which could only be apocalyptic."[12] In *Things Hidden*, he speaks about our being in an intermediary period, where the end of the world is not at hand, but has become a real possibility.[13] As Girard returns to this theme in the aftermath of 9/11, the analysis has changed: "Violence can no longer be checked. From this point of view, we can say that apocalypse has begun."[14] It is true, though, that Girard thinks apocalypse is not solely linked to increasing terror: nuclear threat, ecological threat, and the biological manipulation of the human species are among the "signs of the time" (Matt. 16:3).[15] Even so, it remains crucial to Girard's analysis that violence has reached a new historical stage, an apocalyptic stage, of which terrorism is the most palpable symptom.

The troubling thing about the apocalypse as portrayed in the New Testament is that it seems to entail a stepping back into archaic notions of the sacred: The envisioned mythical dramas that are to unfold before Christ's second coming are the times of God's violent revenge on the infidel and evil, dressed vividly in pictures of cosmic wars.[16] But in Girard's interpretation, there is nothing mythical about it, no magic contained in its prophecies; rather, it is a matter of taking the internal working of the revelation of the cross to its logical conclusion. By unmasking the violent logic of the scapegoat mechanism, and with it the unmasking of the false transcendence of the sacred, the cross has robbed us of the original and most effective way to establish peace and order: "Having a scapegoat means not knowing that we have one.

Learning that we have a scapegoat is to lose it forever and expose ourselves to mimetic conflicts with no possible resolution."[17] As long as humans do not completely renounce mimetic rivalry, potential violence will continue to accumulate; after the Christian revelation this means that cultures are plunged into a permanent sacrificial crisis, with the chaotic threat of war of the all against the all. Hence, Christian revelation entails at once the possibility of the end to all violence and the possibility of apocalypse:

> The system cannot be pulled back by any form of pharmacological resolution [both poison and cure], and the virus of mimetic violence can spread freely. This is the reason why Jesus says: "Do not suppose that I have come to bring peace to earth. I did not come to bring peace, but a sword" (Matthew 10.34). The Cross has destroyed once and for all the cathartic power of the scapegoat mechanism. Consequently, the Gospel does not provide a happy ending to our history. It simply shows us two options: ... either we imitate Christ, giving up all our mimetic violence, or we run the risk of self-destruction. The apocalyptic feeling is based on that risk.[18]

The Christian revelation is indeed risky business – so risky that Paul says that if the rulers of this world had known what they did when they crucified the Lord, they would never have done it (1. Cor. 2:8). The revelation thus brings the sword – not from beyond, but from the internal working of mimetic rivalry: sons against fathers, nations against nations. In this situation scapegoats are needed more than ever before, and, indeed, there has never been a shortage of new ways to camouflage new scapegoats. What has changed, however, is the outcome of violence: it is no longer *generative*; that is, it has lost its power to generate the foundation of culture, order, and peace by transfiguring violence into the sacred.[19] The demystification of violence leaves it with its grim face: "Violence, which produced the sacred, no longer produces anything but itself."[20]

THE HISTORICAL EMERGENCE OF THE APOCALYPTIC SITUATION

Girard fills in the account of apocalypse with more attention to its historical dimensions, especially in his reflections on the Prussian general and military theoretician Carl von Clausewitz, *Battling to the End*. Clausewitz's most famous statement, that war is "merely the continuation of policy by other means," suggests that the means of war can be guided and restricted by its politics. However, what attracts Girard's attention to Clausewitz's theory is the internal tension in his treatise. Although undeniably operating with a notion of politically controlled war, Clausewitz betrays an awareness of the inner logic of war that pulls in the opposite direction. In Girard's rendering, Clausewitz realizes that in principle there are no restrictions that pertain to the nature of war. Clausewitz, however, backs off from this frightening intuition, and instead turns to tamed and rationalized warfare. Nevertheless, Girard thinks it is precisely this unrestricted logic of war – in Clausewitz words, its "escalation to extremes" – that needs to be thought through, right to its logical conclusion. At the heart of war lies the concept of the duel. Despite the Aristocrat ring, Clausewitz's invocation of the duel is meant to focus on reciprocity, in which attacks are followed by counter-attacks, reciprocally bound together by the ambition of compelling the other with all available physical force. Once the duel is put in motion, there is no internal limit to it; for the heightening of force on one side will lead to the heightening of force on the other side. This makes it possible for Girard to claim that the mimetic theory of violent contagion, first elaborated with regard to archaic communities, also applies to international warfare.[21]

From Clausewitz's perspective in the early 1800s, global war is a purely theoretical possibility and is not meant to capture what he conceives as real war. In real war, there are physical and economic limitations, and, more importantly, there are strong political institutions that confine its escalation. As long as there are differentiating principles intact, such as national and political institutions, the escalation to extremes will be prevented. What fascinates and frightens Girard is, however, that Clausewitz's concept of purely theoretical war now seems to fit the reality at hand – and that is precisely due to the corrosion of constituting differences. There is no doubt that in the twentieth century, warfare manifested on a hitherto unknown scale, wars that transcended the nation state, especially through two world wars. But even during the Cold War, however truly threatening it was, fundamental distinctions between the superpowers where not weakened, but rather strengthened.

In Girard's view, the violence we have witnessed in the latest decades has becomes less and less geographically restricted and more and more global in reach. From Girard's perspective, such globalizing tendencies are only secondarily economic or technological in nature; it is primarily an outcome of disintegration of the structures that found cultures: "The true engine of progress is the slow decomposition of the closed worlds rooted in victim mechanisms. This is the force that destroys archaic societies and henceforth dismantles the one replacing them, the nations we call 'modern.'"[22] Globalization is thus a late fruit of the decomposition of the victim mechanism, now working to disintegrate the national state as the decisive military unit. The global reciprocity that prepared this anxiety was already underway during the ideological infusion into the wars of the twentieth century. One can see how reciprocity and rivalry prepared the state of planetary reciprocity: Nazism responded to communism, just as the Chinese economy today responds to the American economy. But as they fight one another, they become more and more alike, like doubles or twins.[23]

Globalization brings us nearer one another, through economic exchange, technology and, not least, communication technology. Bringing people closer to one another might be a good thing – but it can easily turn bad. For the corrosion of differences leads to the state of undifferentiation, which in Girard's thought invariably signals the danger of mimetic crisis. Given the reciprocity inherent in war, such undifferentiation paves the way for violence no longer held in check by political or national borders and conducted with observance of the strict distinctions between military and civilian targets. Girard observes that terrorism has replaced traditional, restricted warfare: "there is the kind of violence that is now seen throughout the world, a terrorism without limits or boundaries." What becomes clear is that there is no contract of war that can any longer bind it; globalization has not meant the strengthening of legal structures, but has instead led to the opposite. The imminent danger is violence's escalation to extremes.

Samuel P. Huntington's "clash of civilizations" is the most famous exponent of the widely held view that differences engender conflicts and violence. Interestingly, Girard proposes a significantly different perspective: "Terrorism is undoubtedly connected to a world 'different' than ours. But what gives rise to it is not this 'difference,' which distances it most from us and renders it beyond our comprehension. What gives rise to it, on the contrary, is an exacerbated desire for convergence and resemblance."[24] Distinctions and differences preserve peace and order – conflicts always increase to the extent that differences disintegrate and the opponents become more like, or "doubles." At the bottom of undifferentiation lies the mimetic desire that draws the opponents toward one another – so also in the case of terrorism: "Far from turning away from the West, they [Islamist terrorists] cannot avoid imitating it."[25] In this age, there is a global transmission of desired objects that has proven decisive for Western countries, particularly as expressed in American culture. To be more precise, Girard naturally points to the wealth and prosperity that Western society enjoys.

But it is also possible to detect how America replied by imitating the attackers. "The war on terror," given religious underpinning by George W. Bush, now starts to look like a counter-attack guided by similar principles.[26] The convergence is dangerous because it opens up the possibility of dangerous escalation. Once triggered by a desire for a scarce good – resources, prosperity, wealth – the dynamics of the rivalry are such that at a certain stage the desired object drops out and the rivalry itself become a matter of prestige in its own right. The triad of desire collapses into a dyadic desire, into what Girard calls metaphysical desire, where there is a fight for totally possessing or destroying the other.[27] Appearing from the inside as absolute opposites, the opponents have become doubles. With no difference to put an end to the rivalry or scapegoat mechanism to channel it, Girard believes it leads to the violent, apocalyptic chaos.

A SUPER-VICTIMARY MACHINE

Historically, Girard claims, the cross has led to the modern concern for victims, for the weak, the marginalized, and oppressed. Indeed, rights independent of capabilities or properties, welfare, charity, and humanitarianism in general has grown out of Christian soil. Nietzsche saw with unprecedented clarity that this was indeed the outcome of Christianity – and protested.[28] Nonetheless, as the lack of conviction in scapegoats fades, the need to find scapegoats has not disappeared. But more than ever before, our era is highly alert to any kind of scapegoating and has developed sophisticated means to detect perpetrators of any sort. If the sacred in archaic society had the status of the absolute, modern ideologies were the secularized prolongation of absolutes. After the fall of communism in Soviet and Eastern Europe, one expected that absolutes would vanish. However, Girard suspects that this is not the case. It is only displaced, and the new candidate is the victimary principle. There is not only no need to dispute the protection of the victim; it has become virtually impossible to challenge: "the defence of victims has become holy: *it is the absolute.*"[29]

At this stage the concern for the victim can be turned into a weapon. If any victim is innocent and pure, all the guilt is now transferred to the persecutors. This prepares the return of a paradoxical form of scapegoating after the fall of sacrificial logic, where violence can be channeled, not toward the victim, but toward any perpetrator:

In short, we integrate the central concern of Judaism and
Christianity into our systems of self-defense. Instead of criticizing
ourselves, we use our knowledge in bad faith, turning it against
others. Indeed, we practice a hunt for scapegoats to the second
degree, a hunt for hunters of scapegoats. Our society's obligatory
compassion authorizes new forms of cruelty.[30]

The great attraction of the "hunt for hunters" is that it absolves the
hunters from consulting their own responsibility for perpetuating
violence. This logic has a strong hold in the modern world, partly
because it takes its cue from the absolute status of the victim,
partly because it gives way to legitimizing violence and channeling
it outside. But just as with archaic scapegoating, it disguises the true
face of violence and wraps it in self-righteousness – it is even almost
impossible to criticize. However, as long as the rights of the victim
are absolute, it can lead to a new spiral of rivalry: "The concern
for victims has become a paradoxical competition of mimetic rivalry,
of opponents continually trying to outbid one another."[31] The
driving force here, what Girard calls a "super-victimary machine,"
is a strange return of the victim mechanism – a return with a
vengeance.[32]

Drawing heavily on Girard's analysis, Charles Taylor shows how
claiming to be a victim serves terrorism, as he writes that,

my being the victim means that you are the victimizer. I am pure.
Claiming victimhood is an assertion of our purity; we all right.
Moreover, our cause is good, so we can fight, inflict a violence that
is righteous: a holy violence. Hence we have a right to do terrible
things, which others have not. Here is the logic of modern
terrorism.[33]

The logic of holy violence works into the hands of terrorists, especially as they perceive themselves as victims. And Girard does not
deny that there is something to it – he even says that Islamic terrorism has been kindled by the arrogance of the West.[34] The important
thing at this point is, however, that such reasoning works to legitim-
ize unrestricted violence against the persecutors. Terrorists' appeal to
such a victimage principle was part of Osama Bin Laden's rhetoric,
but it widely shared with the underlying convictions held by Christian and Jewish terrorists as well – Anders Behring Breivik being no
exception.[35] This tendency is further enhanced by the tendency,

especially among suicide killers, to view themselves as martyrs. They are in their own eyes not only victims, but sacrifice themselves in solidarity with other victims. But as with the victim mechanism, the retrieval of martyrdom is highly paradoxical, even a perversion of the Christian concept; for where nonviolent resistance was central to it, it has now turned into an act of killing.[36] Moreover, such killings are heading in an apocalyptic direction, because global terrorism traverses the line between "good," generative violence, which is channeled through substitutes and ritualization, and "bad" violence directed toward itself and others. When the distinction between generative and destructive violence dissolves, we are thrown into spiral of sacrificial crisis. According to Girard, this leaves us with the prospect of an unbound violence that generates nothing but its own destructiveness, escalating to extremes.

Faced with such apocalyptic prospects, Girard nevertheless denies that he is a pessimist. To Girard, there is no question of the seriousness of the global situation – to argue otherwise only testifies to one's unwillingness to take it in. Nonetheless, since the apocalypse is of human making, it is also within the scope of our abilities to avoid it. To avoid it, one must, however, make a radical change in which we completely renounce the cycle of mimetic violence. But is it realistic that such an attitude will change the current situation? Girard writes: "The apocalypse does not announce the end of the world; it created hope ... Hope is possible only if we dare to think about the danger at hand."[37] Girard rounds off his reflection by citing Hölderlin:

> But where danger threatens
> That which saves from it also grows.[38]

Further Reading

Girard, René *Battling to the End. Conversations with Benoit Chantre*, translated by M. Baker. Michigan: Michigan State University Press, 2010.
Things Hidden Since the Foundation of the World. Research Undertaken in Collaboration with Jean-Michel Oughourlian and Guy Lefort, translated by S. Bann and M. Metteer. London: Continuum, 2003.
Girard, René and Robert Doran "Apocalyptic Thinking after 9/11: An Interview with René Girard," *SubStance* 37 (2008), 20–32.
Pallaver, Wolfgang "Terrorism versus Non-Violent Resistance," *Journal of Religion and Violence* 1 (2013), 218–249.

Endnotes

1 René Girard, Henri Tincq, and Thomas C. Hilde, "What Is Happening Today Is Mimetic Rivalry on a Global Scale," *South Central Review* 19 (2002), 22.

2 Robert Doran, "René Girard's Apocalyptic Modernity," *Comunicacao & Cultura* 11 (2011), 38.

3 René Girard and Robert Doran, "Apocalyptic Thinking after 9/11: An Interview with René Girard," *SubStance* 37 (2008), 21.

4 René Girard, *Deceit, Desire, and the Novel: Self and Other in Literary Structure*, translated byYvonne Freccero (Baltimore: John Hopkins University Press, 1966), pp. 1–2. Cf. Chris Fleming, *René Girard. Violence and Mimesis* (Cambridge: Polity Press, 2004), pp. 10–16.

5 René Girard, *Things Hidden Since the Foundation of the World. Research Undertaken in Collaboration with Jean-Michel Oughourlian and Guy Lefort*, translated by S. Bann and M. Metteer (London: Continuum, 2003), pp. 12–13.

6 Ibid., p. 24

7 Rene Girard, *Violence and the Sacred*, translated by Patrick Gregory (Baltimore: Johns Hopkins University Press 1977). (originally published in French in 1972)

8 Girard, *Things Hidden*, 25.

9 Ibid., 170.

10 René Girard, *I See Satan Fall Like Lightning*, translated by J.G. Williams (New York: Orbis Books, 2001), p. 124.

11 René Girard, *Battling to the End. Conversations with Benoit Chantre*, translated by M. Baker (Michigan: Michigan State University Press, 2010), p. x.

12 Girard, *Things Hidden*, p. 250.

13 Ibid., p. 260. The thought about the intermediary time in terms of the Pauline notion *katéchon* (2. Tess. 2:6–7), that is the power to hold back, restrain evil and put limits to violence. The implication is that the limited time, from revelation up to the end, the powers of the world will hold violence at bay far as long as it can. Cf. Wolfgang Palaver, "Hobbes and the Katéchon: The Secularization of Sacrificial Christianity," *Contagion. Journal of Violence, Mimesis, and Culture* 2 (1995), 61–63.

14 Girard, *Battling to the End*, 210.

15 Girard and Doran, "Apocalyptic Thinking," 21.

16 In his influential study, Mark Juergensmeyer says that it is precisely the image of cosmic war, rather than mimetic rivalry and sacrifice, that lies at the heart of terrorism. *Terror in the Mind of God. The Global Rise of Religious Violence* (Berkley: University of California Press, 2000), pp.171–173.

17 Girard, *Battling to the End*, p. xiv

18 René Girard, *Evolution and Conversion. Dialogues on the Origins of Culture* (London T&T Clark, 2007), p. 237.

19 Girard, *Violence and the Sacred*, 273.

20 Girard, *Battling to the End*, x. Cf. James Warren, *Compassion or Apocalypse. A Comprehensible Guide to the Thought of René Girard* (Washington: Christian Alternative, 2012), p. 311.
21 Girard, *Battling to the End*, pp. 4–6.
22 Girard, *I See Satan Fall*, p. 166.
23 Girard, *Battling to the End*, pp. 40–42.
24 Girard, "What Is Happening," 22.
25 Ibid.
26 Girard, *Battling to the End*, p. 211.
27 Girard, *Things Hidden*, pp. 296–297.
28 Girard, *I See Satan Fall*, p. 172.
29 Girard, *Evolution and Conversion*, pp.257–258.
30 Girard, *I See Satan Fall*, p. 158.
31 Ibid., p. 164.
32 Girard, *Evolution and Conversion*, p. 236. Cf. Stephen L. Gardner "Modernity as Revelation: René Girard's Imagination of the Worst," *Journal of Religion and Violence* 1 (2013), 300.
33 Charles Taylor, "Notes on the Sources of Violence: Perennial and Modern," in J.L. Heft (ed.) *Beyond Violence. Religious Sources of Social Transformation in Judaism, Christianity, and Islam* (New York: Fordham University Press, 2004), p. 36.
34 Girard, *Battling to the End*, 210.
35 Wolfgang Pallaver, "Terrorism versus Non-Violent Resistance," *Journal of Religion and Violence* 1 (2013), 235.
36 Girard and Doran, "Apocalyptic Thinking," 30–31.
37 Girard, *Battling to the End*, p. xiii.
38 Ibid., p. xvii.

7 Rational Choice and Religious Terrorism: Its Bases, Applications, and Future Directions

STEPHEN NEMETH

While for many, the term "rational choice" signifies a normative judgment about an individual's choices, it presents a much different reality for scholars. For social scientists, it refers to a range of models that posit that individuals will be motivated by self-interest and a desire to maximize their sense of well-being or, in the language of economists, their utility. These models have imposed an element of predictability on human behavior, allowing for the scientific study of a range of economic, social, and political processes – including terrorism. In addition, rational choice also has much to offer in the study of religious terrorism, despite the metaphysical dimensions of belief. This chapter discusses the assumptions of the rational choice model, its use in terrorism research and applicability to the study of religious terrorism, objections to the model, and its future applications.

THE RATIONAL CHOICE MODEL

In their simplest form, rational choice models posit that actors seek to maximize their utility. Utility has a variety of definitions within this; most commonly it is thought of as self-regarding behavior. Efforts to maximize wealth or income spring most readily to mind. It can also encompass the satisfaction that comes with the fulfillment of a personal goal or, for the faithful, the attainment of enlightenment, or afterlife. Utility can also be conceptualized in terms of other-regarding behavior. Altruistic actions that help support friends, family, and strangers would also fit within most rational choice models.

In order for actors to maximize their respective utilities, rational choice models require that actors fulfill three basic requirements.[1] First, an individual has to have complete preferences over the set of potential outcomes. This means that a person knows whether they prefer, are indifferent, or dislike the assumed consequences of their decisions. Second, these preferences are transitive. That is, if the individual believes outcome *a* to be superior to outcome *b* and *b* is superior to c, then it holds that outcome *a* is better than outcome *c*. These two conditions allow the individual to make a preference ordering, ranking the outcomes from best to worst and facilitating the third condition, the ability to select their most preferred outcome. As a result, rational choice models allow for human behavior to be generalizable and predictable, and analyzed through econometric techniques.

Because of the differences between the standard conception of rational choice and its use in social science, it is important to point out the misconceptions that result. First, rational choice refers to a description of the decision-making process, not the preferences that an actor is using to make their decision. A terrorist may pursue morally suspect goals; however, they do so by engaging in the rational choice process when weighing their options. Rational choice, then, is about the "logic of consequences" rather than the "logic of appropriateness."[2] Second, the process depicted by the rational choice approach is a generalized description of the basic logic underlying an individual's decisions, not an actual calculation or a cognitive process.

Rational choice also does *not* imply that different individuals will reach the same decision even when given similar situations. Instead, a variety of outcomes may result that reflect different actors' preferences over the outcomes. In terrorism, one organization may value some actions solely due to their destructive potential, perhaps seeking to maximize civilian casualties, while another may prefer actions which are more symbolic than destructive, perhaps because they wish to only engage in property destruction. Furthermore, in those situations where different actors share similar preferences, their unique risk tolerances may cause them to choose different actions. Two terrorist organizations may both wish to overthrow a government, but one may use more risk-acceptant strategies than the other. Lastly, rational choice does not imply that the outcomes are free of error: the outcomes of a rational choice process are only as good as the ability of the actor to find and weigh options.

The picture presented by the classical rational choice approach, that of economic man (*homo economicus*), was quickly challenged from a number of sides. Scholars were quick to note that people were simply not able to fully accomplish the tasks laid out by the standard approach. Rather, individuals face inherent cognitive and processing limits when confronted with information, thus resulting in decision-making that differs from the classical ideal. To account for this, scholars began to suggest that individuals were "boundedly rational;" that is, people engage in cognitive processes that allow them to gather and process enough information to lead to decisions that, while not value-maximizing, are "good enough."[3] This has led to discussions about variation in human decision-making processes and the degree to which the precepts of the rational choice model are followed; these variants are generally referred to as "thick" and "thin" rationality.

Scholars challenged the concept of expected utility maximization as the outcome of the rational choice process. In many instances, the outcomes associated with a particular decision are incommensurable. For example, if an action results in an income loss, how many "units" of religious benefit would balance out or exceed this loss? The solution was to create a *subjective* expected utility in which previously incommensurable costs and benefits can be translated.[4] Debate about how individuals aggregated these costs would later spawn a wide number of alternative and sophisticated decision rules.

RATIONAL CHOICE MODELS IN TERRORISM

The application of rational choice models to terrorism began when William Landes applied Gary Becker's model of crime and punishment to estimate the effects of US counterterrorism policy on the phenomena of aircraft hijacking.[5] In Becker's original model, criminals were assumed to be rational individuals acting on self-interest, who had the ability to choose between legal employment or a life of crime. Crime became a rational choice when its rewards exceeded a.) the probability of punishment, b.) the severity of the punishment, c.) the loss of income from legal work, and several other variables.[6] Efforts to change these variables, such as increasing fines or raising wages, would therefore lead to a decreased likelihood that an individual would turn to crime.

For Landes, a potential hijacker operated along similar principles. The utility of hijacking an aircraft was a function of the offender's wealth as well as the probability that the individual would be apprehended and the monetary costs (to the offender) associated with trial and eventual incarceration.[7] Efforts to increase the probability of apprehension, as was done with the installation of metal detectors in US airports in 1973, and increasing punishments were posited to decrease the occurrence of hijacking. Landes tested his theoretical model using Federal Aviation Administration (FAA) data on all airline hijackings in the United States from 1961 to 1976, demonstrating the real-life effect that each of his variables had on the occurrence of hijacking. In particular, he found that *ex ante* measures, such as screening, were much more effective in reducing the likelihood of hijacking than *ex post* actions, like measures that increased apprehension after the hijacking had already taken place.

These two works also form the parameters of the rational choice model as they apply to terrorists. Like the classic model, terrorist are rational actors seeking to maximize their utility (read political goals) while operating under three basic assumptions.[8] First, terrorists are motivated by stable and consistent political goals. That is, political grievances form the base and motivation for terrorist violence. Second, terrorism is a course of action decided on when other forms of political participation have been blocked. This perspective is consistent with work that views terrorism as an allocation decision made when total resources to the organization are highest, where the costs of illegal acts are low, and where the relative gains for illegality are high.[9] Lastly, terrorism is used insofar as its effectiveness outweighs the effectiveness of other means. A variant of this argument can also suggest that particular forms of terrorism are used over others based on their effectiveness. Given this, terrorists should be discriminating about their attacks and select violence consistent with the risks and consequences involved.

Walter Enders and Todd Sandler would further refine the concept of terrorist rationality by introducing the concept of "substitutability."[10] They suggested that rationality is not simply evident in the targets selected or the means employed. Rationality can also be seen in the ways that terrorists respond to changes in the availability of resources; the behavior of terrorists under conditions of scarcity will differ from their behavior under times of abundance. The nature of operations are predictable; operationally "simple" activities that require few resources, such as bombings, far outpace more complex and resource-intensive activities like hostage-taking and barricading operations. In addition, counterterrorism efforts by the government impact these actions, as they serve to increase the costs of certain acts. As a result, organizations may substitute less costly acts, and even nonviolent activities, for violent ones.

Over this time, rational choice models have been effective in elucidating a wide range of terrorist activities. While most of this focus has been on the factors that determine the number of attacks, others have focused on issues relating to group maintenance, tactical innovation, basing decisions, and many more.[11] A full accounting of these works would be impossible within the parameters of this review, instead see Todd Sandler's "The Analytical Study of Terrorism: Taking Stock" for an appraisal of terrorism research using the rational choice approach and its future directions.[12]

Rationality and Religious Terrorism: The Club Model

When considering religious terrorism however, many quickly dismiss the utility of the rational choice approach. This response is well understood, religious terrorism has often resulted in appalling levels of brutality and has been espoused by people noteworthy for their maximalist rhetoric and their unwillingness to accept any level of political compromise.[13] Surely, individuals following the dictates of a higher power, and acting unbound from "society's law and limitations" demonstrate a different, and noneconomic, logic.[14] Instead, rational choice explanation retains its pride of place as an explanation for terrorist violence and, in essence, suggests that religious and secular terrorism can be considered very similarly.

As Bryan Caplan (2006) observes, the analysis of terrorism – and religious terrorism in particular – contains a paradox.[15] While many may believe in the rewards that accrue to them should they engage in terrorism, so few actually take that step. If individuals did not act in the ways described by the rational choice approach, argues Caplan, terrorism employed by the faithful would be much more common than it is. Religion then, rather than being a competing explanation to rational choice, can be considered a parameter to be evaluated within the model. While reducing religious belief into a dissection of costs and benefits may seem sterile, this approach has allowed us to better understand why individuals and groups may conduct violence that appears both illogical and irreligious.[16] This approach to the study of religion does not deny the value that faith has for many, but instead provides us with a framework to comprehend and, potentially, combat this type of violence.

In this approach, the individual is viewed as a consumer of religion. An individual seeks faith because it is a way to "transcend the usual technological constraints and physical limits of everyday life."[17] This is a rational and appropriate response for individuals, especially as they confront the challenges and questions of everyday life. In economic terms, an embrace of one's faith is a decision that enhances one's expected utility provided that the costs that come with it are sufficiently low. This can be considered a "wise investment" as it does not require a deep devotion to any particular belief but instead a sufficient level of doubt pertaining to the lack of a higher power.[18]

The individual benefits of faith provide one explanation of how rational choice can be used to evaluate religious terrorism. The decision to engage in terrorism can be a rational one if the act of terrorism is believed to be rewarded in the hereafter, is considered a form of altruism, or advances the goals of a larger group. Individual terrorists can certainly believe that their acts will be recognized after their death, parables about the rewards of afterlife and the benefits of noble self-sacrifice are found throughout the major religions of the world. This justification, however, has not been predominant among those terrorists that have been imprisoned or have failed in acts of suicide terrorism. While interviews of incarcerated populations have their drawbacks, it is more likely that the rationale for violent acts is linked to the last two ideas.[19]

Given that these justifications are more communal, it is also necessary to evaluate the role of religion as an entity which both depends upon and benefits the many. Evaluating religious organizations as a provider of benefits is particularly important in those areas where the state is unable to provide basic public goods (products which are considered nonrivalrous and nonexcludable) such as law and order, education, and welfare services. In these types of situations, the religious community becomes a center around which services are both produced and provided. It is this aspect, stressing the costs of coordination and the benefits that faith communities provide to ensure obedience that forms the "club model" approach.[20] This provides an explanation for the violence of organizations like Hamas, Hezbollah, and the Taliban, and their success in conducting suicide terrorism.

To start, the club model recognizes one of the basic problems that confront all organizations – a concept called the "free-rider" problem.[21] This is simply the propensity for people to use a public goods organization for its benefits while providing nothing in return. Organizations attempt to solve this problem by creating costs that separate true believers from opportunists. In religious organizations, these costs can involve direct sacrifice – the destruction of valued resources, distinctive dress and grooming habits, and prohibitions on certain activities.[22] This removes the group, to some degree, from the external world, helps make group activities more valuable, and encourages participation from members.

By screening out participants, the good that the organization provides changes from a public to a club good (a product which is nonrivalrous but excludable). As a result, those who become members – while being called upon to have high levels of commitment and participation – benefit more than those that did not make the group. The beneficiaries then have a reason to contribute to the organization, even despite the risks that come with membership. The high costs demanded through these screening practices also create a signal to the rest of the organization regarding the suitability to potential applicants.[23] It is for these reasons that religious organizations are advantaged in the creation of violence.[24]

This means that the average member of a terrorist organization, be it religious or secular, is likely to be quite different than the background population. Rather than being poor and desperate, the profile of the terrorist supporter and participant are noteworthy for their relative affluence and education.[25] Within the context of the club model, the consequences are sobering: the better the provisions a religious organization is able to provide (the stronger the club), the more loyal the members, and the more likely the group will be to use suicide terrorism. Moreover, stronger clubs will also be more likely to engage in more lethal attacks.

Examples of the benefits that accrue to people within these organizations are not difficult to find. Benefits to recruits and a stipend to recruits' families have been noted in Chechnya.[26] In the Gaza Strip, Nasra Hassan (2001) noted that suicide bombers, and their families, are revered. Images of the perpetrator are emblazoned across the neighborhood, in graffiti, and publications – including a "Martyr of the Month" calendar.[27] The perpetrators' families are feted with celebrations honoring the sacrifice of their family member and are swamped with well-wishers offering them blessings and congratulations, raising their social profile and encouraging others to become suicide bombers. Families also benefit financially. Many of these organizations have developed a social welfare system that provides generous benefits to the family of a suicide bomber long after their death.[28] Jean-Paul Azam notes that suicide terrorism then may be thought of as a form of "intergenerational investment," whereby potential perpetrators view the act of suicide terrorism as a way to create and pass down wealth to benefit their immediate family.[29] This type of payoff may be appealing in areas where economic conditions are poor and might be useful in steering future adherents to the cause.

Because the club model focuses on the material incentives that accrue to adherents, the ways to address religious terrorism may be more straightforward – and closer to policy prescriptions for secular terrorists – than initially thought. Rather than Juergensmeyer's conception of a "cosmic war" that eludes earthly solutions, answers may in fact be possible.[30] One solution lies in creating incentives for defection among members of the club. Destroying bonds of trust should reduce the activity of the group, given that no one will know whether their compatriot is an honest party or not. Efforts in Italy, known as the "Repentance Laws" – so named because they reduced prison sentences in exchange for group information – were successful in reducing instances of both left and right-wing terrorism.[31] The second is to increase the capacity of the government to provide public goods, particularly to the populations that already, or may, engage in terrorist violence. This way the choice to not joining an extremist religious organization becomes rational.

This should in no way suggest that secular terrorism is any simpler to address than religious terrorism. For either type of terrorism, counter-terror efforts are likely to be dogged by the "substitution effect," briefly alluded to above.[32] Like the name suggests, attempts to deter terrorism will lead terrorists to change tactics and to select less well-defended targets. Enders and Sandler found that the imposition of metal detectors led to a decrease in hijackings, yet *increased* hostage-taking. Efforts to fortify embassies led to less attacks against personnel in those facilities, but more assassinations as these individuals were attacked off embassy grounds. Even efforts to punish terrorists, like Reagan's bombing of Libya in 1986, have little discernable effect on broader trends. Instead, punishments led to an increase in low-cost terrorist activity, with the number of higher-cost attacks ultimately reverting back to its "normal" rate.[33] As a result, actions to address the material aspects of religious terrorist organizations may also only temporarily allay the threat of terrorism.

CRITICISMS OF THE RATIONAL CHOICE MODEL

The ubiquity of this approach has not meant it is free from criticism. In one of the best-known critiques of the approach, Abrahms highlights seven common terrorist behaviors that challenge the rational choice model.[34] First, terrorists may not possess complete and transitive preferences over the potential outcomes of their actions. Terrorist statements often indicate an amorphous and inconsistent political ideology in which ideological distinctions and differences do not appear to be honored. In Germany, right-wing terrorist organizations had so fully adopted the rhetoric of the left that law enforcement initially identified these groups as Communists.[35] In Italy, the Red Brigades justified their actions on the basis of a hodgepodge of left and right-wing ideas conceptualized as "revolutionary justice."[36] Some groups have abandoned a previously avowed political platform, often very quickly, in favor of beliefs that were almost contradictory to their original position. The absence of nuance and lack of conviction in both rhetoric and action suggest that terrorists may not have any sort of preference ordering in place by which to make a decision from among potential choices.

Further, terrorist organizations do not appear to be able to make decisions that maximize their utility. Because terrorism rarely achieves its stated goals, most groups – if they bided by utility maximization – would not engage in terrorism to begin with. Instead, terrorism is a first choice, many times triumphing over more peaceful and more effective means of political change. Similarly, when confronted with compromise, many terrorist groups reflexively reject it in favoring of continuing a campaign of violence, even if this action is ultimately destructive to the group's stated end goals.

Finally, in order for the organization to reap any benefits from the act of terrorism, the identity of the perpetrator has to be known. Instead, many groups hide their participation and fail to take credit for terrorist operations.[37] This puzzle is pervasive; Abrahms (2008, 89) notes that around 64 percent of global terrorist attacks since 1968 – and three quarters of attacks since September 11th – have been conducted by unknown or anonymous perpetrators. Such behaviors are at odds with the assumption of utility maximization.

Rather, Abrahms (2008) suggests that the incentive structure for terrorists do not center on the organization's political goals, but rather that individuals join and persist in organizations on the basis of group solidarity.[38] In other words, groups are not rational in the classical sense, as organization-wide political objectives do not form the basis of the organization's utility function. Instead, the personal relationships and social benefits that a group imparts forms its utility function. One cause for this rests in the terrorist recruitment process: groups rely on preexisting social contacts for new members and, once that member joins, locks them into the organization. This breaks the recruits' connections with the outside world, thus cementing their loyalty to the organization and their fellow members. Moreover, these strong social bonds will cause the organization to pursue actions that keep the connections intact, even while sacrificing larger operational goals. This suggests that actions that make terrorism less politically fruitful will be ineffective. Smarter counterterrorism strategies should focus on social networks between members and break the connections that make terrorist organizations socially desirable.

FUTURE DIRECTIONS

From the early work of Becker and Landes, the study of terrorism has evolved and become increasingly complex, in many ways responding to the growth and complexity of the threat itself.[39] While challenges to the rational choice model do exist, its overall health is excellent as evidenced by new developments in the field. While there are many, I will limit my discussion to two recent developments: the application of game-theoretic models to capture intraorganizational dynamics and the growing use of spatial methodology.

Game-theoretic models offer a strategic component to rational choice models. That is, game theory approximates the interactions of two (or more) rational choice actors. Rather than simply deciding what is the best course of action for the player, actors within a game have to decide what is utility-maximizing while also accounting for the possible decision of another actor. As such, it is good for understanding the interplay between terrorist groups and governments, competing terrorist organizations, or competing factions within a terrorist organization.

This work has already yielded impressive findings. Ethan Bueno de Mesquita and Eric Dickson argue that terrorist organizations, delineated as extremist or moderate, vie for leadership of an aggrieved population.[40] Extremists, seeking control of the population, engage in acts of violence to provoke one of two government responses – discriminating or undiscriminating. Discriminating counterterror does not radicalize the population; indiscriminate counterterror, on the other hand, is counterproductive because it radicalizes the population and emboldens extremists, thus leading to increased mobilization for the organization and greater levels of violence. States, however, are in a dilemma as crackdowns may be the only perceived effective way to deal with terrorism. This may perhaps explain why religious terrorist organizations often pursue strategies that appear self-defeating and may understand why religious terrorist organizations often gain the support of those defined as nonreligious.[41]

Looking at intragroup dynamics, Jacob Shapiro and David Siegel study the dichotomy of poor operatives working for large, well-funded, organizations.[42] They posit that a principal-agent process is at work: leaders delegate to middlemen the funds for operations and, because of operational security, cannot track the way funds are spent. Benefiting from a lack of oversight, middlemen skim from the funds given to them, leaving operatives very little in the way of resources. This greed will, in some instances, cause leaders to cease funding attacks, simply because the costs of skimming are too great. Concerns about skimming are universal – religious terrorist organizations, despite their professed piety, have no more honor among their operatives than do secular organizations. Rather, as Shapiro notes, these concerns are more related to how groups are organized – either as hierarchies or through other forms – rather than their ideology.[43]

The second major development in the field has been the application of geographic information systems (GIS) approaches. The refinement of GIS methodology and a renewed focus on data collection – at increasingly smaller units of aggregation – presents an exciting new area of focus for terrorism researchers. This also allows the insights of rational choice theory to be applied within countries, as the risks of terrorism differ based on the characteristics found at a subnational level.[44] This honors the influence of the rational choice perspective, but applies it in a more realistic way – reflecting the influence of local, as opposed to national, conditions. Insights from the club model, especially those bearing upon the heightened level of commitment among these types of organizations, should be manifested in geographic data. A validation of the club model would see religious terrorist organizations more likely to strike "difficult" targets and areas that are systematically distinct from other types of organizations.

CONCLUSION

Understanding terrorism, and religious terrorism, through the lens of rational choice theory has greatly aided our knowledge of its formation, its prevalence, and its potential staying power. Certainly, criticisms exist; aspects of terrorist behavior remain anomalous to discussions about utility maximization. Others may argue that rational choice appears to be too calculating and utilitarian to be applied to a system of belief that provides comfort to billions. In sum however, the usefulness of the rational choice approach lies in its parsimony and explanatory power, allowing us to understand why religion may serve as an appeal to violence and why so few may heed its call.

Suggested Readings

Max Abrahms, "What Terrorists Really Want: Terrorist Motives and Counterterrorism Strategy," *International Security* 32(2008), pp. 78–105.

Eli Berman, *Radical, Religious, and Violent: The New Economics of Terrorism.* Cambridge: MIT Press, 2009.

Mark Juergensmeyer, *Terror in the Mind of God: The Global Rise of Religious Violence*. Berkeley: University of California Press, 2003.

Todd Sandler, "The Analytical Study of Terrorism: Taking Stock," *Journal of Peace Research* 51(2014), pp. 257–271.

Jacob Shapiro, *The Terrorist's Dilemma*. Princeton: Princeton University Press, 2013.

Endnotes

1 Herbert Simon, "A Behavioral Model of Rational Choice," *Quarterly Journal of Economics* 69(1955), pp. 99–118; Anthony Downs, *An Economic Theory of Democracy* (Boston: Addison-Wesley Publishing Company, 1957).

2 James March, *A Primer on Decision Making*. (New York: Free Press, 1994).

3 Herbert Simon, *Administrative Behavior: A Study of Decision-Making Processes in Administrative Organizations*. (New York: Macmillan, 1947); Herbert Simon, *Models of Man: Social and Rational*. (New York: Wiley, 1957).

4 John von Neumann and Oskar Morgenstern, *Theory of Games and Economic Behavior*. (Princeton: Princeton University Press, 1944).

5 William Landes, "An Economic Study of U.S. Aircraft Hijacking, 1961–1976," *Journal of Law and Economics* 21(1978), pp. 1–31; Gary Becker, "Crime and Punishment: An Economic Approach," *Journal of Political Economy* 76(1968), pp. 169–217.

6 Becker, "Crime and Punishment."

7 Landes, "An Economic Study of U.S. Aircraft Hijacking, 1961–1976."

8 Max Abrahms, "What Terrorists Really Want: Terrorist Motives and Counterterrorism Strategy," *International Security* 32(2008), pp. 78–105.

9 Todd Sandler, John Tschirhart, and Jon Cauley. "A Theoretical Analysis of Transnational Terrorism," *American Political Science Review* 77 (1983), pp. 36–54.

10 Walter Enders and Todd Sandler, "The Effectiveness of Antiterrorism Policies: A Vector-Autoregression-Intervention Analysis," *American Political Science Review* 87(1993), pp. 829–844.

11 Brian Lai, "'Draining the Swamp': An Empirical Examination of the Production of International Terrorism, 1968–1998," *Conflict Management and Peace Science* 24(2007), pp. 297–310; Patrick Brandt and Todd Sandler, "What Do Transnational Terrorists Target? Has it Changed? Are We Safer?" *Journal of Conflict Resolution* 54(2010), pp. 214–236; Michael Horowitz, "Nonstate Actors and the Diffusion of Innovations: The Case of Suicide Terrorism," *International Organization* 64(2010), pp. 33–64; Navin Bapat, "Understanding State Sponsorship of Militant Groups," *British Journal of Political Science* 42(2012), pp. 1–29.

12 Todd Sandler, "The Analytical Study of Terrorism: Taking Stock," *Journal of Peace Research* 51(2014), pp. 257–271.

13   See Mark Juergensmeyer, *Terror in the Mind of God: The Global Rise of Religious Violence.* (Berkeley: University of California Press, 2003).

14   Ibid., p. 221.

15   Bryan Caplan, "Terrorism: The Relevance of the Rational Choice Model," *Public Choice* 128(2006), pp. 91–107.

16   Ibid., Laurence Iannaccone and Eli Berman, "Religious Extremism: The Good, the Bad, and the Deadly," *Public Choice* 128(2006), pp. 109–129; Eli Berman and David Laitin, "Religion, Terrorism, and Public Goods: Testing the Club Model," *Journal of Public Economics* 92(2008), pp. 1942–1967; Eli Berman, *Radical, Religious, and Violent: The New Economics of Terrorism.* (Cambridge: MIT Press, 2009).

17   Laurence Iannaccone and Eli Berman, "Religious Extremism: The Good, the Band, and the Deadly," *Public Choice* 128(2006).

18   Ibid., p. 113.

19   Jerrold Post, Ehud Sprinzak, and Laurita Denny, "The Terrorists in Their Own Words: Interviews with 35 Incarcerated Middle Eastern Terrorists," *Terrorism and Political Violence* 15(2003), pp. 171–184; Ariel Merari, Ilan Diamant, Arie Bibi, Yoav Broshi, and Giora Zakin, "Personality Characteristics of 'Self Martyrs'/'Suicide Bombers' and Organizers of Suicide Attacks," *Terrorism and Political Violence* 22 (2009), pp. 87–101.

20   Iannaccone and Berman, "Religious Extremism Berman and Laitin, Religion, Terrorism, and Public Goods"; Eli Berman, *Radical, Religious, and Violent.*

21   Mancur Olson, *The Logic of Collective Action: Public Goods and the Theory of Groups.* (Cambridge: Harvard University Press, 1965).

22   Iannaccone and Berman, "Religious Extremism Berman and Laitin, Religion, Terrorism, and Public Goods"; Berman, *Radical, Religious, and Violent.*

23   Thomas Hegghammer, "The Recruiter's Dilemma: Signalling and Terrorist Recruitment Tactics," *Journal of Peace Research* 50(2013), pp. 3–16. It is important to note that this also occurs within secular groups as well. Martha Crenshaw (1985) notes the use of "severe initiation costs" as a way of assessing a recruit's commitment to the cause. Martha Crenshaw, "An Organizational Approach to the Analysis of Political Terrorism," *Orbis* 29(1985), p. 485.

24   Berman and Laitin, "Religion, Terrorism, and Public Goods."

25   Nasra Hassan, "Letter from Gaza: An Arsenal of Believers," *The New Yorker*, 19 November 2001; Alan Krueger and Jitka Maleckova, "Education, Poverty, and Terrorism: Is There a Causal Connection?" *Journal of Economic Perspectives* 17(2003), pp. 119–144; Ethan Bueno de Mesquita, "The Quality of Terror," *American Journal of Political Science* 49(2005), pp. 515–530.

26   Valery Tishkov, *Chechnya: Life in a War-Torn Society.* (Berkeley: University of California Press, 2004).

27   Hassan, "Letter from Gaza", p. 39.

28   Iannaccone and Berman, "Religious Extremism ."

29 Jean-Paul Azam, "Suicide Bombing as Intergenerational Investment," *Public Choice* 122(2005), pp. 177–198.

30 Juergensmeyer, *Terror in the Mind of God*, p. 10.

31 Franco Ferracuti, "Ideology and Repentance: Terrorism in Italy." In Walter Reich, ed. *Origins of Terrorism*. (Washington D.C.: Woodrow Wilson Center Press, 1998), pp. 59–64.

32 Enders and Sandler, "The Effectiveness of Antiterrorism Policies."

33 Bryan Brophy-Baermann and John Conybeare, "Retaliating Against Terrorism: Rational Expectations and the Optimality of Rules Versus Discretion," 38(1994), pp. 196–210.

34 Abrahms, "What Terrorists Really Want."

35 Ibid., p. 88.

36 Luigi Manconi, "The Political Ideology of the Red Brigades." In Raimondo Catanzaro, ed. *The Red Brigades and Left-Wing Terrorism in Italy*. (London, UK: Pinter, 1991), pp. 115–143.

37 See Aaron Hoffman, "Voice and Silence: Why Groups Take Credit for Acts of Terror," *Journal of Peace Research* 47(2010), pp. 615–626.

38 Abrahms, "What Terrorists Really Want."

39 Becker, "Crime and Punishment: An Economic Approach"; Landes, "An Economic Study of U.S. Aircraft Hijacking, 1961–1976."

40 Ethan Bueno de Mesquita and Eric Dickson, "The Propaganda of the Deed: Terrorism, Counterterrorism, and Mobilization," *American Journal of Political Science* 51(2007), pp. 364–381.

41 Post, Sprinzak, and Denny, "The Terrorists in Their Own Words."

42 Jacob Shapiro and David Siegel, "Underfunding in Terrorist Organizations," *International Studies Quarterly* 51(2007), pp. 405–429.

43 Jacob Shapiro, *The Terrorist's Dilemma*. (Princeton: Princeton University Press, 2013).

44 Claude Berrebi and Darius Lackdawalla, "How Does Terrorism Risk Vary Across Space and Time? An Analysis Based on the Israeli Experience," *Defence and Peace Economics* 18(2007), pp. 113–131; Richard Medina, Laura Siebeneck, and George Hepner, "A Geographic Information Systems (GIS) Analysis of Spatiotemporal Patterns of Terrorist Incidents in Iraq 2004–2009," *Studies in Conflict and Terrorism* 34(2011), pp. 862–882; Stephen Nemeth, Jacob Mauslein, and Craig Stapley, "The Primacy of the Local: Identifying Terrorist Hot Spots Using Geographic Information Systems," *Journal of Politics* 76(2014), pp. 304–317.

8 Terror as Sacrificial Ritual? A Discussion of (Neo-)Durkheimian Approaches to Suicide Bombing

LORENZ GRAITL

INTRODUCTION

With the global proliferation of suicide bombings, Emile Durkheim's theory of altruistic suicide from 1897 has seen a new renaissance. For Durkheim this kind of voluntary death is the result of "over-integration" into society and is thus not repudiated, but highly praised. Several scholars refer to Durkheim's seminal work, *Suicide*, although their use of its terms often diverges from its original use. This results in quite diverse interpretations of these concepts. Durkheim's theory of altruistic suicide was based on his view of "lower societies." Applying it to present-day phenomena is therefore linked with a number of challenges. Can the concept be separated from its nineteenth century social evolutionist baggage? How can social integration be operationalized? How can integration be distinguished from altruistic motives? How big is the social acceptance of these deaths really? Apart from Durkheim's *Suicide*, fewer authors use the concepts of gift and sacrifice developed by other authors from the Durkheimian school. With few connections to the research on terrorism and political violence, Durkheim's theories on ritual and ceremony are used frequently in media studies. Though not without critique, they are also applied to secular contexts. Dayan and Katz for instance regard media events as quasi-religious ceremonies that serve an integrating and community-creating function.[1] Acts of terror have also been described as media events; however, they perform a diametrically opposed function due to their disruptive and chaotic nature. Acknowledging the multidimensional character of events that are perceived in various ways by different audiences, one can ask whether extreme violence like suicide bombings or beheadings can be fit into the category of Durkheimian ritual.

DURKHEIM AND THE STUDY OF SUICIDE BOMBING

The history of modern suicide bombing started in Lebanon in the early 1980s. The military success achieved by Hezbollah in their fight against US and Israeli troops was responsible for the adoption of this tactic by other groups. Those who tried to duplicate Hezbollah's success were ideologically diverse. During the 1980s and 1990s they included both secular-nationalist organizations like the Syrian Social Nationalist Party (SSNP), the Kurdish Workers' Party (PKK) in Turkey, and the Liberation Tigers of Tamil Eelam in Sri Lanka, as well as Islamic Nationalists like Hamas and Islamic Jihad in Palestine. In that era suicide bombings were largely restricted to the Middle East and Sri Lanka. This changed dramatically from the year 2000 on. The majority of suicide missions were now being perpetrated by groups with a Salafi–Jihadi ideology such as al-Qaeda and the Islamic State (IS) who use the tactic much more frequently and much more indiscriminately in their selection of targets. To the present day, 5,430 attacks have occurred in more than 40 countries.[2] In 2015 alone, 636 of these attacks were committed – the highest number in any year so far.[3]

When trying to explain why people are willing to end their lives for the purpose of killing others, scholars often refer to Durkheim's *Suicide*, first published in 1897. Trying to demonstrate the theoretical value of his own sociological approach, Durkheim discusses all major contemporary explanations for voluntary death. For Durkheim, "nonsocial" factors like mental illness, alcohol consumption, climate, seasons, and imitation have little or no significance. Instead, the reason why people deliberately seek death is the result of two forces: social integration and social regulation. In each case of the social factor, both its overabundance as well as the lack of it, result in suicide. On the basis of this assumption, Durkheim constructs four different types of suicide. Anomic suicide is caused by a lack of "social regulation" and appears during divorce, loss of employment, or societal economic crises, which are "disturbances of the collective order,"[4] where people's activities become random and disorderly followed by their distress.[5] The complementary type is fatalistic suicide, which is brought about by excessive social regulation. Durkheim mentions very young husbands, childless wives, and slaves as examples.[6] Egoistic suicide is the consequence of insufficient social integration that family, church, or state fail to provide.[7] A man loses interest in life, when "the bond (. . .) attaching him to society is (. . .) slack."[8] The opposite is true for altruistic suicide,[9] which according to Durkheim is caused by exalted integration. Whereas "modern societies" are breeding grounds for egoistic suicide, "lower societies are the theatre par excellence of altruistic suicide."[10] Durkheim did acknowledge the heterogeneity of non-Western societies, but nevertheless regarded them as earlier developmental stages of the most advanced countries, in accordance with the social evolutionist paradigm dominant at his time.[11] In contrast to Europe where taking one's own life is contradicted by the "cult of human personality,"[12] "lower societies" are characterized by a "rudimentary individuation,"[13] where the people are enmeshed in a "collective personality "[14] and the dominant morality disdains the value of life.[15] Examples of altruistic suicide in Europe are largely restricted to Christian martyrs in previous centuries[16] and the military, whose structure and moral is similar to "lower societies."[17] Yet, even in the army this archaic remnant is in the process of disappearing completely in the ongoing modernization process.[18] Durkheim mentions an extensive list of examples for this form of socially sanctioned suicide – from the ancient Celts and Goths to various cases in North America, Africa, Asia, and Oceania. While the social causes of voluntary sacrifice are always the same, Durkheim further distinguishes three subtypes based on the degree of societal compulsion. The first one is "obligatory altruistic suicide," performed as a duty. Durkheim mentions cases of widow burning in India (known as *sati*) as well as further examples of "following into death" by widows, servants, and followers in other parts of the world.[19] In other instances, self-sacrifice is less explicitly demanded by the surrounding society. This subtype is called "optional altruistic suicide"[20]. Durkheim illustrates it with questionable tales of "the Japanese" who are allegedly willing to slit their bellies for the slightest reasons, and the Dakota and Creek who are said to seek death over minor disappointments.[21] Finally, there are suicides that are performed "purely for the joy of sacrifice."[22] Society does not require them, yet sees them as highly praiseworthy. Durkheim calls these acts "acute altruistic suicides" and states that India is their "classical soil."[23] Mystical reasons motivate the Hindu Brahmin to leap into the floods of the Ganga, the Indian Jain to starve himself to death,[24] and the Japanese Buddhist to let himself be immured into a cave so that he can "strip himself of his personal being in order to be engulfed in something which he regards as his true essence"[25]. For Durkheim, altruistic suicide is thus a phenomenon which is rare in Europe, but the predominant form of self-killing in non-Western societies. It is caused by over-integration. Whereas the degree of social obligation to give up one's life can vary, altruistic suicide is usually accepted and praised by society.

Durkheim's *Suicide* remains one of the most famous sociological classics of all times. Many studies on suicide still reference this seminal work and often attempt to empirically verify its hypotheses or to answer its initial questions with new theoretical models. Although Durkheim gave a detailed description of altruistic suicide, the concept itself attracted little scholarly attention in the first 100 hundred years after its development.[26] It was only after the rise of suicide bombings in the early 2000s that the concept has been discussed again by many scholars.[27]

Several authors suggest differentiating between a micro-, meso-, and macro-level when posing research questions concerning suicide bombing.[28] Thus the main questions researchers are trying to answer are: why are individuals willing to kill themselves and many others? Why do groups decide to utilize this tactic and to what extent do these actions receive societal support? Durkheim's theory of altruistic suicide could potentially be used for all of these levels. A few studies in the field refer to Durkheim to explore certain topics in addition to their main arguments.[29] Other authors try to explain the phenomenon with Durkheim's work as their main theoretical frame.[30]

One of the most cited works on suicide bombing is *Dying to Win* by political scientist Robert Pape (2005). His main argument is that groups send attackers on these missions out of strategic decision-making. Suicide bombings overwhelmingly occur in situations where a group fights against an occupying enemy in the form of a democratic state whose population has another religion. His chapter on the "individual logic" relies heavily on Durkheim whose models of suicide are "highly illuminating with respect to suicide terrorism."[31] For Pape altruistic suicide is perpetrated by integrated individuals in small groups and whose acts are approved by society.[32] While a small number might have egoistic or mixed motivations, Pape argues the majority of today's suicide bombers belong in this category of suicide.[33] This is supported by four arguments. First, most countries where suicide bombings occur frequently do not have a high national suicide rate. This is brought forward to show that suicide attacks are not part of any cultural inclination toward suicide in general. Second, Pape refutes the thesis that these attacks are part of a suicide trend caused by war and crisis, a condition which Durkheim would call anomic. In most cases, the overall suicide rate did not rise in the relevant conflict-torn regions. Third, according to Pape, of all the 462 suicide bombers between 1980 and 2003, 212 or 46 percent died as part of a joint mission against the same target at the same time.[34] Finally, the altruistic motive depends on social approval, and the organizations are "generally an integral part of society"and the local society usually honors the deceased attackers as martyrs.[35] Before assessing the accuracy of these arguments, it is helpful to take a look at "Altruism and Fatalism" by Pedahzur, Perliger, and Weinberg (2003).[36] This study is one of several works approaching suicide attacks that uses not only Durkheim's model of over-integration, but also his idea of fatalism as a form of excessive regulation.[37] Using *Haaretz* as the main source for data collection, Pedahzur et al. present a sample of 80 Palestinian suicide bombers as well as a comparison group of 743 perpetrators of violent acts where death was not sought. The acts were committed between April 1993 and February 2002.[38] Previous experience in terrorist acts, type of education, ideological affiliation, age, marital status, socioeconomic background, and gender were the variables of interest.[39] The empirical data was then compared with social conditions described for altruistic and fatalistic suicide. Pedahzur et al. refer mainly to secondary sources on these topics,[40] and less to Durkheim's *Suicide* itself. In comparison with the control group, suicide bombers in the sample had a higher engagement in previous terrorism acts (80 percent), were more often educated in religious schools (82.8 percent) and were more often affiliated with "religious-fundamentalist" organizations (88.4 percent). These findings are then interpreted as evidence that suicide bombers are better integrated into tight-knit organizations through their previous activities. Furthermore, the stronger religious orientation is said to correspond with Durkheim's type of acute altruistic suicide.[41] In addition, the suicide attackers in the sample are younger, less often married, have less family ties and have a lower socioeconomic status than nonsuicidal terrorists. These results were interpreted by Pedahzur et al. as fatalistic components, with the future of the bombers being "geared towards helplessness and vagueness."[42] Since the social condition of the suicide attackers is both altruistic and fatalistic, the authors suggest that their death should be categorized as a new type called "fatalistic altruistic suicide." Durkheim himself introduced the idea of mixed types.[43] Due to his disinterest in fatalism, he only discussed blends of egoism, anomie, and altruism. Thus, it would only seem logical to construct mixed types based on fatalism. Pedahzur et al.'s use of the term seems, however, to be far from Durkheim's conception and, partially, even the secondary literature. Reinterpreting or reformulating concepts and categories is of course legitimate and often necessary, but authors should be precise where in their texts such reinterpretations or modifications are occurring.[44] In Pedahzur et al.'s study, it would not have been necessary to frame the empirical results in Durkheimian terms. The authors identify concurrent fatalism and altruism which often do not match the description in *Suicide*. In their sample, a large number of bombers are bachelors without a dense family network, whereas Durkheim mentioned husbands who were married too young as an example of the forces of fatalism. Absence of family ties would actually be proof of lower levels of integration, which would be at odds with altruism. Even though it is true that the reward of paradise is relevant for religiously motivated Palestinian suicide attackers, the authors' interpretation of those acts as acute altruistic suicide, the "suicide of martyrs"[45] does not harmonize with the repressive tendencies of fatalism since Durkheim described this type as purely voluntary without any social pressure. Whether drifting away from the original concepts as in the case of Pedahzur et al.'s use of the term fatalism or using a more "literalist" approach, studies trying to employ Durkheim to make sense of suicide bombing have to deal with the following challenges: reconciling the Durkheim's evolutionist conceptualization with modern ideas, operationalizing social integration, differentiating de facto integration from altruistic motivation, and assessing the level of societal approval.

Durkheim regarded altruistic suicide as characteristic of "lower societies" and "primitive peoples," which included historical cultures in Europe such as the Celts, various contemporary small-scale societies outside of Europe, as well as countries like India, China, and Japan. Being a work of "armchair anthropology"[46], the description of those societies in *Suicide* can be criticized. Johnson states that Durkheim's sources are "dubious, being confined to the impressions of ancient authors, early anthropologists, historians, and travelers."[47] This does not mean that all of his examples are mere inventions. However, they are often presented in a distorted or exaggerated way. *Seppuku* in Japan, for example, was committed for a wide variety of motivations.[48] In India, the immolation of a widow was less compulsory than presented by Durkheim and the practice was not unequivocally accepted as there had been opposition to it for several centuries.[49] Even at the time of his writing, the distinction that Durkheim made between modern egoistic suicide and archaic altruistic suicide was questionable. Already in 1894, Steinmetz, another sociologist relying on similar sources when he wrote about *"Suicide among Primitive Peoples,"* came to the conclusion that "the motives are generally the same as those which lead to suicide in all civilized societies."[50] Thus applying this model of a "primitive society" to contemporary societies like Sri Lanka,

Turkey, or Arab countries is not only a-historical, but also based on flawed assumptions. Even in the nineteenth century, voluntary death in non-Western society was often sought for purely individual reasons, and not always perceived as sacrifice for the collective. Though Pedahzur et al. do not use the evolutionist notion of primitives, they use a temporal distinction between postindustrial societies and traditional societies going through transitions, as in the case of Palestine, where the terms altruistic and fatalistic suicide are most applicable.[51] Johnson's 1965 article is named as a source for this conception of fatalism; however, he does not use these characterizations of societies.[52] Without ignoring existing socioeconomic differences between societies, such contrasts could not fully explain the nature of suicide bombing, as many contemporary perpetrators were socialized in Germany, Great Britain, the United States, and other postindustrial societies.

Another difficulty in applying Durkheimian theoretical models is how to operationalize "social integration." Its description in *Suicide* remains rather vague and it is difficult to offer an exact definition. Measuring and determining an abnormally high level of social integration would pose an even greater challenge. Even if scientific consensus existed, collecting data might be highly unreliable as it is difficult to gather unbiased information. The bombers' family might glorify or victimize the person, whereas press reports could sensationalize and demonize an otherwise ordinary biography. In reality, data is often lacking and is frequently interpreted in preexisting discursive frames. Thus, the empirical findings presented as proof for "over-integration" are not always convincing. Pape (2005: 185) argues that suicide attackers are highly integrated since about half of them embark on their mission in teams. Zevallos argues that this is less of an indicator for actual altruism but more a tactical decision made by the organization.[53] Indeed, Pape later contradicts his earlier observation when he writes that "national suicide bombers are often walk-in volunteers who join groups individually" and who "most frequently carry out their attacks individually."[54] Future studies could explore to what extent social integration occurs. This could mean investigating the intensity and quality of relationships among family, friends, extended local networks, and even online communities. For Merari it is less the larger society that is relevant but more the social milieu of the "terrorist group itself." Yet, despite the fact that they are often highly cohesive, only a small number of all armed groups worldwide have resorted to suicide attacks.[55] When over-integration does not necessarily result in altruistic sacrifice, the reverse is also true.

Taylor (1982) has already brought forward the argument that altruistic suicide is not linked to any society in particular.[56] It is not always the result of excessive integration; instead it is frequently caused by "over-attachment."[57] Therefore, the dimension of subjective meanings of voluntary death, as advocated by Douglas (1967) or Young (1972), should more rigorously be taken into consideration.[58] Many studies, however, assume that altruistic motivations as sacrifice for the greater good automatically coincide with high-integration and neglect that they can also appear in situation of moderate and even low levels of integration. The fact that sacrifice occurs in the name of a collective raises the question of whether such acts are always recognized by society. Pape writes that "social approval is central to the logic of altruistic suicide as Durkheim conceived it."[59] For Pape, the perpetrator "willingly accepts a voluntary death precisely because society supports and honors the act."[60] Zevallos is doubtful about community support and argues that public commemorations are often paid for by terrorist organizations and that murals and shrines are no evidence for a culture of martyrdom.[61] Nevertheless, organizations like PKK, LTTE, or Hamas operating in a national context and presenting themselves as defenders from the "outside enemy" always have had a certain degree of community support. In spite of this, Palestinian society, for example, also had a relevant opposition to suicide bombing and the support for this tactic changed over time and in relation to the development of the conflict.[62] General and automatic approval can thus not be observed. The degree of societal acceptance is certainly much lower in regions like Iraq, Syria, or Pakistan where suicide bombings by Jihadi-Salafist groups frequently target almost the entire population. Most Sunni Muslims in Pakistan as well as targeted minorities have no reason to support groups that blow up schools or mosques. This is expressed in a survey in Pakistan in which the statement "Suicide bombers are people who are frustrated and outcasts in their societies" registered an approval rate of 63.7 percent.[63] Jihadi–Salafi suicide bombers are also venerated as martyrs, but less by the surrounding society and more within their own organization and in an often de-territorialized milieu of sympathizers in many different countries.

THE RITUAL DIMENSION OF SUICIDE BOMBING AND VIOLENCE

When trying to explain the phenomenon of suicide bombing, most scholars restrict themselves to Durkheim's *Suicide*. Strenski (2003), however, argues that Durkheim's *Elementary Forms of the Religious Life* (1912) as well as Mauss and Hubert's *Sacrifice: Its Nature and*

Functions (1899), Mauss' *The Gift* (1920) and Halbwachs' *The Causes of Suicide* (1930) are also necessary in understanding the bombers' motivations.[64] Using these works of the Durkheimian school, Strenski interprets what he calls "human bombers" in Palestine as sacrificial gifts to their religion and their nation. Labeling those acts as suicide neglects the social meanings that are attributed to them. Durkheim himself was struggling with the question of how certain cases of voluntary death such as war heroes could be reconciled with his own definition of suicide: "Because altruistic suicide, though showing the familiar suicidal traits, resembles especially in its most vivid manifestations some categories of action which we are used to honoring with our respect and even admiration, people have often refused to consider it as self-destruction (...)"[65]

In his further discussion of such examples, he is unable to answer the question of which variants of heroic deaths should be excluded from the definition of suicide: "When does a motive cease to be sufficiently praiseworthy for the act it determines to be called suicide?".[66] This problem was answered by Maurice Halbwachs, a student of his, whose solution to the problem is "[c]uriously (...) more Durkheimian than Durkheim" according to Strenski.[67] Instead of focusing on an objective definition of suicide alone,[68] Halbwachs reflects the social perception of self-chosen death. Concerning suicide Halbwachs writes, "society fails to recognize it, repudiates it. Society has not desired this".[69] Sacrifice, on the contrary, is distinguished by its ritual character. Unlike suicide, which usually takes place in hidden places and rebels against social norms, sacrifice takes place in the "midst of a community" and is highly honored.[70] If a part of society would question the efficacy of the sacrifice, it would lose its ritual character and become an ordinary suicide.[71] Based on the works of the Durkheimians, Strenski sees suicide bombings as an offering to Palestine, and the Palestinians have to reciprocate this gift by continuing the national struggle. Asad disagrees with the description of Islamic terms by Strenski as well as with the literal interpretation of sacrifice as "making something holy" based on Durkheim's broad conception of the sacred.[72] Asad further stresses the modern character of Islamist concepts like *istishhād*[73], and that one has to "work through the concepts the people concerned actually use".[74] A look at the last wills and testaments of suicide bombers reveals that their rhetoric frequently echoes Halbwachs' analytical distinction between suicide and sacrifice. Islamist and Salafi–Jihadi groups also use terms like "offering" and "sacrifice" in their English- and German-language (translated) media productions. Influenced by secular nationalism, a website linked to Hamas posted a headline announcing that its cadres "will sacrifice their lives for the welfare of their people."[75]

The fruits of sacrifice are also a frequent motive in the *nasheeds* (hymns) of IS. A song by German-born former rapper Denis Cuspert praises the *mujahidin* in Chechnya for blowing "the Russians" apart and states that: "In the protection of the forests, surrounded by angels, they give for Shari'ah their blood and their life"[76] (YouTube 2013). Similarly, the well-known IS hymn declares "The Islamic States has arisen by the Jihad of the pious," who "have offered their souls"[77]. The perspective of the Durkheimian school – emphasizing ritual, gift, and sacrifice – can thus remain useful in explaining religious and political violence. The Durkheimian perspective could also be extended to include secular nationalism in general[78] or the suicide bombings by nonreligious groups like the DHKP-C in Turkey who exercise "sacrificial Marxism."[79] The terms from the discursive universe of armed groups, of course, never fully coincide with scientific meta-categories like "sacrifice" or "martyrdom." Schalk (2009) has worked on the many different terms with which the Tamil Tigers, and their leader Pirapā-karaṇ, in particular, describe heroic death. One of the descriptions used is *tarkoṭai* (gift of oneself), an altruistic, disinterested gift distinct from the image of mandatory sacrifice in animal sacrifice. Schalk also points to a difference in the conception of martyrdom by the LTTE leadership and Catholic priests close to the movement.[80] This is another reminder that societies are never monolithic in their views.

As the works from the Durkheimian school date back to the late nineteenth and early twentieth centuries, they do not analyze how modern rituals and violent acts are frequently not only geared toward people who are physically present, but toward a media audience. From a neo-Durkheimian perspective Dayan and Katz (1994) develop a theory of media events that they see as preplanned acts that are televised live and break daily routine.[81] Their ceremonial character gives those media events a community-creating function.[82] This approach has been criticized by Couldry (2005) as functionalist with the integrating effect of media events being illusory. Instead he advocates a "Post-Durkheimian" approach to "media rituals," the latter being "forms of media communication that construct the 'myth of the mediated centre.'"[83] In a volume edited by Hepp, Krotz, and Couldry (2010), several authors, including Katz, try to rethink and to extend the original approach of media events taking new mediatization and globalization processes under consideration.[84] Dayan and Katz (1994) had limited their definition of media events to conquests, coronations, and competitions, such as the first visit of the Egyptian President Sadat to Israel in 1977, the funeral of John F. Kennedy, or the Olympic Games.[85] Apart from those "ritual media events" there are also conflictual media events including terror attacks, natural disasters, and war.[86] Weimann had already argued in 1987 that terror attacks should be regarded as media events as they, too, are often carefully orchestrated, preplanned, televised live, and contain elements of dramatic story-telling.[87] The spectacular terrorist acts of his time like plane hijackings constitute a fourth genre of media events, which he calls coercion. In his opinion the theatrical acts of terrorism "fulfill important social functions similar to those of the more conventional rituals".[88] While acknowledging that the dramas of this time were co-produced by media and terrorists, it seems that he only had a western audience in mind when he wrote this. The question is whether extreme violence, the beheadings, and suicide bombings by IS, for example, are not disruptive and ritual at the same time, just directed at different audiences. In targeting the enemy societies, the aim is to intimidate and destabilize the social order, whereas one's own community should become more cohesive[89] in the perceived shared experience of victory and in the celebration of martyrdom.

CONCLUSION

As was shown in this chapter, the ideas of Durkheim and the Durkheimian school can be used in numerous ways to describe religiously (and politically) motivated violence such as suicide bombings, plane hijackings, or beheadings. Even when scholars use the same chapter of a classic work, they rarely agree on how to interpret and to apply its concepts. With Durkheim's writings on totemism in mind, Kuper writes that even though the old master was discredited for his ethnographic inaccuracies, his abstract ideas still remain powerful[90].[91] Inspiration by Durkheim's work can still be fruitful, if a critical rereading is adopted and if the applicability of the concepts is empirically verified.

Suggested Readings

Durkheim, Emile, *Suicide*. London: Routledge and Kegan Paul, 1951(fr. 1897).

Halbwachs, Maurice, *The Causes of Suicide*. London: Routledge and Kegan Paul, 1978 (fr. 1930).

Hubert, Henri, and Mauss, Marcel *Sacrifice: Its Nature and Functions*. University of Chicago Press, 1964 (fr. 1899).

Mauss, Marcel, *The Gift: Forms and Functions of Exchange in Archaic Societies*. London: Routledge, 1990 (fr. 1920).

Pape, Robert, *Dying to Win. The Strategic Logic of Suicide Terrorism*. New York: Random House, 2005.

Pedahzur, Ami; Perliger, Arie, and Weinberg, Leonard, "Altruism and Fatalism: The Characteristics of Palestinian Suicide Terrorists," *Deviant Behavior: An Interdisciplinary Journal* 24, 2003, 405–423.

Strenski, Ivan, "Sacrifice, Gift and the Social Logic of Muslim 'Human Bombers,'" *Terrorism and Political Violence* 15.3, 2003, 1–34.

Endnotes

1. Dayan, Daniel and Katz, Elihu, *Media Events. The Live Broadcasting of History*. Harvard University Press: Cambridge, Massachusetts, 1994.

2. CPOST, Suicide Attack Database, October 12, 2016 http://cpostdata .uchicago.edu/search_results_new.php (accessed April 27, 2017).

3. Ibid.

4. Durkheim, Emile, *Suicide*. London: Routledge and Kegan Paul, 1951 (fr. 1897), p. 246.

5. Ibid, p. 259.

6. Ibid, p. 276. Although the term "fatalistic suicide" is mentioned only once in a footnote because Durkheim considered it to be insignificant, he repeatedly discusses examples which could also be categorized under this type (Johnson, Barclay, "Durkheim's one Cause of Suicide," American Sociological Review 30.6, 1965, 877).

7. Durkheim, *Suicide*, p.208.

8. Ibid, p. 214–215.

9. As Whitt (2006) has discovered, the term altruistic suicide had already been used by Hopkins (1880), who dealt with the problem from a normative position. Hopkins, J., "A consideration of suicide," *Popular Science Monthly* 16, 1880: 789–803;Whitt, Hugh, "Durkheim's Precedence in the Use of the Terms Egoistic and Altruistic Suicide: An Addendum," *Suicide and Life-Threatening Behavior* 36.1, 2006, 125–127. Whether Durkheim had read Hopkins' article remains unknown as he does not quote the earlier author. There are two sections in *Suicide* that are reminiscent of Hopkins, which could indicate that Durkheim was familiar with his work.

10. Durkheim, *Suicide*, p. 227.

11. Durkheim acknowledges a multilinear model of evolution as opposed to the one developed by the earlier sociologist Auguste Comte. Nevertheless he often reverts back to an argumentation of unilinear development (Kuper, Adam, "Durkheim's Theory of Primitive Kinship," *The British Journal of Sociology* 36.2; 1985, pp. 227–228, Girtler, Roland, *Kulturanthropologie: eine Einführung*. Münster: LIT Verlag, 2006, p. 30).

12. Durkheim, *Suicide*, p. 334.

13. Ibid, p. 221.

14. Ibid, p. 228.

15. Ibid, p. 240, 348.

16. Ibid, p. 227.

17   Ibid, p. 228–239.

18   Ibid, p. 237.

19   For an historic account of these practices see: Fisch, Jörg, *Burning Women: A Global History of Widow Sacrifice from Ancient Times to the Present.* Oxford: Seagull Books, 2006.

20   Durkheim, *Suicide*, p. 223.

21   Ibid, p. 222.

22   Ibid, p. 223.

23   Ibid.

24   This practice is called Santhara or Sallekhana in the Jain religion and still occurs today (Tukol, T. K., *Sallekhana is Not Suicide*. Ahmedabad. LD Institute of Indology, 1976; Laidlaw, James, "A Life Worth Leaving: Fasting to Death as Telos of a Jain Religious Life," *Economy and Society* 34.2, 2005, 178–199.

25   Durkheim, *Suicide*, p. 225.

26   Young, Lung-Chang, "Altruistic Suicide: A Subjective Approach," *Sociological Bulletin* 21.2, 1972, 103–121, Blake, Joseph, "Death by Handgrenade: Altruistic Suicide in Combat," *Suicide and Life-Threatening Threatening Behavior*, Vol 8.1, 1978, 46–60, Riemer, Jeffrey, "Durkheim's 'Heroic Suicide' in Military Combat," *Armed Forces & Society* 25.1, 1998, 103–120.

27   Abrutyn, Seth, and Mueller, Anna S., "When Too Much Integration and Regulation Hurts: Reenvisioning Durkheim's Altruistic Suicide," *Society and Mental Health* September 8, 2015: 1–16; Leenaars, Antoon and Wenckstern, Susanne, "Altruistic Suicides: Are They the Same or Different from Other Suicides?" *Archives of Suicide Research* 8, 2004, 131–136; Maris, Ronald, Berman, Alan, and Silverman, Morton (eds.), *Comprehensive Textbook of Suicidology*. New York: Guilford, 2000; Merari, Ariel, *Driven to Death. Psychological and Social Aspects of Suicide Terrorism.* Oxford: Oxford University Press, 2010; Pape, Robert, *Dying to win. The Strategic Logic of Suicide Terrorism.* New York: Random House, 2005; Pedahzur, Ami, *Suicide Terrorism.* Cambridge: Polity, 2005; Stack, Steven, "Emile Durkheim and Altruistic Suicide," *Archives of Suicide Research* 8.1, 2004, 9–22; Townsend, Ellen, "Suicide Terrorists: Are They Suicidal?," *Suicide and Life-Threatening Behavior* 37.1, 2007, 35–49.

28   Hafez, Mohammed, *Suicide Bombers in Iraq. The Strategy and Ideology of Martyrdom.* Washington: US Institute of Peace, 2007; Merari, Ariel, *Driven to Death. Psychological and Social Aspects of Suicide Terrorism.* Oxford: Oxford University Press, 2010; Moghadam, Assaf, *The Globalization of Martyrdom. Al Quaeda, Salafi Jihad, and the Diffusion of SuicideAttacks.* Baltimore: JHU Press, 2008; Pape, Robert, *Dying to win. The Strategic Logic of Suicide Terrorism.* New York: Random House; 2005, Pedahzur, Ami and Martin, Susanne, Suicide Attacks, 2015 www.academia.edu/10588202/Suicide_Attacks (accessed October 10, 2015).

29   Pape, *Dying to Win*; Merari, Ariel, *Driven to Death. Psychological and Social Aspects of Suicide Terrorism.* Oxford: Oxford University Press, 2010.

30 Bakken, Nicholas W., The Anatomy of Suicide Terrorism. A Durkheimian Analysis. University of Delaware, 2007, www.ifpo .org/wp-content/uploads/2013/08/Bakken_Suicide_Terrorism.pdf (accessed 7 October, 2015); Holdredge, Philipp Thomas, A Durkheimian Explanation for Suicide Terrorism, 2007, www.hamilton.edu/levitt/ insights/durkheim-suicide%20terrorism%20paper.pdf (accessed 12 July, 2010); Snellens, Dana S., "A Durkheimian Analysis of the Development of Terrorism and the Motives of Suicide Bombers," *Social Cosmos* 3.1, 2012, 9–13.

31 Pape, Dying to Win, p. 179.

32 Ibid., p. 176.

33 Ibid., p. 180–186.

34 Ibid., p. 185.

35 Ibid., p. 187.

36 In Ami Pedahzur's important book *Suicide Terrorism* (Cambridge: Polity, 2005), Durkheimian categories do not have as prominent of a place as in the article that is discussed here.

37 See also: Bakken, The Anatomy of Suicide Terrorism; Holdredge, A Durkheimian Explanation for Suicide Terrorism; Snellens, "A Durkheimian Analysis of the Development of Terrorism and the Motives of Suicide Bombers."

38 Pedahzur, Ami; Perliger, Arie and Weinberg, Leonard, "Altruism and Fatalism: The Characteristics of Palestinian Suicide Terrorists," *Deviant Behavior: An Interdisciplinary Journal* 24, 2003, p. 412–413.

39 Ibid., p. 413.

40 e.g., Johnson, Barclay, "Durkheim's One Cause of Suicide," *American Sociological Review* 30.6, 1965, 875–886; Young, Lung-Chang, "Altruistic Suicide: A Subjective Approach," *Sociological Bulletin* 21.2, 1972, 103–121.

41 Pedahzur et al. "Altruism and Fatalism," p. 408–410, 417.

42 Ibid., p. 420.

43 Durkheim, *Suicide*, p. 277–294. As Hamlin and Brym 2006 have observed, Durkheim's mixed types are based on the individual's emotional state before the act and not on the social conditions that he had previously described (Hamlin, Cynthia Lins, and Brym, Robert J., "The Return of the Native: A Cultural and Social-Psychological Critique of Durkheim's Suicide Based on the Guarani-Kaiowá of Southwestern Brazil," *Sociological Theory* 24.1, 2006, 42–57). Durkheim's ego-altruistic type would be a logical contradiction as excessive and insufficient integration cannot appear at the same time (Johnson, "Durkheim's One Cause," p. 877).

44 See for example Abrutyn and Mueller's (2015) attempt to re-conceptualize altruistic suicide: Abrutyn, Seth, and Mueller, Anna S., "When Too Much Integration and Regulation Hurts: Reenvisioning Durkheim's Altruistic Suicide," *Society and Mental Health* September 8, 2015: 1–16.

45 Pedahzur et al., "Altruism and Fatalism," p. 408.

46 Couldry, Nick, Media Rituals: Beyond Functionalism, 2005, http:// eprints.lse.ac.uk/52494/1/Couldry_Media_rituals_beyond_functional ism_2005.pdf (accessed October 3, 2015).

47   Johnson, "Durkheim's One Cause," p. 880.
48   Pinguet, Maurice, *Voluntary Death in Japan*. Cambridge: Polity, 1993;
     Seward, Jack, *Hara-kiri: Japanese Ritual Suicide*. Rutland: Tuttle, 1968.
49   Sharma, Arvind, *Sati. Historical and Phenomenological Essays*. New
     Delhi: Motilal Banarsidass Publ., 1988.
50   Steinmetz, Sebald Rudolf, "Suicide among Primitive Peoples." *Ameri-
     can Anthropologist* 7.1, 1894, p. 59.
51   Pedahzur et al., "Altruism and Fatalism," p. 408.
52   In 1965 post-industrialism was still a new idea and it was certainly
     not used by Durkheim himself. As mentioned above, Johnson was
     highly critical of Durkheim's characterization of non-Western
     societies.
53   Zevallos, Zuleyka, What would Durkheim Say? Altruistic Suicide in
     Analyses of Suicide Terrorism. *Proceedings of the Annual Conference
     of The Australian Sociological Association: Sociology for a Mobile
     World*, 2006, http://researchbank.swinburne.edu.au/vital/access/ser
     vices/Download/swin:25063/SOURCE1 (accessed 7 October 2015).
54   Pape, Robert, and Feldman, James, *Cutting the Fuse: The Explosion of
     Global Suicide Terrorism and How to Stop It*. University of Chicago
     Press, 2010, p. 57.
55   Merari, *Driven to Death*, p. 204.
56   Taylor, Steve, *Durkheim and the Study of Suicide*. London: Macmillan,
     1982, p. 91.
57   Ibid.
58   Douglas, Jack, *The Social Meanings of Suicide*. Princeton University
     Press, 1967; Young, Lung-Chang, "Altruistic Suicide."
59   Pape, *Dying to Win*, p. 187.
60   Ibid.
61   Zevallos, What would Durkheim Say?, p. 7.
62   Merari, *Driven to Death*, pp. 295–303.
63   Kazim, Syed Faraz et al., "Attitudes toward Suicide Bombing in Paki-
     stan," *Crisis* 29.2, 2008, p. 83.
64   Strenski, Ivan, "Sacrifice, Gift and the Social Logic of Muslim 'Human
     Bombers,'" *Terrorism and Political Violence* 15.3, 2003, 1–34.
65   Durkheim, *Suicide*, p. 239.
66   Ibid., p. 240.
67   Strenski, "Sacrifice, Gift and the Social Logic of Muslim 'Human
     Bombers,'" p. 7.
68   Durkheim, *Suicide*, p. 41–46.
69   Halbwachs, *The Causes of Suicide*, p. 306.
70   Ibid., p. 307.
71   Ibid. As discussed before, present-day martyrdom is rarely accepted by
     an entire collective, whether it has a national, ethnic, or religious basis.
72   Asad, Talal, *On Suicide Bombing*. Columbia University Press, 2007,
     pp. 42–50.
73   Which can be translated as self-sacrifice.
74   Ibid. p. 52, p. 44.

75 The Palestinian Information Center, Hamas: Our Cadres Will Sacrifice Their Lives for the Welfare of Their People, http://english.palinfo.com/ site/pages/details.aspx?itemid=61488 (accessed October 10, 2015).

76 Chechenya Nasheed, YouTube video, 6: 27, Posted by "Ghura-bal3i1Ithnillah," January 12, 2013. www.youtube.com/watch?v= TOt4_wLPbqw (accessed November 6, 2015). Literal translation from the German lyrics by the author.

77 My Ummah, Dawn Has Appeared Best Jihadic Nasheed امتي قد لاح ح فجر English subtitles, YouTube video, 4:31, Posted by "Hafiz Tila," January 7, 2015. www.youtube.com/watch?v=RYjt1-TEQk4 (accessed November 6, 2015). Quotes from the English subtitles of the Arab language song. I assume that the hymn was translated by an IS member or sympathizer.

78 Marvin, Carolyn, and Ingle, David. *Blood Sacrifice and the Nation: Totem Rituals and the American Flag.* Cambridge University Press, 1999.

79 Bargu, Banu, *Starve and Immolate: The Politics of Human Weapons.* Columbia University Press, 2014, p. 239.

80 Schalk, Peter, "Die Lehre des heutigen tamilischen Widerstandes in Īlam/Laṅkā vom Freitod als Martyrium". *ZfR* 17, 2009, p. 79.

81 Dayan, and Katz, *Media Events.*

82 Ibid.

83 Hepp, Andreas and Couldry, Nick, "Introduction: Media Events in Globalized Media Cultures," In: Couldry, Nick, Hepp, Andreas and Krotz, Friedrich eds. *Media Events in a Global Age.* London: Routledge, 2010, p. 5

84 Couldry, Nick, Hepp, Andreas and Krotz, Friedrich eds. *Media Events in a Global Age.* London: Routledge, 2010.

85 Dayan and Katz, *Media Events.*

86 Hepp and Couldry, "Introduction: Media Events," p. 12.

87 Weimann, Gabriel, "Media Events: The Case of International Terrorism," *Journal of Broadcasting & Electronic Media* 31.1, 1987, p. 25–27.

88 Ibid. 27.

89 This might or might not be a myth as Couldry argues (Couldry "Media Rituals").

90 Kuper, Adam, "Durkheim's Theory of Primitive Kinship," *The British Journal of Sociology* 36.2, 1985, 224–237.

91 See for example Marvin and Ingle's work *Blood Sacrifice and the Nation* on American nationalism based on a reinterpretation of totemism.

9 Imitations of Terror: Applying a Retro Style of Analysis to the Religion-Terrorism Nexus

JAMES R. LEWIS

My day's work started a little before five o'clock yesterday, when I began helping Ed Sanders mix heating oil with the ammonium nitrate fertilizer ... We stood the 100-pound bags on end one by one and poked a small hole in the top with a screwdriver, just big enough to insert the end of a funnel ... It took us nearly three hours to do all 44 sacks, and the work really wore me out ... Finally, I ran the cable and switch from the detonator through a chink from the cargo area into the cab of the truck.

[We then drove to the site, and] George and I headed for the building in the car, with Henry following in the truck ... until we found a good spot to park. [Finally, we left and hit the detonator.]

[T]he pavement shuddered violently under our feet. An instant later the blast wave hit us – a deafening 'ka-whoomp,' followed by an enormous roaring, crashing sound, accentuated by the higher-pitched noise of shattering glass all around us.

Overturned trucks and automobiles, smashed office furniture, and building rubble were strewn wildly about – and so were the bodies of a shockingly large number of victims. Over everything hung the pall of black smoke burning our eyes and lungs and reducing the bright morning to semi-darkness ... we gaped with a mixture of horror and elation at the devastation.

All day yesterday and most of today we watched the TV coverage of rescue crews bringing the dead and injured out of the building. It is a heavy burden of responsibility for us to bear, since most of the victims of our bomb were only pawns who were no more committed to the sick philosophy or the racially destructive goals of the System than we are. But there is no way we can destroy the System without hurting many thousands of innocent people – no way. It is a cancer too deeply rooted in our flesh. And if we don't destroy the System before it destroys us – if we don't cut this cancer out of our living flesh – our whole race will die.

Nevertheless, every time the TV camera focuses on the pitiful, mutilated corpse of some poor girl – or even an FBI agent – being pulled from the wreckage, my stomach becomes tied in knots and I cannot breathe. It is a terrible, terrible task we have before us.

Passages from a Timothy McVeigh letter? Excerpts from the diary of Terry McNichols? A fictionalized version of events written in the aftermath of the Oklahoma City bombing on 19 April 1995? While the parallels to the bombing of the Oklahoma City federal building are eerie, this prophetic description of events comes from the 1978 novel, *The Turner Diaries*.[1] The narrative of this piece of dark fiction is built around an apocalyptic race war that culminates in the extermination of all non-White peoples. The tale is told through the eyes of Earl Turner, a White revolutionary who eventually bombs the Pentagon in a final act of suicidal martyrdom. Not coincidently, Timothy McVeigh made a living selling survival items and copies of *The Turner Diaries* at gun shows.

An underground 'classic' within North America's White racialist subculture, *The Turner Diaries* supplies both a rationale and a prophetic blueprint for White supremacist terrorists. While not especially well-written, there is some strange appeal about this narrative that has helped inspire a number of different right-wing extremists to take direct, violent action against 'the System'. The bombing of the Oklahoma Federal Building is merely the most dramatic case in point. Also of note are the activities of The Order, a.k.a. The Silent Brotherhood, a group of White revolutionaries similarly inspired by *The Turner Diaries*. In 1983–84, The Order engaged in a crime wave, mostly in the West, preparatory (they anticipated) to launching attacks on the federal government. Between 1984 and 1986, members of the Order were captured and tried, and its leader, Robert Matthews, was killed in a shootout with the FBI.

While William L. Pierce, the presumed author of the *Diaries*, might not have intended such literalistic readings of his fiction, it is clear that he did envision a future race war for which he wished his Aryan brethren to be prepared. Although not fitting the stereotype of the robed and bearded recluse familiar from Hollywood adaptations of Judeo–Christian scriptures, he was, in a sense, a modern prophet. The major difference was that, rather than simply predicting events, Pierce provided what might be termed a 'mythological' model that would eventually inspire a number of quasi-ritualistic acting out of events.

MYTHOLOGY

The related topics of myth and ritual have attracted the systematic attention of both anthropologists and religious studies scholars since the beginnings of those disciplines in the nineteenth century. However, while earlier researchers were especially interested in finding commonalities among myths (as well as rituals) – an approach referred to as comparative mythology – this approach has fallen into disfavor in recent decades. Contemporary approaches tend to emphasize both the differences among myths[2] as well as the embedded character of religion,[3] in part because of a more general revolt against prior universalizing approaches, particularly as these earlier approaches were represented in the work of Mircea Eliade.[4] In the present chapter, I will utilize a selection of these earlier understandings of myths as the basis for interpreting the mythic/ritualistic characteristics that many terrorist acts seem to exhibit. This is not, I should emphasize, the same as presenting a comprehensive interpretation of terrorism. (Nor should my utilization of a handful of notions from Eliade be interpreted as advocacy for the entire Eliadean system.) In the later part of the paper, I will present a rethinking of this older approach in terms of more recent research and theorizing, particularly as old and new overlap in the notion of 'imitation'.

One of the problems with myth is that it has multiple meanings, one of which is 'falsehood', as when 'myth' and 'reality' are utilized as contrasting terms. Within the discipline of religious studies, a handy brief definition is 'sacred story' – which does not immediately judge any given myth as being historically either true or false. Another problem is that there are numerous theories of myth that are often not compatible with each other.

One popular approach to mythology, a depth psychological approach embodied in the works of Carl Jung and Joseph Campbell, has wide appeal outside of academia. This approach views myths as representing purely psychological meanings.[5] In Jung's words, 'myths are original revelations of the preconscious psyche, involuntary statements about unconscious psychic happenings, and anything but allegories of physical processes'.[6] The academic mainstream has largely rejected this school of thought, at least as a comprehensive theory of mythology – though Jung's notion that reports of flying saucers represent psychological projections is still referred to favorably.[7]

Early studies of mythology focused on texts of mythic narratives (e.g., classical mythology) and tended to speculate about the meaning of myths independently of cultural context. By the early twentieth century, this approach had come under sustained criticism from the influential anthropologist, Bronislaw Malinowski. Based on his fieldwork among Trobriand Islanders, Malinowski described myth as

> not merely a story told but a reality lived ... Myth fulfills in
> primitive culture an indispensable function: it expresses, enhances,

and codifies belief; it safeguards and enforces morality: it vouches for the efficiency of ritual and contains practical rules for the guidance of man. Myth is thus a vital ingredient of human civilization; it is not an idle tale, but a hard-worked active force; it is not an intellectual explanation or an artistic imagery, but a pragmatic charter of primitive faith and moral wisdom.[8]

For the present discussion, the two functions of mythology I want to draw from Malinowski are that (1) myths can legitimate (i.e., act as 'charters' for) certain actions, as well as for certain aspects of the existing social order. Additionally, (2) they can provide paradigms or models that we are able to imitate, both in formal rituals as well as in everyday behavior. These two aspects of mythology are, obviously, closely related.

I also want to draw on parts (though not his entire model) of Victor Turner's notion of 'social drama'. In *Dramas, Fields, and Metaphors*, Turner argues that when conflict situations escalate to the point of breaking through routine coping mechanisms, social groups as well as individual social actors tend to fall back on myths, metaphors and other dramatic structures provided by their respective cultures. The metaphor or narrative structure selected out of the collectivity's 'storehouse' of symbols then provides the pattern for coping with the disruptive situation.

Articulating the social drama idea within his earlier theorizing about the dynamic polarity between structure and anti-structure, Turner portrays the choice of symbolic structures as a non-mechanistic process in which many options are possible. Yet his examples, such as the confrontation between Thomas Becket and King Henry II,[9] also imply that, once embraced, the chosen narrative tends rigidly to structure one's actions, to the point where an historical actor will follow out even a tragic plot. It is not difficult to see how this kind of an analysis can be stretched to encompass the impact of *The Turner Diaries* on the Oklahoma City Bombing, as well as to some of the other activities influenced by Peirce's novel.

In any given conflict, it is not predetermined which narratives or symbolic structures will be brought forward to serve as paradigms for action. Explicitly religious groups and individuals will, for example, often draw upon their respective scriptural and historical traditions for legitimacy as well as for models of action. Though not usually regarded as a terrorist event,[10] a particularly poignant example of this can be found in the Branch Davidian tragedy, and in the efforts of the group's leader,

David Koresh, to understand himself, the 1993 law enforcement attack
on his community, and the subsequent siege in terms of biblical models.

'THE BIBLE WAS WRITTEN FOR OUR TIME'

To provide a brief backdrop for readers unfamiliar with the Branch
Davidian attack: on the 28th of February 1993, a force of seventy agents
of the Bureau of Alcohol, Tobacco and Firearms (ATF) raided the Branch
Davidian community situated outside of Waco, Texas. The raid turned
into a shootout between federal agents and Branch Davidians. The
resulting standoff developed into a fifty-one-day siege that ended on
the 19th of April when the FBI (which had taken over the siege from
the ATF) launched a new attack on Mt. Carmel (the Davidian complex).
Agents of the federal government used military equipment to batter
holes in buildings through which they injected noxious gas in an
attempt to force the Davidians outside. A fire ignited in the buildings
and over eighty members died.

The Branch Davidians were biblically based, but the Bible was
interpreted through the revelations of a living prophet. Though Koresh's
assumption of a prophetic mantle might seem a radical departure from
traditional Christianity, in principle it was not strange for the Adventist
tradition out of which the Branch Davidians had sprung – a tradition
that recognized living prophets. Thus, the theological innovations introduced by their leaders were recognized as legitimate because God was
continually revealing new truths through His prophets.[11] One of Koresh's revelations that was especially important for understanding his
response to the attack on Mt. Carmel was that the Bible was literally
'written for our time'.[12]

In a live radio interview conducted shortly after the ATF raid,
Koresh told his audience that 'We are now in the fifth seal'.[13] The fifth
seal is described in Revelation 6:9–11:

> And when he had opened the fifth seal, I saw under the altar the
> souls of them that were slain for the word of God, and for the
> testimony which they held: And they cried with a loud voice,
> saying, How long, O Lord, holy and true, dost thou not judge and
> avenge our blood on them that dwell on the earth? And white robes
> were given unto every one of them; and it was said unto them, that
> they should rest yet for a little season, until their fellow servants
> also and their brethren, that should be killed as they were, should be
> fulfilled.

Not unlike McVeigh's reading of *The Turner Diaries*, Koresh was reading the Bible like a script that told him what was going to happen next, and that also gave him instructions on what to do. He took the 'souls of those who had been slaughtered' as referring to the six community residents who had died during the initial ATF raid. They were being told to 'wait a little season'. However, they were also being told that they were 'soon to be killed'. Two biblical scholars particularly interested in apocalypticism, Phillip Arnold and James Tabor, contacted the FBI and tried to convey the seriousness of the situation. They especially feared that the Davidians might – believing they should follow out the next step in the biblical script God had provided – provoke a violent denouement (in the form of what today might be called a 'martyrdom operation') in order to push the situation along to the sixth seal, the Day of Judgement.[14]

Despite Koresh's outward confidence, it was clear that he was confused. Although the Endtime scenario in Revelation called for the events described in Revelation 6:9–11 to take place, he had previously anticipated all of this happening in another time and place. Additionally, despite the seeming applicability of these particular verses, many other things had happened that did not seem to match up with the biblical text.

As analyzed by Tabor and others, the dynamics of interpreting contemporary events in terms of the biblical text involve three principal factors:

1. The text of the Bible, which is fixed.
2. The interpreter, who attempts to understand and apply the text to events.
3. The fluid context in which the individual or group finds itself.[15]

Although the Bible acts as a roadmap that cannot be changed, there is a high degree of flexibility in applying the text to actual events. The interpreter is always interpreting. The two scholars thus felt they might be able to intervene in Koresh's interpretive world and offer an alternative scenario.

After receiving a token okay from the FBI, Arnold and Tabor arranged to speak on a radio program they knew the Davidians listened to in order to put forward an alternative interpretation of Revelation – one in which the remaining members of the community did not have to die. Specifically, they discussed the 'little book' that is the subject of Chapter Ten of Revelation. Arnold and Tabor knew Koresh regarded himself as the figure in that text who receives a book containing the 'mystery of God' as 'declared to his servants the prophets' (10:7).

On the 14th of April, two weeks after the radio program and five days before the FBI attack, Koresh declared the waiting period over. God had commanded him to write a book unveiling the meaning of the Seven Seals. Arnold and Tabor were elated, convinced Koresh would be true to his word and come out peaceably after he had finished his exposition of the seven seals. Unfortunately, the FBI, tired of what they derisively referred to as 'Bible babble', were equally certain this was just one more delaying tactic and went ahead with the assault.

On the evening of the 19th of April, following the final fiery holocaust, Jeffrey Jamar, the FBI agent in command at Mt. Carmel, asserted on the *Larry King Show* and *Nightline* that, through the agency's classified surveillance techniques, the FBI had 'incontrovertible evidence' that Koresh not only had not started working on his manuscript, but that he never intended to do so. This confident claim was, however, either based on misinformation or an audacious lie. The Davidian prophet had, in fact, finished his exegesis of the first seal. One of the few survivors of the attack, Ruth Riddle, had typed up the first chapter of Koresh's hand-written manuscript on the 18th of April. On the day of the fire, she escaped with a computer disk in her jacket containing a record of this manuscript.[16]

IMITATION

Most of us are familiar with religious conservatives who appeal to their traditions as models for many of their actions. This pattern is, in fact, so familiar that we typically do not ask deeper kinds of questions about it. However, with a little reflection, we can see that there is a distinction between obeying overt commands found in religious traditions (e.g., obeying the Ten Commandments) and quite another to model our actions after religious figures (e.g., imitating Mohammed's actions described in the hadith literature). One might say that it is natural to look for and to imitate divine models; however, it appears that our drive to imitate[17] goes much deeper.

One of the building blocks of Rene Girard's theory of violence (discussed in Espen Dahl's chapter in the present volume) is that, beyond such basics as thirst and hunger, we quite literally learn what to desire by modeling our behavior after other people in our environment – Girard's notion of mimetic desire.[18] At a different, more general level, our drive to imitate plays a central role in Richard Dawkins's discussion of 'memes' (which he views as analogous to 'genes') as the fundamental units of culture – memes that are passed around within a society and subsequently down through the generations as a consequence of this drive to imitate. In Dawkins's words,

> Examples of memes are tunes, ideas, catch-phrases, clothes fashions, ways of making pots or of building arches. Just as genes propagate themselves in the gene pool by leaping from body to body via sperms or eggs, so memes propagate themselves in the meme pool by leaping from brain to brain via a process which, in the broad sense, can be called imitation.[19]

Dawkins' theory has attracted plenty of criticisms, but not the part of his system about the universal propensity of human beings to imitate each other, which is the foundational observation on which his theory is built.

However, to take this analysis down to an even more fundamental level, imitation is an essential component of childhood learning, and 'plays a constitutive role in the early development of an implicit sense of the self as a social agent'.[20] Our ability to imitate has been linked to specific neurons in the brain,[21] and research has even been carried out on how newborns imitate adult facial expressions; e.g.,

> Andrew Meltzoff and M. Keith Moore performed a study on twelve 21-day-old infants to assess their ability to imitate certain facial expressions, including sticking out the tongue and opening the mouth. The infants were able to imitate accurately the facial expressions of the researchers ... These studies indicate that facial imitation is present at a very early age and is seemingly innate.[22]

In addition to providing the basis for learning and development, human beings have universally viewed perceived similarities as involving more than coincidental connections. Thus in his classic discussion of magic in *The Golden Bough*, James Frazer discusses two forms of magic found across the globe, one of which is imitative magic. As an example of this type of magic, the magician might undertake a ritual in which she pours water on the ground while imitating thundering noises in an effort to evoke rain during a drought. Or, to consider another common pattern – one for which Frazer provides a number of examples from disparate cultures[23] – an individual creates an image of an enemy which he then destroys in an effort to harm that enemy. The underlying idea here is that imitating the desired result in a ritual establishes a magical link with the natural world or with another person which in turn evokes a similar response.

This line of analysis brings us back around to the topic of mythology. In addition to theorizing myths as social charters, Malinowski also emphasized the notion that 'the really important thing about the myth is its character of retrospective, ever-present live actuality. It is to a native neither a fictitious story, nor an account of a dead past; it is a statement of a bigger reality still partly alive'.[24] He repeated this point over and over again in his writings because so much prior work in the field of mythology had been focused on the sacred stories of ancient Greece and Rome, which had been studied as textual artifacts, abstracted from their original socio-cultural matrices.

These ideas from Frazer and Malinowski are, in effect, brought together in Eliade's theorizing about the invocation of a still-living mythic past in the context of rituals – rituals which, more often than not, imitate the activities of the gods that took place in mythic time (*in illo tempore*; a Latin phrase meaning 'in that time'). What Eliade added was the notion that archaic peoples were prompted to invoke this sacred past (this *illud tempus*; 'that time') because of their desire for 'significance, permanence, beauty and perfection as well as escape from their sorrows'[25] – a desire that would be fulfilled by living 'among the gods' during rituals.[26] Ritual imitation thus enables communities to establish magical or mystical links with the immortal power of the gods.

> In imitating the exemplary acts of a god or of a mythic hero, or simply by recounting their adventures, the man of an archaic society detaches himself from profane time and magically re-enters the Great Time, the sacred time.[27]

Presumably, acting out the plots of sacred stories outside of rituals would accomplish the same goal, as noted earlier in the discussion of Victor Turner's social dramas. Though not the focus of most of his work, Eliade also viewed mythic narratives as more general models for human behavior.[28]

One might well question the applicability of this kind of schema to Timothy McVeigh's attack on the Oklahoma Federal Building, the motive for which was said to be revenge. Perhaps the connection was simply one of being inspired by the fictional attack in Pierce's narrative – though I would certainly not be the first to suggest that fiction can often function as mythology.[29]

This pattern's relevance for the Branch Davidians, on the other hand, is transparent. For Koresh in particular, the dramatic present time of the attack and then the siege had been so completely absorbed into the sacred time of scripture that he was attempting to anticipate what would happen next by studying the Book of Revelation.

Another straightforward example we can consider here are conservative Islamists. For example, Sunni terrorists are often, though not invariably, from a Salafi background.[30] Salafis attempt to strictly model all of life after the examples set by the first three generations of Muslims – especially the companions of Muhammad and the Prophet himself as they are presented in the Qu'ran, the hadith (hadith are the traditional stories about, and sayings of, Muhammad) and the sira (early hagiographies of the Prophet). This formative period of Islam has, in effect, come to function as a kind of historicized *illud tempus* (or, one might say, a mythologized history).

> [The Prophet] must be emulated in every detail. Salafis also follow the guidance of the Prophet's companions (the salaf), because they learned about Islam directly from the messenger of God and are thus best able to provide an accurate portrayal of the prophetic model.[31]

Salafi Muslims go so far as to imitate such details as the way the Prophet dressed and how he cleaned his teeth. 'Even minor particulars of appearance, everyday behavior and divine worship are covered by the hadith and, for those who take them seriously, are seen as significant'.[32]

Salafis feel that they are applying self-explanatory principles from the Qur'an and the hadith rather than 'interpreting' them. Jihadists in the Salafi tradition or from other literalist strands of Islam are similarly adamant about grounding their actions in early Muslim tradition:

> All strategies are predicated on the principle that every action carried out in the struggle – including military strategies, priorities for attacks, and the selection of targets – should be inspired by the life of Muhammad and have the support of the Qu'ran, hadith or *sira*.[33]

Thus, for example, the so-called 9/11 Handbook – a four-page document in Arabic containing instructions for the hijackers – refers to 'Muhammad's military practices as a legitimating and inspirational model',[34] and provides very detailed directions, such as recommending that 'everyone should grit his teeth as our forefathers used to do before engaging in battle'.[35] Thus contemporary jihadists view their current struggle,

> as a continuation of the struggles of the Prophet and his companions. For example, al-Qaeda's attacks are called 'raids'

(*ghazawāt*), just as Muhammad's campaigns in the seventh
century. Its suicide attacks are labelled 'martyrdom operations'
(*al-'amaliyyāt al-istishhādiyya*), and are thus being related to the
classical concept of martyrdom (*istishhād*), as well as to the
martyrs (*shuhadā'*) who fell on the battlefields during the early
days of Islam. The execution of these attacks is thoroughly
ritualised and, despite the innovative character of these
'martyrdom operations,' they are continuously related to
contemporaries of Muhammad who 'sought martyrdom' on the
battlefields. Al-Qaeda's attacks are presented as acts of 'worship'
(*'ibāda*) and as re-enactments of the raids of the Prophet (from
Pieter Nanninga's al-Qaeda chapter in the present volume).

For movements like al-Qaeda, the time of Muhammad and his righteous
companions has clearly become an *illud tempus*, a 'sacred reservoir of
timeless truths',[36] providing paradigms through which the faithful
understand and respond to contemporary situations. Just as Eliade had
described the impact of ritually re-enacting the sacred past of myths,
viewing one's present actions as aligned with the paradigms found in
accounts of the Prophet and his early community allow actors to 'blur
the present movement with paradigmatic events of the past'.[37]

CONCLUSION

As I was careful to note earlier, this essay was not an attempt to put
forth a comprehensive theory of religion and terrorism. Rather, my
purpose was to explore earlier theorizing about myths – especially some
of the ideas discussed by Mircea Eliade – and bring them to bear on the
mythic/ritualistic characteristics that certain terrorist acts appear to
embody. I was particularly interested in theorizing this sort of behavior
in terms of the characteristically human drive to imitate – a seemingly
innate drive that begins to become active shortly after birth.

One of the important explanatory elements that Eliade adds to the
understanding of our attraction to the imitation of paradigms found in
sacred narratives is our need for meaning:

If we suspend Eliade's sometimes overly abstract terms and
mystical concepts, ... he says simply that humans by nature desire
to establish for themselves a meaningful place in which to dwell and
live their lives. They want to feel part of a larger whole, rooted,
centered, and, on occasion, freed from the confinements and
mediocrity of the everyday and the commonplace.[38]

Contemporary observers have speculated about why some individuals, particularly young people from Muslim backgrounds, leave relatively comfortable situations at home to join al-Qaeda or the Islamic State (briefly discussed toward the end of Scott Atran's chapter and Pieter Nanninga's al-Qaeda chapter in the present volume). What many analyses often miss is the powerful attraction exercised by movements that claim to have actually re-established the Islamic community as it was during the days of Muhammad. For individuals who accept those claims, joining either al-Qaeda or Islamic State would be not unlike leaving the present and traveling back to the time of the Prophet and his earliest companions – and, in effect, becoming one of the righteous companions by imitating the paradigms laid down in the Muslim *illud tempus*. This is not, of course, a complete answer to the question of why Muslim youth might run away to Syria and Iraq, but I would argue that it supplies a potentially useful supplement to explanations based purely on sociological, political and economic variables.

Endnotes

1 Andrew Macdonald [William L. Pierce], *The Turner Diaries* (Washington, DC: National Vanguard Books, 1978).
2 Robert A. Segal, *Theorizing About Myth* (Amherst: University of Massachusetts Press, 1999), p. 148.
3 See the discussion in Michael Stausberg, 'Prospects in Theories of Religion', *Method and Theory in the Study of Religion* 22 (2010), p. 226.
4 E.g., Mircea Eliade, *The Myth of the Eternal Return: Cosmos and History*, Transl. Willard Trask (Princeton: Princeton University Press, 1971).
5 In this regard, refer, e.g., to Segal, *Theorizing*, pp. 67–97 and pp. 135–141.
6 Carl G. Jung, *The Archetypes and the Collective Unconscious*, Transl. R.F.C. Hull (Princeton: Princeton University Press, 1968), p. 154.
7 Carl. G. Jung, *Flying Saucers: A Modern Myth of Things Seen in the Sky*, Transl. R.F.C. Hull (Princeton: Princeton University Press, 1978).
8 Bronislaw Malinowski, 'Myth in Primitive Psychology' (orig. 1926), in Ivan Strenski, *Malinowski and the Work of Myth* (Princeton: Princeton University Press, 1992), pp. 81–82.
9 Victor Turner, *Dramas, Fields, and Metaphors: Symbolic Action in Human Society* (Ithaca: Cornell University Press, 1974), Chapter Two.
10 However, it should also be noted that the ATF accused the Davidians of plotting a terrorist attack on the citizens of Waco, Texas; this was, in fact, one of the pretexts on which the ATF raid was launched. In the words of one ATF official, the Davidians 'were going to come out and attack the citizens of Waco'. Cited in James R. Lewis, 'The Mount

Carmel Holocaust: Suicide or Execution?' in James R. Lewis and Carole M. Cusack, eds., *Sacred Suicide* (Surrey, UK: Ashgate, 2014), p. 235.

11   The situation is not unlike that of the Church of Jesus Christ of Latter-day Saints – popularly known as Mormons – who recognize the President of the Church as a living prophet, empowered to reveal new truths.

12   Cited in Eugene V. Gallagher, 'Theology Is Life and Death: David Koresh on Violence, Persecution, and the Millenium', in Catherine Wessinger, ed. *Millennialism, Persecution, and Violence: Historical Cases* (Syracuse: Syracuse University Press, 2000), p. 86.

13   Cited in James D. Tabor, 'Religious Discourse and Failed Negotiations', in Stuart A. Wright, ed. *Armageddon in Waco: Critical Perspectives on the Branch Davidian Conflict* (Chicago: University of Chicago Press, 1995), p. 265.

14   James R. Tabor, 'The Waco Tragedy: An Autobiographical Account of One Attempt to Avert Disaster', in James R. Lewis, ed., *From the Ashes: Making Sense of Waco* (Lanham, MD: Rowman & Littlefield, 1994), pp. 15–17.

15   Tabor, 'Religious Discourse', p. 270.

16   This brief exposition has appeared in a number of places, including as an appendix in Tabor and Gallagher 1995.

17   To avoid confusion, it should be noted that imitation is not mimicry: 'Mimicry is literal, an attempt to render as exact a duplicate as possible. Imitation is not so literal as mimicry the offspring copying its parent's behavior imitates, but does not mimic, the parent's ways of doing things'. Merlin Donald, *Origins of the Modern Mind: Three Stages in the Evolution of Culture and Cognition* (Cambridge, Massachusetts: Harvard University Press, 1991), p. 16.

18   Jean-Michel Oughourlian, 'From Universal Mimesis to the Self Formed by Desire', in Scott R. Garrels, ed., *Mimesis and Science: Empirical Research on Imitation and the Mimetic Theory of Culture and Religion* (East Lansing: Michigan State University Press, 2011), pp. 41–54.

19   Richard Dawkins, *The Selfish Gene* (Oxford: Oxford University Press, 2nd ed. 1989,), p. 173.

20   Jean Decety and Thierry Chaminade, 'The Neurophysiology of Imitation and Intersubjectivity', in Susan Hurley and Nick Chater, eds., *Perspectives on Imitation: From Neuroscience to Social Science* (Cambridge, Massachusetts: MIT Press, 2005), p. 133.

21   E.g., Giacomo Rizzolatti, 'The Mirror Neuron System and Imitation', in Hurley and Chater, *Perspectives*, pp. 55–76. It should be noted that the significance of mirror neurons has also been disputed. Refer in this regard to Gregory Hickok, *The Myth of Mirror Neurons* (New York: Norton, 2014).

22   James A. Van Slyke, *The Cognitive Science of Religion* (Surrey, UK: Ashgate, 2011), pp. 101–102. While I have not, in the past, been attracted to the cognitive-evolutionary perspective, what I have come to appreciate about this approach is the counterbalance it provides to some of the more extreme anti-universalizing voices within religious

studies – voices that level the charge of *essentialism* whenever a researcher discusses transcultural patterns.

23   Sir James George Frazer, *The Golden Bough: A Study in Magic and Religion* (Hertfordshire, UK: Wadsworth: 1993; rpt. 1922), pp. 12–13.

24   Malinowski, 'Myth', p. 100.

25   Daniel L. Pals, *Nine Theories of Religion* (New York: Oxford University Press, 3rd ed., 2015), p. 247.

26   Pals, *Nine Theories*, p. 237.

27   Mircea Eliade, *Myths, Dreams and Mysteries*. Trans. Philip Mairet. (New York: Harper & Row, 1967), p. 23.

28   Robert A. Segal, 'Are There Modern Myths?' in Bryan Rennie, ed., *Changing Religious Worlds: The Meaning and End of Mircea Eliade* (Albany: State University of New York Press, 2001), p. 26.

29   E.g., Thomas C. Sutton and Marilyn Sutton, 'Science Fiction as Mythology', *Western folklore* 28:4 (1969), pp. 230–237; Yusuf Nuruddin, 'Ancient Black Astronauts and Extraterrestrial Jihads: Islamic Science Fiction as Urban Mythology', *Socialism and Democracy* 20:3 (2006), pp. 127–165.

30   Just so that there is no misunderstanding on this point, please note that the great majority of Salafis are peaceful. For an authoritative treatment of Salafism, refer to Meijer 2009.

31   Quintan Wiktorowicz, 'Anatomy of the Salafi Movement', *Studies in Conflict & Terrorism* 29 (2006), p. 209.

32   Mary Habeck, *Knowing the Enemy: Jihadist Ideology and the War on Terror* (New Haven: Yale University Press, 2006), p. 45.

33   Habeck, *Knowing*, p. 137.

34   Bruce Lincoln, *Holy Terrors: Thinking about Religion after September 11* (Chicago: University of Chicago Press, 2003), p. 10.

35   Cited in Hans G. Kippenberg and Tilman Seidensticker, eds., *The 9/11 Handbook: Annotated Translation and Interpretation of the Attackers' Spiritual Manual* (London: Equinox, 2006), p. 16.

36   Lincoln, *Holy*, p. 35.

37   Lincoln, *Holy*, p. 12.

38   David Cave, 'Eliade's Interpretation of Sacred Space and Its Role Toward the Cultivation of Virtue', in Rennie, *Changing*, p. 238.

10 The LTTE: A Nonreligious, Political, Martial Movement for Establishing the Right of Self-Determination of Īlattamiḷs

PETER SCHALK

Vēluppiḷḷai Pirapākaraṇ (1954–2009) led a *de facto* state, which was defended between 1972 and 2009 by an urban guerrilla movement and, later, by a regular military force, which built institutions and advanced territorial control in the north and east of Sri Lanka. From 1987, the Liberation Tigers of Tamil Eelam (known as the LTTE or simply "Tamil Tigers") saw itself as a national liberation movement with the right of self-determination, in accordance with UN A/Res/42/159. The LTTE was not recognized, however, as a state by the international community as it was not considered to comply with demands for human rights. The state of Sri Lanka regarded the LTTE as a creation of terrorists and denied that Īlattamiḷs (supporters of the Tigers' goal) had the right of self-determination. Furthermore, their fight to be recognized did not suit the geopolitical interests of other countries such as India and the United States.

Vēluppiḷḷai Pirapākaraṇ died in armed struggle against the Sri Lanka Armed Forces on May 18, 2009 in Muḷḷivāykkāl, where the LTTE was destroyed, but a transnational resistance movement against the Government of Sri Lanka (GoSL) has remained in place, which strives by political means for the recognition by the UN of the right of self-determination for Īlattamiḷs in the north and east of Sri Lanka.[1]

This paper argues that religion was, and is, of no concern for the Tamil Tiger Movement. Vēluppiḷḷai Pirapākaraṇ's rationale for negotiating and fighting for secession was the concept of a universal right to self-determination for people like the Īlattamiḷs. After failed negotiations to establish this right against the will of the GoSL, India, and the rest of the world, Vēluppiḷḷai Pirapākaraṇ guided his cadres in armed struggle by teaching a nonreligious, political, and martial martyrology.[2]

*

We start with the term "nonreligious," which I apply to Vēluppiḷḷai Pirapākaraṇ's political program – a move that seems contradictory, given that the language of Vēluppiḷḷai Pirapākaraṇ is teeming with traditional Tamil_ religious terms (the meaning of which – and, more importantly, the *changes in meaning* – can be clarified by historians). The term *māvīrar* – "great hero" – was regularly compared by the Tiger Movement to the English word "martyr." It is the English definition, rather than the Tamil, that has a religious connotation. Even the English meaning is polysemous, however: "martyr" can be used nonreligiously in modern society to refer to a person who is suffering. In Tamil, the concept of *māvīrar* evokes no religious overtones; rather, it references a person who attains *vīraccāvu*, or "death as a hero" in battle.

Vēluppiḷḷai Pirapākaraṇ's extensive published writings in Tamil were, of course, influenced in terms of language and content by the situation in which they were produced. It was an extreme situation known as total war, which was fought uncompromisingly on both sides from the mid-1970s onwards,[3] preceded by wars of words between Tamil and Sihala speakers, which began in the early twentieth century. We can talk of a progressive radicalization of formulations of lexemes in this war of words, and especially in the language of Vēluppiḷḷai Pirapā- karaṇ, which led to semantic shifts and variations – to deviations in language use. Deviance here is understood as a conscious, deliberate linguistic shift in the form of bold formulations in the context of polit- ical agitation. They reflect and depend, of course, on a deviance of politics in a state of emergency. In the case of Vēluppiḷḷai Pirapākaraṇ, this consisted of a radical displacement of concepts from a religious to a nonreligious semantic field. One might connect Vēluppiḷḷai Pirapākaraṇ to Indian religions, for example, because of his use of the Tamil term *aram* (Sanskrit: *dharma*), but this refers to the concept of universal human rights in Pirapākaraṇ's thinking.[4]

*

In several interviews, Vēluppiḷḷai Pirapākaraṇ testified that he was convinced that self-determination was possible, but could not *necessar- ily* be realized tomorrow. It was felt to be an unpredictable, uncertain, or contingent idea in his generation. It was only in the distant future that one could be sure that the independent nation state of Tamilīlam would come into being – "one day." In other words, it was only from this long- term perspective that self-determination was "noncontingent."

In a tradition stemming from Immanuel Kant, "contingency" can be said to be projected on to circumstances, objects, and events. Some theologians speak of the world as contingent and of God as not contingent. From a historical-scientific point of view, the world is, of course, not contingent, but there is a disconcerting *experience* connected to the imagined possibility of the nonexistence and nonnecessity of the world, which can be called the *experience of contingency*. The term contingency belongs to the human world of experiencing the world subjectively, rather than to the object world.[5]

Coming back to Vēluppiḷḷai Pirapākaraṇ, one of his reflections consists of the following:

> It is sure that one day Tamilīlam will arise. It is sure that you also, our people, will obtain release. It is sure that our country as an egalitarian society will flourish. With this hope and determination of spirit we shall without hesitating march heroically on our way for liberation.[6]

Vēluppiḷḷai Pirapākaraṇ and the followers around him lived daily with a subliminal and latent experience of contingency. He taught them a historical determinism, in which actions "must" lead to the goal.[7] He is well known to have stated: "History is my guide (*valikāṭṭi*)."[8] He then took up the role of *valikāṭṭi* himself via the affirmation of allegiance to him.[9] This confidence in history (which can be understood as heritage/memory[10]) and in himself eliminated the potential for failure, meaning that only one outcome was possible: success. Complexity was reduced, which created confidence in Pirapākaraṇ.

Pirapākaraṇ practiced yet another way to reduce this worrying experience of uncertainty. The environment in which he lived was influenced deeply by religions like Caivam (Shivaism), Vaiṇavam (Vaishnavism), Mukammatiya camayam (Islam), Kiṟittavu camayam (Christianity), and Pauttam (Buddhism).[11] These faiths represented values, which were claimed to be "sacred." In this environment, religious concepts had an emotional and cognitive surplus, which could reduce uncertainty; they referred to experiences of a transcendent world in which worrying experiences of contingency were lessened. Vēluppiḷḷai Pirapākaraṇ was aware of this and borrowed ideas from this world of religious concepts. Such an activity might not seem particularly original, when one considers the ways in which some politicians indulge in religious rhetoric; Pirapākaraṇ, however, dismissed the idea that any element of his Tiger Movement was religious. Its ideology and practice left no place for religion among its combatants.[12] This nonreligious ideology encompassed a territorial, linguistic, historical, and cultural nationalism, as well as a moral call for dedication and ritual practice in the name of patriotism.[13] We are faced with a peculiar relationship: Pirapākaraṇ's language was characterized by diverse references to traditional religious concepts, which are to be understood in the context of a nonreligious semantic field. He referred, for example, to his fallen warriors using bold images of godly or divine ascetics who had abandoned life in battle; the death ritual, however, did not allude to Caivam or Christianity at all, and no priest or pastor performed the ritual. Pirapākaraṇ wrote:

> To be courageous to annihilate oneself for the happy living of others is godly asceticism (*teyvīkat turavaram*). The godly births (*teyvīkap piravikaḷ*) are the Black Tigers indeed.[14]

This quotation appears deeply religious, given that "godly" is used twice, as well as "asceticism," but a Hindu or Christian interpretation of this text presupposes that that original signifieds are "attached" or "pasted" to the signifiers; a frequent fallacy.[15]

First, we should realize that we are encountering martial martyrdom. The combatants give their lives in the act of killing, but this does not correspond with our modern, idealized image of a Catholic martyr like Maximilian Kolbe. Martial martyrdom is different. Some would say that it is not martyrdom at all. Such a view is pious, but not historical. Martial martyrdom was – and is – widespread around the globe, but nonreligious, martial martyrdom is rare.

Second, we can interpret the term "godly" in the same way as "sacred" (see below). When it comes to the word *turavaram*, or "asceticism," this can be defined as a relinquishing, rejection, and renunciation of the pleasures of life. Here, Vēluppiḷḷai Pirapākaraṇ has taken imagery from Caivam and/or Christianity (where these religions refer to outer and inner asceticism as precursors for the salvation of the soul in heaven) but he has applied it to the rigorous exercises required for *cūya oḷukkam*, or "self-discipline," which all common combatants – the special task-force groups like the Black Tigers, the Leopards, and ninja-groups – have to go through in their military careers. Their lives do not end in heaven, but in a grave and in memorialization by the living; there is nothing else beyond.

The concept of discipline is understood as self-discipline. As basic guidance, there is a code of conduct, which elaborates the six necessary characteristics (*paṇpukaḷ*) that mark a warrior. One of them is the mental preparation to take cyanide and to wear a *jakkaṭ* if required. This term is a Tamilization of the English "jacket," which refers to a belt bomb worn around the waist, together with a vial of cyanide around the neck, as reminders of the need to accomplish *the* task. By using the religious term "asceticism" for this self-discipline – and for other rules of conduct for the achievement of warrior discipline – Pirapākaraṇ implicitly expresses the idea that *true* asceticism is warrior discipline, or that warrior discipline has the status of Caiva and Christian asceticism. A genuine religious ascetic from the fold of Indian religions would be useless as warrior because of his egocentricity ("lonely rhinoceros"). What can be done with such an ascetic in a ninja group of assassinators who are completely dependent on each other? It would be fair to say that Pirapākaraṇ found Caiva and Christian imagery of ascetics to be fascinating because of the dedication and discipline that is evoked; he was not, however, a dedicated Hindu, a guru who turned his warriors into Caiva ascetics.[16] In other words, he changed the signified of the signifier "asceticism" from "dedication to a god" to "dedication to the right of self-determination."

One of the six rules of conduct instructed the combatants to keep away from premarital sex, alcohol, and smoking. Gambling was also rejected. These were all activities that could affect concentration on, and dedication to, working for this right. They had no religious purpose, such as saving the soul. *Arppi* – "dedication" – has the religious connotation of sacrifice, but it was de-religionized by Vēluppiḷḷai Pirapākaraṇ. The dedication was to achieving the right – if not by negotiation, then through armed struggle.

The Tiger Movement's nonreligious ideology and practice was not imposed on civilian society, which cultivated traditional religion with the consent, and even support, of the Tiger Movement.[17] The Tamil Tigers were not anti- or areligious, but nonreligious, like the French Foreign Legion. Religions were not eliminated, but only suspended from, or factored out of, the lives of the combatants. If a combatant left and returned to his/her home for a visit, s/he could practice his/her religion. Religion was understood as privatized in the Tiger Movement system. A combatant in service is not a private person. This factoring out of religion functioned to prevent conflict based on religious and sectarian attitudes, which would weaken the common battlefront. It was administrative and pragmatic, but not antireligious.

*

Now, when I use the term "nonreligious," I often envisage what the Tiger Movement envisages. Nonreligious is "non-Caiva" and "non-Christian," and, thus, also "nontranscendent."

There are lively discussions happening that ascribe hidden religious agendas to the Tiger Movement, such as the view that a Great Hero is a martyr who has acted in imitation of Christ, or the supposition that an active combatant is like a Caiva ascetic.[18] How can he, in his deeply religious culture, reduce the experience of the contingency of his political project to a nontranscendent idea?

I refer to my analysis of religious concepts in the language of Vēluppiḷḷai Pirapākaraṉ[19] and will expand on only one idea here – namely, *puṇita* ("sacred/holy" or "pure") – as exemplary of his handling of religion.[20] In Sri Lanka and Tamilnāṭu, there is a common basis for theological concepts in Tamil for both Caivam and Christianity.[21]

The sacred is a revelation of transcendence, from the perspectives of Caivam and Christianity. There is no sanctity without divine transcendence. Vēluppiḷḷai Pirapākaraṉ says that independence is a sacred right (see below), which would imply, in the case of a Caiva/Christian interpretation, that he envisages this right to be given by the divine.

What does Vēluppiḷḷai Pirapākaraṉ think of as sacred? "Sacred" is, for him, independence, for example, which follows after using the right to secede contained in the right of self-determination:

> Independence is not trading of goods through bargain; it is a sacred right (*oru puṇitamāṉa urimai*) that is won through the spill of blood.[22]

Vēluppiḷḷai Pirapākaraṉ does not think like a Christian, Jew, Caiva, or Muslim. The indisputability of the right is justified differently by him.

Before we expand on this point, let us note that in his statement, Vēluppiḷḷai Pirapākaraṉ does not say that this right is made sacred through the shedding of blood; rather, it has been achieved through such bloodshed. So, we still do not know why this right should be considered sacred. There is something missing, which is highlighted on a regular basis in other statements by Vēluppiḷḷai Pirapākaraṉ.[23] Let us examine one of his reflections to find out why this right is not only one among others, but is, allegedly, a sacred right:

> What do we demand? Why are we fighting? We want to live with peace and honour and independence (*cutantiram*) from others in our land, historically our habitat, and our homeland where we were born and where we grew up. We are also humans (*namum maṉitarkaḷ*); a human society with fundamental human rights (*maṉitarkaḷukkāṉa aṭippaṭai urimaikaḷai koṇṭa oru maṉita camūkam*). We are a separate ethnic community with a separate

cultural life and history. We demand that we should be accepted as a human society with distinctive characteristics. We have the right to decide our political life by ourselves. On the basis of this right, we would like to establish a system of government where we rule ourselves.[24]

Here, it is made clear that Pirapākaraṉ appeals to a universal law, according to which a "people" is self-determining. This is a fact written into the Charter of Human Rights, which the Tiger Movement signed in 1988 as a non-state, armed group, like many other such groups in the world, which wanted to assert themselves as liberation movements.[25] It is noteworthy that he does not mention religion as one of the properties that make the Tamils a "people."[26] Indeed, the usual Tamil words for religion – *camayam* and *matam* – are missing from all his Pirapākaraṉ's collected reflections.[27] Furthermore, other religions prevalent in the area are never mentioned by name. His cultural nationalism was deliberately designed without religion in mind. It is based on common territory, a common language, and the common past of the Īlattamils.

Vēluppiḷḷai Pirapākaraṉ was aware that he must show the United Nations that the Īlattamils were not only Tamils, but represented a universal value through which they could be considered a "people," in the sense of the Charter of Human Rights. He must also show that this "people" stayed together, in spite of inner conflicts. Pirapākaraṉ does not play the nationalist card in the text above.[28] Here, it is striking that he talks of "the people," not of *tēciyam* ("nation"), in conjunction with "human society" and "fundamental human rights." The text emphasizes not that the Tamils are special, but that they are universally human. He strives to universalize what, otherwise, is specific, even appealing to the reader: "We are also human beings." It follows, therefore, that Īlattamils also have human rights. He appeals for the right of self-determination in the name of humanity. He speaks for the whole, not just for some. Who could resist that?

Now, we can return to the term "sacred." Vēluppiḷḷai Pirapākaraṉ used "sacred" not just in a persuasive way, like in commercial advertising and sports reports. The emotional surplus of religious terms can be used for the purpose of mobilization, but also to convey insight. We know this cognitive moment in religious terms as "transcendence," but we find transcendence converted into universality in Vēluppiḷḷai Pirapākaraṉ's thinking.

In this context, Pirapākaraṉ's introductory sentence is interesting. He explains that independence is not a tradable commodity.[29]

Immanuel Kant's understanding of morality is that it should not have a price; and what is priceless has dignity.[30] Kant's influence on Pirapākaraṇ was mediated through the language of the international human rights lobby – especially through Amnesty International, which positioned Kant's account of moral principles as an *a priori* product of pure reason that was universal.[31] He formed his consciousness under the intrusive influence of the global human rights lobby. There is no doubt that the global human rights lobby had a major impact on the Tiger Movement via Paris. The pillar of this lobby was that morality is only moral if standards were universal. This idea is the legacy of Immanuel Kant. Indeed, this Kantian concept goes even further: morality is only moral if it applies as an absolute necessity to all people. His view of universality even extends beyond humans, being applicable to all other rational beings.[32]

Immanuel Kant taught that the meaning and origin of all moral concepts is *a priori*, and that in this *Reinigkeit* ("purity") of their origin lies their dignity. "Purity" is a property that is ascribed to the sanctity of the transcendent, whereas the "impure" relates to the imminent. *Puṇita* can also be interpreted as purity. For Immanuel Kant, purity is the *a priori* character of reason, and equals universality (and, implicitly, the impure is the empirical). To this, we can add Immanuel Kant's his formulation of the categorical imperative, which sees morality as a universal governing:

> *Handle nur nach derjenigen Maxime, durch die du zugleich
> wollen kannst, dass sie ein allgemeines Gesetz werde* ("Act only
> according to that maxim whereby you can wish at the same time
> that it becomes a universal law").[33]

We can conclude that if a god does not exist, it is obvious that it is not necessary for one to be invented because there is already a replacement for him: the universality of values, which makes norms liable. In this sense, Immanuel Kant might say that the categorical imperative is pure not because a god has bestowed it, but because it represents the universal value of pure reason, which is exempt from the impure of the contingent empirical.

Vēluppiḷḷai Pirapākaraṇ changed the signified of the signifier "right of self-determination." The idea that "the right to self-determination for a people is sacred" now no longer equals "the right to self-determination for a people is given by the transcendent divine and is therefore invulnerable;" instead, self-determination becomes a universal value, and is therefore incontestable. Vēluppiḷḷai Pirapākaraṇ says "sacred," but envisages "universal."

We also have to consider Vēluppiḷḷai Pirapākaraṇ's statement that his national community fought for its right and shed its blood. He does not expand on this idea, but today's Tamil Resistance Movement has done so. It says that the bloodshed should be understood in the context of a redistributive conception of justice, which, in turn, is regarded as universal. Through their suffering, the Tamil people have earned the right to independence as compensation for this suffering. Pirapākaraṇ did not use the phrases "redistributive justice" or "remedial justice." These technical terms were introduced by human rights activists as a response to the acknowledgment by the United Nations of the massive human rights violations made by the GoSL during the last phase of the war in 2009.[34] These violations have been characterized by some human rights activists as genocide.[35] The awareness of genocide was followed by a demand for a redistributive/remedial justice in the form of the establishment of a state, similar to what the Israelis were given in 1948, following the genocide of the Israelis by the Germans. The Holocaust experience and the subsequent legal claims have been internationalized.[36]

*

To summarize, the concept of the sacred right of independence as used by Vēluppiḷḷai Pirapākaraṇ is not related to a divinity through which an experience of contingency is reduced in the process of promoting the claim for this right; rather, it refers to the universality of human rights, which also reduces this experience of contingency, because universality is beyond all experience of contingency. References to universality are regarded as invulnerable, incontestable, and liable.

We might use powerful words like "outermost," "absolute," "final," and "ultimate" when we speak of our highest values. Vēluppiḷḷai Pirapākaraṇ uses "sacred," but this has no reference to the divine or, generally speaking, to the transcendent. It has, however, a strong emotional surplus in the context of the deeply religious culture in which he was active. He preserved the emotional part of such religious terms. We might use "ultimate" or "absolute," considering the nonreligious context. We could replace all occurrences of "sacred" with "ultimate" in his texts. However, his use of religious terms is his way of radicalizing his message.

His appeal to the transcendence of religious terms is reframed and directed toward something else, which becomes liable; namely, universal human rights. It would, of course, be illogical to say that he sacralizes human rights.

Within the current Tamil Resistance Movement, Vēluppiḷḷai Pirapākaraṉ's martial lingo was discontinued after May 2009. It was too personal. In the diaspora, the right to self-determination for Īlattamils is handled by established international law experts. This right is considered *jus cogens* – a "mandatory law" – and as a universal and customary international legal principle that is *erga omnes* in character: absolute rights "towards all." As far as I understand Vēluppiḷḷai Pirapākaraṉ, this is exactly what he wanted, but his dependence on the bombastic and pompous language of the heroic traditions of the Dravidian movement – the radicalization of words in the war and the temptation to exploit the surplus of religious termini – drove him to make loans from religious vocabulary; but not always. He could get by without these loans, as shown by a reflection directed toward Western diplomats, politicians, and human rights activists:

> On the moral level (*tārmīka aṭippaṭaiyil*) we stand on a decisive fundament. The aim of our struggle is just (*niyāyamāṉatu*). It is in accordance with international ethics of humanity (*carvatēca maṉita aṟatirkku icaivāṉatu*). Our people have the right of self-determination (*taṉṉāṭci urimaikku*). They are eligible to found a state of their own (*taṉiyaracu*). According to international law (*carvatēca caṭṭatiṉ*) this right cannot be rejected by anybody.[37]

In conclusion, the deviance in the language of Vēluppiḷḷai Pirapākaraṉ was developed in a situation of total war, and in a specific cultural environment in which religious concepts still encompassed a cognitive reference and emotional excess. As a result of his defeat in the war, his linguistic juggling with bold concepts failed. However, his goal did not; it is now pursued nonviolently by a transnational resistance movement, which accuses the GoSL of genocide. The ultimate goal is to gain redistributive/remedial justice in the form of recognition by the United Nations of the right to self-determination.[38] The final explanation for the Tiger Movement engaging in armed struggle is not that it followed the demands of a religion, but that it wanted to establish the right to self-determination for the Īlattamils, who had been refused this in previous negotiations. The Tiger Movement was a model case of a nonreligious, national, armed movement. Religion was of no concern; a nonreligious, political, martial martyrology was taught to its combatants.[39]

Endnotes

1 See Peter Schalk, "On Resilience and Defiance of the Īlamtamil Resistance Movement in a Transnational Diaspora," in V̄olkhard Krech, Marion Steinicke, eds., *Dynamics in the History of Religions between Asia and Europe: Encounters, Notions, and Comparative Perspectives* (Leiden, Netherlands: Brill, 2012), pp. 391–411.

2 Peter Schalk, "Martyrdom," in *Religions of the World: A Comprehensive Encyclopaedia of Beliefs and Practices* (ABC/Clio: 2010), pp. 1814–1819; Peter Schalk, "Memorialisation of Martyrs in the Tamil Resistance Movement of Īlam/Laṁkā," in Axel Michaels, ed., *State, Power, and Violence: Ritual Dynamics and the Science of Ritual III* (Wiesbaden, Germany: Harrassowitz Verlag, 2010), pp. 55–73.

3 Armed encounters with the GoSL started in the early 1970s, not in 1983.

4 *cintaṇai* 63:4, in Peter Schalk, *Die Lehre der Befreiungstiger Tamilīlams von der Selbstvernichtung durch göttliche Askese: Vorlage der Quelle Überlegungen des Anführers (talaivariṇ cintaṇaikaḷ)* (Uppsala, Sweden: Acta Universitatis Upsaliensis, 2007), p. 244.

   See also Schalk, *Die Lehre*, pp. 119–122 and Peter Schalk, "Ist die LTTE eine hinduistische Sekte?" in *Südasien: Zeitschrift des Südasienbüro* 5 (1998), pp. 18–19.

5 On the concept of contingency, see Niklas Luhmann, *Funktion der Religion* (Frankfurt am Main, Germany: Suhrkamp, 1977); Peter Vogt, *Kontingenz und Zufall: Eine Ideen- und Begriffsgeschichte* (Berlin, Germany: Akademie Verlag, 2011).

6 *talaivariṇ cintaṇaikaḷ* 31:1, in Schalk, *Die Lehre*, p. 223.

7 See Schalk, *Die Lehre*, p. 127f.

8 *talaivariṇ cintaṇaikaḷ* 8:1, in Schalk, *Die Lehre*, p. 209.

9 Schalk, *Die Lehre*, p. 38.

10 For the polarization between history and heritage in relation to both parties, see Peter Schalk, *Cāvilum vālvōm, "Auch im Angesicht des Todes werden wir leben": Īlamtamile sein im Krieg und in der Fremde* (Dortmund, Germany: Internationaler Verein Emigrierter Tamilischer Schriftsteller e.V., 2006), pp. 123–149.

11 For an overview of the religions of Sri Lanka, see Schalk, *Cāvilum vālvōm*, pp. 94–122. On Caivam in Sri Lanka and the diaspora, see Peter Schalk, *God as Remover of Obstacles: A Study of Caiva Soteriology among Īlam Tamil Refugees in Stockholm, Sweden (Acta Universitatis Upsaliensis, Historia Religionum 23)* (Uppsala: Acta Universitatis Upsaliensis, 2004).

12 See N. Malathy, *A Fleeting Moment in My Country: The Last Years of the De-Facto State* (Atlanta, GA: Clear Day Books, 2012), p. 118.

13 See Schalk, *Cāvilum vālvōm*, pp. 150–160; Schalk, *Die Lehre*, pp. 27–32.

14 Schalk, *Die Lehre*, pp. 93–96; 102–104; *cintaṇai* 36:4 in Schalk, *Die Lehre*, p. 227.

15 Peter Schalk, "Konsten att dö: om den ritualiserade fridöden bland Īlavar på ön Īlam," in *Riter och ritteorier, religionshistoriska diskussioner och teoretiska ansatser* (Stockholm: Nya Doxa, 2002), pp. 157–215; Schalk, "Memorialisation," pp. 60–71.

16 William Harman, "The Militant Ascetic Traditions of India and Sri Lanka," in Pratap Kumar, ed., *Contemporary Hinduism* (Durham, NC: Acumen, 2013), pp. 252–256.
17 See Malathy, *A Fleeting Moment in My Country*, p. 117.
18 For further ascriptions of this kind, see Schalk, *Die Lehre*, p. 138.
19 Schalk, *Die Lehre*, pp. 77–131; Schalk, "Konsten att dö," pp. 192–198.
20 See also Schalk, *Die Lehre*, p. 123f.
21 Bror Tilliander, *Christian and Hindu Terminology: A Study in the Mutual Relations with Special Reference to the Tamil Area* (Uppsala, Sweden: Uppsala University, 1974).
22 *talaivariṉ cintaṉaikaḷ* 19:4, in Schalk, *Die Lehre*, p. 264.
23 Schalk, *Die Lehre*, p. 200; p. 249.
24 *talaivariṉ cintaṉaikaḷ* 72:3, in Schalk, *Die Lehre*, p. 295.
25 Olivier Bangerter, "Internal Control: Codes of Conduct within Insurgent Armed Groups," *Occasional Paper of the Small Arms Survey* 31 (2012), 6.
26 Schalk, *Die Lehre*, pp. 153–386.
27 On these ideas, see Peter Schalk, "Tamilische Begriffe für Religion," in Peter Schalk, ed., *Religion in Asien? Studien zur Anwendbarkeit des Religionsbegriffs,(Acta Universitatis Upsaliensis, Historia Religionum 32)* (Uppsala, Sweden: Acta Universitatis Upsaliensis, 2012), pp. 80–124.
28 *talaivariṉ cintaṉaikaḷ* 72:3, in Schalk, *Die Lehre*, p. 295.
29 *talaivariṉ cintaṉaikaḷ* 19:4, in Schalk, *Die Lehre*, p. 264.
30 Immanuel Kant, "Grundlegung der Metaphysik der Sitten," in *Kants gesammelte Schriften, Band 4* (Berlin, Germany: Preußische Akademie der Wissenschaften, 1911), p. 411.
31 Stephen Hopgood, "Moral Authority, Modernity and the Politics of the Sacred," *European Journal of International Relations* 15 (2009), pp. 229–255.
32 Kant, "Grundlegung der Metaphysik der Sitten," p. 389.
33 Ibid., p. 421.
34 Schalk, "On Resilience," p. 394f; *Report of the Secretary-General's Internal Review Panel on United Nations Actions in Sri Lanka* (2012), available at www.un.org/News/dh/infocus/Sri_Lanka/The_Internal_Review_Panel_report_on_Sri_Lanka.pdf, accessed 10 July, 2015; *Report of the Secretary-General's Panel of Experts Report on Accountability in Sri Lanka* (2011), available at www.un.org/News/dh/infocus/Sri_Lanka/POE_Report_Full.pdf, accessed 10 July 2015.
35 NESoHR, *"Damit wir nicht vergessen": Massaker an Tamilen 1956-2008 (mit einer Einführung von Professor [em.] Dr. Peter Schalk)* (Heidelberg, Germany: Draupadi Verlag, 2012).
36 Anon., "Remedial Sovereignty," on *TamilNet*, available at www.tamilnet.com/art.html?catid=79&artid=34499, accessed 10 July 2015.
37 *talaivariṉ cintaṉaikaḷ* 24:2, in Schalk, *Die Lehre*, p. 219. This rendering is repeated in *talaivariṉ cintaṉaikaḷ* 63:4.
38 Schalk, "On Resilience."
39 See Schalk, "Memorialisation."

11 The Role of Religion in al-Qaeda's Violence

PIETER NANNINGA

The role of religion in al-Qaeda's violence has been strongly debated since the attacks of 11 September 2001. In public debates, religion has often been assigned an explanatory role. In scholarly literature on al-Qaeda, interpretations have diverged. In a study on suicide attacks from 2005, for example, Robert A. Pape downplays the role of religion in explaining al-Qaeda's violence. 'For al-Qaeda, religion matters', he writes, 'but mainly in the context of national resistance to foreign occupation'.[1] Assaf Moghadam, in contrast, emphasised that al-Qaeda's long-term mission is 'fundamentally religious', namely 'to wage a cosmic struggle against an unholy alliance of Christians and Jews'.[2] Others have offered variations on these arguments, for example by distinguishing between al-Qaeda's 'almost purely political' immediate objectives and its 'distinctively Islamic' ultimate aims.[3]

This chapter aims at providing a more nuanced understanding of the role of religion in al-Qaeda's violence by relating the topic to insights from religious studies. In debates on the religious dimension of terrorism, several scholars in this field have argued that religion should not be isolated from other factors, such as politics. Only in particular contexts, they claim, can religion play a certain – though usually not a primary – role in terrorist attacks.[4] Other scholars, foremost among them William T. Cavanaugh, have gone a step further by arguing that any attempt to attribute an independent role to something called 'religion' in explaining violence is inconsistent, as there is no coherent way to isolate religion from its (alleged) secular counterpart.[5]

Based on the statements of the leaders of 'al-Qaeda Central' – the group around Bin Laden in Afghanistan and Pakistan in the period between 1996 and 2011 – this chapter argues that it is not very fruitful to ask whether religion, as an abstract category, has played a role in al-Qaeda's violence.[6] Instead, it claims that it is more interesting to examine why the question on the role of religion in jihadist violence has been so prevalent over the last one and a half decades.

'THIS WAR IS FUNDAMENTALLY RELIGIOUS'

Al-Qaeda emerged as a diverse, dynamic and decentralised network of jihad fighters out of the war against the Soviet forces in Afghanistan in the 1980s. In the mid-1990s, the leaders of the network shifted the focus of their jihad to the West, which they underlined in a statement declaring war on 'the Americans' in 1996. Since that moment, al-Qaeda's war against the West has been presented as a thoroughly religious war. It is a struggle between the 'people of Islam' and the 'Zionist-Crusader alliance and their allies', the statement from 1996 states.[7] Bin Laden expressed himself even more explicitly about five years later, shortly after al-Qaeda had struck at its enemy on its own soil on 11 September 2001, by claiming that 'this war is fundamentally religious'. It is a conflict between the Muslims and the 'Crusader people of the West', he wrote, and the enmity between them 'is one of faith and doctrine'.[8]

The conflict as presented by al-Qaeda in its statements between 1996 and 2011 is a worldwide religious conflict. According to al-Qaeda's leadership, the worldwide Muslim community (*umma*), spearheaded by its 'jihadist vanguard', is engaged in a struggle with a coalition of enemies, which consists of the Western world and its allies, among whom are the alleged 'treacherous rulers' of the Muslim world. This conflict is not a mere conflict, however. In Bin Laden's words, the current struggle is only one episode of the timeless conflict between 'truth and falsehood' that will continue until Judgement Day.[9]

The current situation in this conflict is deplorable, al-Qaeda's leaders emphasise. The lands of Islam are being occupied by 'infidel forces' and Muslims are being oppressed and humiliated in Afghanistan, Iraq, Saudi Arabia, Palestine and elsewhere. According to al-Qaeda, Muslims themselves are to blame for this situation. They have deviated from the 'pure Islam' of the first generations of Muslims ('the pious predecessors', *al-salaf al-sāliḥ*), which is the cause of their misery. Bin Laden states: 'We have reached this miserable situation because many of us lack the correct and comprehensive understanding of the religion of Islam'.[10] Therefore, al-Qaeda's leaders argue over and over again, Muslims should return to the correct creed (*'aqīda*) and method (*manhaj*).[11] This includes the waging of jihad in the way of God (*fī sabīl Allāh*), which, according to al-Qaeda's statements, is obliged to liberate Muslim lands from the occupation by 'infidel forces'.

Al-Qaeda claims that it does follow the 'pure Islam' of the first generations of Muslims. Its violence is also presented as such: as a continuation of the struggles of the Prophet and his companions. For example, al-Qaeda's attacks are called 'raids' (*ghazawāt*), just as Muhammad's campaigns in the seventh century. Its suicide attacks are labelled 'martyrdom operations' (*al-ʿamaliyyāt al-istishhādiyya*), and are thus being related to the classical concept of martyrdom (*istishhād*), as well as to the martyrs (*shuhadāʾ*) who fell on the battlefields during the early days of Islam. The execution of these attacks is thoroughly ritualised and, despite the innovative character of these 'martyrdom operations', they are continuously related to contemporaries of Muhammad who 'sought martyrdom' on the battlefields. Al-Qaeda's attacks are presented as acts of 'worship' (*ʿibāda*) and as re-enactments of the raids of the Prophet.[12]

Thus, according to al-Qaeda's representations, its struggle is a thoroughly religious struggle. But what, exactly, is the meaning of the term 'religion' in al-Qaeda's discourse? One of the central terms in this respect is the term '*dīn*'. While this term is usually translated as 'religion', al-Qaeda uses it to denote 'God's religion': Islam.[13] Accordingly, in al-Qaeda's discourse, *dīn* is closely related to *imān* ('faith'), and its opposite is not the 'secular' as it is often perceived in the West, but rather 'unbelief' (*kufr*). This refers to unbelief in God's *dīn*, i.e., Islam, and thus includes both so-called atheists and groups that would be defined as 'religious' in Western discourse, such as Jews and Christians.

In al-Qaeda's representations of the perceived conflict, the precise beliefs of the enemies themselves are not very relevant. For example, while al-Qaeda often refers to the Christian background of its Western adversaries by calling them '*naṣārā*' (a Qurʾanic term used for 'Christians') or '*ṣalībiyyūn*' ('crusaders'), it also speaks about the West 'that disbeliefs in religion (*dīn*)'.[14] This may sound paradoxical in Western discourse, but, from al-Qaeda's perspective, 'Christians' and 'disbelievers in *dīn*' belong to the same category of unbelievers (*kuffār*), whose common characteristic is that they do not adhere to Islam, or they even oppose it. This places Bin Laden's remark that the conflict is 'fundamentally religious' in a different perspective. It is not a war between different religions or a war that is religious as opposed to a secular war, but rather it is a war between the followers of *dīn*, i.e., Muslims, and *kuffār*.

In this war, al-Qaeda presents itself as the defender of Islam and the *umma*. Its leaders explicitly resist the idea that their struggle has anything to do with politics or terrorism. Regarding politics, they do distinguish between religion and politics (*siyāsa*) in their statements. Whereas the importance of the former is emphasised, the latter is usually denounced. In al-Qaeda's discourse, the field of politics is predominantly associated with the domain of unbelief, and especially with the West. Alleged Western institutions and concepts such as parliaments and democracy are rejected because they include the upholding of man-made laws and therefore oppose God's sovereignty.[15] Moreover, politics is related to oppression and hypocrisy, both by the West and by its alleged puppet regimes in the Muslim world.

The U.S.-led 'war on terror' is perceived as a prime symbol of Western double standards. Interestingly, al-Qaeda's leaders have not always rejected the labelling of their actions as 'terrorism' (*irhāb*). In several statements, they indicate that it is an obligation to 'terrorise' the enemies (cf. Q. 8:60), which leads Bin Laden to the conclusion that 'our terrorism against America is praised terrorism'.[16] However, the way in which the term 'terrorism' is used by Western leaders is condemned as highly hypocritical. 'Those who maintain that this is a war against terrorism', Bin Laden asked shortly after the 11 September attacks, 'what is this terrorism that they talk about at a time when people of the *umma* have been slaughtered for decades?'[17] About three years later he concluded: 'Destruction is called freedom and democracy, while resistance is terrorism and intolerance'.[18]

Thus, although al-Qaeda claims to wage a religious war, the meanings it attributes to the concepts of religion, politics and terrorism diverge from those that are dominant in the West. Religion, politics and terrorism do not have universal, trans-historical meanings. They are cultural constructions that are being negotiated by specific actors – among whom are al-Qaeda's leaders and operatives – in their particular contexts.[19] This has consequences for discussing the role of religion in al-Qaeda's violence.

THE CASE OF 'RELIGIOUS VIOLENCE'

Despite the rhetoric of al-Qaeda's leaders, it is evident that al-Qaeda's violence cannot be solely attributed to something called 'religion'. To understand al-Qaeda's attacks, one should look at the specific backgrounds and motivations of both the organisers and perpetrators in their particular contexts. The question remains, however, whether religion has *contributed* to al-Qaeda's violence.

There is plenty of empirical material that shows that particular constructs of beliefs which actors consider religious can contribute to violence. For instance, my research on the farewell videos of al-Qaeda's suicide bombers demonstrates that al-Qaeda's message of a worldwide religious conflict provided these men with a sense of agency and empowered them as the alleged followers of pure Islam who defend the *umma* against its enemies.[20] However, this is something different than designating al-Qaeda's suicide attacks as 'religious violence' or claiming that religion, as an abstract category, has contributed to these attacks. Attributing a specific role to religion is arbitrary, as a closer look at al-Qaeda's statements illustrates. I will provide two examples.

First, to legitimise their war against the West, al-Qaeda's leaders have frequently emphasised the 'crimes' of the U.S. and European states in the Muslim world. In a letter that was posted online in November 2002, for example, Bin Laden explains to the Americans why al-Qaeda is fighting them. According to Bin Laden, the Americans 'occupy our countries', 'steal our wealth and oil' and 'starved the Muslims of Iraq' by means of their sanctions. They have supported Israel, Russia and India in slaughtering Muslims in Palestine, Chechnya and Kashmir, respectively, as well as collaborated with governments in the Middle East that are oppressing Muslims. In addition, the United States is not ruled according to God's law (*sharī'a*), but it permits usury, intoxicants, gambling and immorality, and exploits women like consumer products. Finally, the Americans are hypocritical: 'Let us not forget one of your major characteristics: your duality in both manner and values; your hypocrisy in both manner and principles. All manners, principles and values have two scales: one for you and one for everybody else'.[21]

Bin Laden thus provides various reasons for al-Qaeda's war against the United States Seemingly 'religious' arguments are being used side by side with arguments that we could label 'historical', 'political' and 'economic'. To put it more precisely, these 'religious' and 'non-religious' factors are strongly intertwined and cannot be separated consistently. To focus on the case of America's 'occupation' of Muslim lands that Bin Laden refers to in his letter, the presence of U.S. troops in Saudi Arabia since the Gulf War of 1990–1991 has been one of al-Qaeda's prime concerns in this respect. The United States is 'plundering its riches, dictating to its rulers, humiliating its people, terrorising its neighbours and turning its bases in the Peninsula into a spearhead through which to fight the neighbouring Muslim peoples', Bin Laden and his associates wrote as early as 1998.[22] Presupposing a Western religious-secular divide, this formulation could lead us to the conclusion that the 'occupation' of Saudi Arabia should be considered a non-religious (i.e., political, economic) argument for al-Qaeda's resistance against the West. This is indeed what Robert A. Pape argues in his analysis of al-Qaeda's suicide attacks. However, from al-Qaeda's perspective, the occupation of the Arabian Peninsula is a thoroughly religious issue. In accordance with authoritative jurisprudence on the waging of jihad, al-Qaeda argues that the occupation of the lands of Islam by unbelievers makes the waging of jihad an individual duty for each Muslim in order to liberate these Muslim lands.[23] Accordingly, Bin Laden states in his letter to the Americans: 'God, the Almighty, legislated the permission and option to avenge this oppression. Thus, if we are attacked, then we have the right to strike back'. This is 'commanded by our religion', he warns the Americans, so 'do not expect anything for us but jihad, resistance and revenge'.[24]

The question thus arises whether occupation should be considered a 'religious' legitimation for al-Qaeda's violence or not. Each answer to this question would be arbitrary, as this would presuppose a clear, unambiguous distinction between a 'religious' and a 'secular' sphere. Yet conceptualisations of these spheres differ across place and time and are the product of specific historical and cultural contexts, as we already noticed when discussing al-Qaeda's conceptualisation of religion.[25] So, although the presence of U.S. troops in Saudi Arabia has definitely contributed to al-Qaeda's violence, any conclusion as to whether something called 'religion' has contributed to its attacks is inconsistent.

Second, this observation is underlined by the meanings that al-Qaeda's leaders have attributed to the attacks themselves.[26] As noted above, al-Qaeda's leaders perceive the state of the *umma* as miserable. Central terms characterising the *umma* in their statements are 'weakness' (*wahn*) and 'humiliation' (*dhull*), as well as phrases about the 'honour' (*'ird*) and 'dignity' (*karāma*) of Muslims that is being violated. Jihadists, in contrast, are presented as the ones who are ashamed of the fate of the *umma* and restore its honour by revenging the crimes of the enemies. In the words of its leaders, al-Qaeda's attacks are the way 'to honour our *umma*', 'to eradicate the humiliation and unbelief that has overcome the land of Islam' and 'to remove the weakness, feebleness and humiliation which the *umma* is experiencing currently'.[27] The perpetrators of al-Qaeda's violence expressed themselves in comparable terms. For instance, one of the 11 September attackers states in his farewell video: 'I take no pleasure in a life of humiliation, and my heart has demanded from me that I live honourably in compliance with my Lord's religion'. Thus, he devoted himself to the jihad, he explains, 'so that I might kill Americans and other enemies of Islam and avenge my brothers' blood'. He avenged the dishonouring of his community, and 'went out to die with honour', as he concludes his statement.[28] Al-Qaeda's violence is seen as honourable and, regardless of its results in numbers of casualties, it is thought to contribute to the restoration of the dignity of the *umma*.

Research on violence has shown that al-Qaeda's emphasis on humiliation, honour and revenge is far from exceptional in this respect.[29] Particularly in cultures with a strongly developed sense of honour, public insult and humiliation (i.e., the violation of honour), can result in feelings of shame that, in turn, may fuel violence. In these cases, violence can be experienced as redeeming the honour of the insulted individual or group.

These insights are important when considering the importance of tribal structures and values in the context in which the concept of jihad originated. In seventh-century Arabia, loyalty to the community (*'aṣabiyya*), and especially the tribe, constituted the basis of the social structure. The honour of individuals was strongly related to the kinship group, and when the kinship group was humiliated, revenge was considered crucial to restore its honour. Often violence was seen as the appropriate means to do so. The early Muslims largely adopted these ideas of loyalty, honour and revenge, but primarily applied them to the *umma* rather than to the kinship group. It was now the reputation of the *umma* that had to be protected and, in case of humiliation, revenged.[30] This was the context in which the notion of jihad was developed, as a result of which it is closely connected to virtues such as loyalty, honour and revenge in early Islamic sources.[31] Evidently, these sources cannot be translated one-to-one into the twenty-first century. The honour code of the earliest Muslims has been transformed, redefined and renegotiated throughout the centuries. Yet shame and honour undeniably still play an important role in authoritative sources on jihad, as well as in the regions where many jihadists come from and operate.[32]

Just as in the example of occupation, it is impossible to determine whether feelings of humiliation, honour and revenge should be regarded as religious motivations of al-Qaeda's violence or not. In al-Qaeda's discourse, humiliation, honour and revenge are inseparably connected to concepts such as the *umma* and jihad, and thus seen as part of their struggle for Islam. However, presupposing a distinction between religion and the secular, it could also be argued that honour and revenge are tribal values and should therefore be seen as secular motivations. In this case too, any decision would be arbitrary. Rather than maintaining an artificial boundary between 'religious' concepts such as jihad and *umma* and 'tribal' values such as honour and revenge, both could better be seen as part of the cultural repertoire from which jihadists draw to motivate, shape, justify and give meaning to their violence.

Thus, while the alleged occupation of Muslim lands and feelings of humiliation, honour and revenge have definitely contributed to al-Qaeda's violence, it is not very fruitful to ask whether the same is true for the abstract category of 'religion'. Instead, it is more interesting to ask why questions on the role of religion in al-Qaeda's violence have been so prevalent over the last one and a half decade.

THE PREVALENCE OF 'RELIGIOUS VIOLENCE'

Focusing on the West, William T. Cavanaugh has argued that the artificial distinction between religion and the secular has been so often applied to violence because it reconfirms and authorises Western self-definitions as secular, rational and modern in opposition to a religious, fanatical and uncontrolled 'other'. According to Cavanaugh, so-called secular violence is generally associated with Western states and ideals. Religious violence, in contrast, is typically perceived as a product of non-Western and especially Muslim forms of culture. While secular violence is seen as rational, functional and controlled, religious violence is viewed as fanatical and unrestrained. This dichotomy might authorise secular violence in the name of Western nation states that is deemed necessary to contain religious fanatics. Hence, to oversimplify Cavanaugh's well-informed argument, the 'myth of religious violence' is maintained in the West because it works.[33]

As we have noticed above, the dichotomy that is being upheld in al-Qaeda's statements is not between secular and religious violence, but rather between the violence of infidels (against Islam) and the violence of al-Qaeda's mujahidin who stand up for their religion. Despite these differences, Cavanaugh's insights can be also applied to al-Qaeda.

In al-Qaeda's statements, the enemies' violence is inherently connected to its alleged unbelief. To focus on al-Qaeda's representations of the West, the latter's lack of *dīn* has resulted in the absence of 'principles and manners'. This explains the alleged hypocrisy of Western Middle East policies. According to al-Qaeda's leaders, Western rhetoric about democracy, human rights and freedom is hollow. Bin Laden states: 'To you, values and principles are something you merely demand from others, not that which you yourself must adhere to'. For example, he claims, 'the freedom and democracy that you call for is for yourselves and for the white race only. As for the rest of the world, you impose upon it your monstrous, destructive policies and governments'.[34] Western unbelief has led to policies that are solely characterised by self-interest and an attitude of materialism, according to al-Qaeda's statements. Westerners aim at earthly gains, as is illustrated by its policies in the Muslim world which includes the stealing of wealth and oil. Moreover, they are attached to earthly life, as a result of which its troops, who have nothing to fight for, are lacking morale, are afraid of death and prefer to bomb from a distance while its forces 'remain safe and sound'.[35] Therefore, al-Qaeda's leaders emphasise, the enemies may appear superior because of their technologies and equipment, but once it comes down to morale and faith, they are easily defeated.[36] Thus, Western violence in the Muslim world reflects its unbelief: it is hypocritical, cowardly, aimed at material gain and lacking any conviction.

For al-Qaeda, the West serves as an 'other' against which al-Qaeda defines itself. In its statements, the enemies' unbelief is contrasted with the pure faith, method and creed of the mujahidin. Western self-interest is opposed to the attitude of al-Qaeda's fighters, who are being guided by values such as loyalty and honour instead. While the West oppresses Muslims, al-Qaeda's mujahidin are presented as the ones standing up for the *umma*. Their fights are not aimed at self-enrichment and earthly gains, but they are symbols of heroism, honour, manliness and purity. They do not cling to worldly existence, but abandon their earthly positions and possessions to dedicate themselves to the struggle in the way of God. They renounce material life and are willing to sacrifice themselves for the sake of their religion, which makes them highly motivated and will bring them victory in the end.[37]

The disbelief of the enemies and its resulting hollowness, hypocrisy and terrorism enables al-Qaeda to present itself as the true followers of Muhammad and its attacks as sanctioned resistance. The distinction between Islam and unbelief serves al-Qaeda's self-definition as the vanguard of the *umma* and legitimises its violence as part of the timeless war between truth and falsehood. The result is a compelling appeal to the Muslim youths al-Qaeda aims at.

Al-Qaeda's message of the humiliated *umma* encompasses broadly shared grievances and anti-Western sentiments among Muslims from all over the world. Al-Qaeda connects these grievances and concerns by presenting them as part of a worldwide religious conflict, which facilitates and invigorates its (potential) supporters to identify with their fellow Muslims, and therefore with al-Qaeda's mujahidin who stand up for their brothers and sisters in need. Besides, al-Qaeda's emphasis on the pure Islam increases its appeal. As we have noticed, al-Qaeda anchors its message in perceived authentic Muslim traditions, which makes it applicable in every situation regardless of specific cultures, nations or ethnicities.[38] At the same time, however, the 'authentic' Islamic traditions are being applied in new situations, and therefore provided with new meanings. The result is a hybrid and dynamic ideology that is distinctly globalised, but nevertheless easily blends with local customs and traditions.[39] By claiming and being perceived to be genuinely Islamic, yet at the same time being adapted to modern, local and global contexts, al-Qaeda's message can be attractive for people from divergent backgrounds. It offers young Muslims throughout the world a model to assist their humiliated fellow believers. It gives them a sense of agency and an empowering role as the defenders of *umma* who, just like the Prophet, can revive the glory of Islam. Al-Qaeda's message, in short, offers young people from different regions in the world a way to give meaning to their lives that is experienced as authentically Islamic, but at the same time thoroughly modern, and therefore both empowering and fitting their needs and experiences.[40]

CONCLUSION

The prevalence of the question of whether religion has contributed to al-Qaeda's violence is understandable, not in the last place because of al-Qaeda's emphasis on the religious nature of the conflict, which has also reinforced Western perceptions on the issue. However, the question is not the right question, as it assumes a coherence that the concept of religion does not have. Religion does not have a trans-historical essence, but means different things to different observers. For example, while religion is often opposed to the secular in Western discourse, al-Qaeda distinguishes religion, i.e., Islam, from unbelief. What constitutes religion depends on particular historical and cultural contexts. Therefore, it is impossible to consistently distinguish between religious and non-religious violence or to argue that something called 'religion' contributes to, let alone causes violence. Particular beliefs, values and practices that are deemed religious by the actors may fuel violence in specific circumstances. Yet these beliefs, values and practices cannot be consistently labelled 'religious' from an analytical point of view.

Rather than studying the role of religion in violence, we should explore why wars and violence are so often perceived as being religious wars and religious violence. In the case of al-Qaeda, this shows that the opposition between the infidel enemies and the mujahidin served al-Qaeda's self-definition as a group of authentic Muslims who defend the *umma* in the footsteps of the prophet Muhammad. The dichotomy has reconfirmed and authorised al-Qaeda's alleged superiority over an infidel 'other', and therefore legitimised its violence in the name of the pure Islam of the Prophet and its suffering followers in the twenty-first century.

Endnotes

1 Robert A. Pape, *Dying to Win: The Strategic Logic of Suicide Terrorism* (New York: Random House, 2005), 104.

2 Assaf Moghadam, 'Suicide Terrorism, Occupation, and the Globalization of Martyrdom: A Critique of *Dying to Win*', *Studies in Conflict and Terrorism* 29:8 (2006), 707–729 esp. 718. See also Idem, *Globalization of Martyrdom: al-Qaeda, Salafi Jihad, and the Diffusion of Suicide Attacks* (Baltimore: The John Hopkins University Press, 2008).

3 Mark Sedgwick, Al-Qaeda and the Nature of Religious Terrorism, *Terrorism and Political Violence* 16:4 (2004), 795–814.

4 Cf. R. Scott Appleby, *The Ambivalence of the Sacred: Religion, Violence, and Reconciliation* (Lanham; Rowman & Littlefield Publishers, Inc., 2000); Mark Juergensmeyer, *Terror in the Mind of God: The Global Rise of Religious Violence* (Berkeley: University of California Press, 2003[2]); James W. Jones, *Blood that Cries out from the Earth: The Psychology of Religious Terrorism* (Oxford: Oxford University Press, 2008); and Charles Selengut, *Sacred Fury: Understanding Religious Violence* (Lanham; Rowman & Littlefield Publishers, Inc., 2008[2]).

5 William T. Cavanaugh, *The Myth of Religious Violence: Secular Ideology and the Roots of Modern Conflict* (Oxford: Oxford University Press, 2009).

6 The term 'al-Qaeda' is used here to refer to 'al-Qaeda Central' only, and thus excludes al-Qaeda's so-called affiliates or franchises in, among others, the Maghreb, the Arabian Peninsula and Iraq. The period under discussion here runs from al-Qaeda's declaration of war against the Americans in 1996 to Bin Laden's death in 2011.

7 Osama bin Laden, *I'lān al-jihād 'alā al-Amrīkiyyīn al-muhtalīn li-Bilād al-Haramayn* ['Declaration of Jihad against the Americans Occupying the Land of the Two Holy Places'], *Al-Quds al-'Arabi*, 23 August 1996, www.tawhed.ws/r?i=1502092b, accessed May 2014.

8 Untitled letter by Osama bin Laden, *Al-Jazeera*, 3 November 2001, transl. in Bruce Lawrence, *Messages to the World: The Statements of Osama bin Laden* (London: Verso, 2005), 133–138, esp. 134–135.

9 Untitled audio Statement by Osama bin Laden, *Al-Jazeera*, 4 January 2004, transl. in Lawrence, *Messages to the World*, 212–32, esp. 217. See also the statement of an unknown voice-over in a video by al-Qaeda's media group al-Sahāb Media, *Al-qawl qawl al-sawārim: ghazwa al-mu'adhin Abū Gharīb al-Makkī* ['The Word is the Word of the Swords: the Raid of the Muezzin Abu Gharib al-Makki'], 4 September 2008, https://archive.org/details/AsSahab-TheWordIsTheWordOfTheSwords1, accessed December 2015, 0:20–0:41'.

10 Bin Laden, 4 January 2004, transl. in Lawrence, *Messages to the World*, 227.

11 Statement by Ayman al-Zawahiri in al-Saḥāb Media, *Ḥiṣād 7 sanawāt min al-ḥurūb al-ṣalībiyya* ['The Results of Seven Years of the Crusades'], 17 September 2008, https://archive.org/details/AsSahab-ResultsOf7YearsOfTheCrusades, accessed December 2015, 1:11:08–1:13:13.

12 Hans G. Kippenberg, 'Defining the Present Situation of Muslims and Re-enacting the Prophet's Ghazwas', in Idem and Tilman Seidnsticker (eds.), *The 9/11 Handbook: Annotated Translation and Interpretation of the Attackers' Spiritual Manual* (London: Equinox Publishing Ltd., 2006) 47–58; Pieter Nanninga, 'The Liminality of "Living Martyrdom": Suicide Bombers' Preparations for Paradise', in Peter Berger and Justin Kroesen (eds.), *Ultimate Ambiguities: Investigating Death and Liminality* (New York: Berghahn Books, 2015), 79–96.

13 For a more nuanced discussion on the (multiple) meanings of *dīn*, see L. Gardet, 'Dīn', *Encyclopaedia of Islam* (Leiden: Brill Online, 2012²).

14 On the latter, see a statement by a leading al-Qaeda ideologue, the Saudi Attiya Allah, in al-Saḥāb Media, *Ḥiṣād 7 sanawāt*, 35:33–37:25.

15 See, for example, Ayman al-Zawahiri, 'Advice to the Community to Reject the Fatwa of Sheikh Bin Baz Authorizing Parliamentary Representation', n.d., transl. in Gilles Kepel and Jean-Pierre Milelli, *Al Qaeda in its Own Words*, transl. Pascale Ghazaleh (Cambridge: The Belknap Press of Harvard University Press, 2008), 192–192.

16 Statement by Osama bin Laden in al-Saḥāb Media, *Badr al-Riyāḍ 1* ['The Full Moon of Riyadh 1'], 4 February 2004, https://archive.org/details/moon_BR, accessed December 2015, 19:00–19:08.

17 Bin Laden, 3 November 2001, transl. in Lawrence, *Messages to the World*, 135.

18 Video statement by Osama bin Laden, *Risāla ilā al-shaʿb al-Amrīkī* ['Message to the American People'], *Al-Jazeera*, 30 October 2004, transl. at www.aljazeera.com/archive/2004/11/200849163336457223.html, accessed December 2015.

19 It is important to emphasise that even within al-Qaeda's statements these meanings diverge and are dependent on the historical context of a particular statement, on the individual uttering it and on the audiences that are being addressed.

20 Pieter Nanninga, *Jihadism and Suicide Attacks: Al-Qaeda, al-Sahab and the Meaning of Martyrdom*, (PhD Thesis University of Groningen, 2014).

21 Untitled statement by Osama bin Laden, 6 October 2002, transl. at www.theguardian.com/world/2002/nov/24/theobserver, accessed December 2015.

22 World Islamic Front for Jihad against the Jews and Crusaders, *Bayān al-Jabha al-Islāmiyya al-ʿĀlamiyya li-jihād al-yuhūd wa-l-ṣalībiyyīn* ['Statement of the World Islamic Front for Jihad against Jews and Crusaders'], *Al-Quds al-ʿArabi*, 23 February 2008, www.library.cornell.edu/colldev/mideast/fatw2.htm, accessed December 2015.

23   On the concept of jihad, see David Cook, *Understanding Jihad* (Berkeley: University of California Press, 2005).

24   Statement Bin Laden, 6 October 2002. For a more elaborate legitimation of al-Qaeda's jihad, see World Islamic Front, *Bayān al-Jabha al-Islāmiyya al-ʿĀlamiyya*.

25   Cf. Talal Asad, *Genealogies of Religion: Discipline and Reasons of Power in Christianity and Islam* (Baltimore: The John Hopkins University Press, 1993); and Idem, *Formations of the Secular: Christianity, Islam, Modernity* (Stanford: Stanford University Press, 2003).

26   Cf. Nanninga, *Jihadism and Suicide Attacks*.

27   Untitled audio statement by Osama bin Laden, 14 February 2003, transl. excerpts in in Lawrence, *Messages to the World*, 186–206, esp. 195; Statement by Bin Laden in al-Saḥāb Media, *Tadmīr al-mudammira al-amrīkiyya Kūl* ['The Destruction of the American Destroyer [USS] Cole 2'], summer 2001, https://archive.org/details/AsSahab-StateOfTheUmmah2, accessed December 2015, 27:55–28:35; Statement by Mustafa Abu al-Yazid in al-Saḥāb Media, *Jihād wa-istishhād: al-qʿāid Abū al-Ḥasan* ['Jihad and Martyrdom: Commander Abu al-Hasan'], 8 July 2008, https://archive.org/details/Jihad-wa-Esishhad, accessed December 2015, 3:27–4:44.

28   Statement by Ahmad al-Haznawi in al-Saḥāb Media, *Waṣāyā abṭāl ghazawāt Nīw Yūrk wa-Wāshintun: Aḥmad al-Haznāwī* ['The Wills of the Heroes of the Raids on New York and Washington: Ahmad al-Haznawi'], 15 April 2002, https://archive.org/details/Haznawi, accessed December 2015, 50:27–54:53.

29   Cf. Anton Blok, 'Introduction', in Idem, *Honour and Violence* (Cambridge: Polity Press, 2001), 1–13.

30   Timothy Winter, 'Honor', *Encyclopaedia of the Qurʿan 2* (Leiden: Brill Academic Publishers, 2002), 447–448.

31   Reuven Firestone, *Jihad: The Origin of Holy War in Islam* (Oxford: Oxford University Press, 1999), 30–36.

32   See, for example, Philip Carl Salzman, *Culture and Conflict in the Middle East* (New York: Humanity Books, 2008).

33   Cavanaugh, *The Myth of Religious Violence*, esp. 225–230.

34   Untitled statement Bin Laden, 6 October 2002.

35   It is interesting to note in this respect that the term *dīn* is also used as the opposite of *dunya*, 'world' or 'the domain of material life'. Cf. Gardet, 'Dīn'.

36   Cf. Statement by Osama bin Laden in al-Saḥāb Media, *Waṣāyā abṭāl*, 39:59–40:39; Statement by an unknown voice-over in al-Saḥāb Media, *Jihād wa-istishhād*, 0:23–2:59.

37   Attiya Allah vividly expressed this mirror imaging by describing the conflict as a conflict 'between truth and falsehood', 'between the people of monotheism (*tawḥīd*) and the people of *kufr*', 'between the sons of Islam and the sons of (...) the materialistic and atheistic (*mulḥid*) West who disbelieve in *dīn*' and 'between the pure and oppressed ones who (...) worship God on His earth as He ordered and loves and the unjust despots, the people of excess, shamelessness, immorality and treason'.

Hence, he concludes, 'our concept of war is the loftiest and most just of concepts, because it is based on fear of God, on God's will and on helping his *dīn*'. al-Saḥāb Media, *Ḥiṣād 7 sanawāt*, 35:33–37:25.

38 Cf. Olivier Roy, *Globalized Islam: The Search for a New Ummah* (New York: Columbia University Press, 2004), 257–287.

39 See, for example, David Leheny, 'Terrorism, Social Movements, and International Security: How Al Qaeda Affects Southeast Asia', *Japanese Journal of Political Science* 6:1 (2005) 87–109; and Madawi Al-Rasheed, 'The Local and the Global in Saudi Salafi-Jihadi Discourse', in Roel Meijer (ed.), *Global Salafism: Islam's New Religious Movement* (London: Hurst & Company, 2009), 301–320.

40 For a more elaborate version of this argument, see Nanninga, *Jihadism and Suicide Attacks*.

12 Meanings of Savagery: Terror, Religion and the Islamic State

PIETER NANNINGA

In 2004, the jihadist ideologue Abu Bakr Naji wrote a treatise titled *Management of Savagery* in which he outlined a long-term strategy to defeat the mujahidin's enemies. Through a lengthy campaign of constant violence; through causing terror and chaos, territories could be gained where, eventually, the caliphate could be re-established.[1]

The Islamic State is often seen as having followed Naji's blueprint. Founded in 2006 as the Islamic State of Iraq, the group rose to prominence after the withdrawal of American troops from Iraq and the outbreak of the Syrian civil war. In the spring of 2013, it announced its expansion into Syria and, under the name of the Islamic State of Iraq and al-Sham, it conquered large territories in the Sunni-dominated areas of both countries. Prompted by its successes and determined to rebuild the early-Islamic empire and fulfil apocalyptic prophecies, it announced the reestablishment of the caliphate on 29 June 2014, proclaiming its leader, Abu Bakr al-Baghdadi, as the new caliph. One decade after the publication of Naji's tract, the 'promise of God' had been fulfilled.[2] The Islamic State had established itself after countless acts of brutal violence, many more of which would follow in subsequent years.[3]

In most literature on the topic, the Islamic State's violence has been perceived along the lines of Naji's strategy: as a means of terror. Accordingly, the group's violence has been mainly interpreted as a means to spread fear and chaos among the target audience, be it the enemies' forces, the local population in the self-proclaimed caliphate or people in other targeted societies.[4] This perspective is significant, but insufficient. As research on violence has shown, violence is not only a means to an end. Acts of violence are also expressive actions that embody cultural meanings for the participants and 'say' something to the audience.[5] Accordingly, the Islamic State's violence should also be studied in its cultural context and by examining its meanings for the actors involved.

In this chapter, I will examine the cultural meanings of the Islamic State's violence for its participants. In doing so, I will pay particular attention to the role of religion, which, according to some authors, is especially relevant in cases of theatrical, symbolic violence.[6] For this purpose, I will focus on two cases of symbolic violence by the Islamic State against Western targets: the videotaped beheadings of four American and British journalists and aid workers in 2014 and the Paris attacks of 13 November 2015. Based on these two cases, I will argue that Muslim traditions provide one of the sources that the Islamic State draws from to create spectacular acts of symbolic violence that are not just a means of terror, but also performances in which the actors display for others the meaning of their social situation.[7]

'STRIKING THE NECKS OF THE ENEMIES'

Between 19 August and 3 October 2014, the Islamic State's most important media outlet, al-Furqān Media, released four videos that showed the executions of the American journalists James Foley and Steven Sotloff, and the British aid workers David Haines and Alan Henning, respectively.[8] Each video shows a captive kneeling in the sand somewhere in the hills near Raqqa, dressed in an orange jumpsuit with his hands tied behind his back. Behind him stands a masked, black-dressed executioner, who would become known as 'Jihadi John' and was later identified as the Londoner Mohammed Emwazi. After both the captive and 'Jihadi John' have delivered a short statement on the reasons for the killing, 'Jihadi John' pushes the hostage to the ground, puts his knife to the victim's throat and starts to saw. The camera cuts away and then the decapitated body of the victim is shown, lying on his stomach, his severed head placed on the middle of his back.

What motivated the Islamic State to commit these killings? According to its media publications on the events, the primary motivation for the executions were the US-led airstrikes against the group, which had started exactly eleven days before the release of the first video. The Islamic State frames the executions as retaliation for these actions, for example by starting each of the beheading videos with a short clip of US President Obama, British Prime Minister David Cameron or a news reporter commenting on the bombings. The airstrikes are also the main theme of the statements delivered by both the captives and their executioner, the latter of whom states: 'Just as your missiles continue to strike our people, our knife will continue to strike the necks of your people'.[9] The same is argued in the third issue of the Islamic

State's online magazine *Dabiq*, which offers eight arguments for the beheading of James Foley, all of which have to do with US policies in the region.[10]

Thus, the beheadings could be perceived as statements about the Western airstrikes against the group, aimed at producing shock and horror in the West to retaliate against the 'shock and awe' campaign of the United States and its allies. The killings followed the blueprint of Naji's *Management of Savagery*, which states: 'hostages should be liquidated in a terrifying manner, which will send fear into the hearts of the enemy and its supporters'.[11] Along these lines, the executions emphasised that more bloodshed would follow as long as the airstrikes continued. The last scenes of the four videos functioned as horrifying cliff-hangers in this respect, showing the executioner together with the next hostage who would be executed if the West would not 'back off and leave our people alone', as Emwazi phrases it.[12]

Yet, whereas the main context of the executions could be labelled as 'political', factors that could be designated as 'religious' also play a role. From the Islamic State's perspective, the beheadings, as well as the airstrikes they allegedly retaliated against, are part of a worldwide religious conflict. Since the Islamic State announced the reestablishment of the caliphate, it has presented itself as the defender of Muslims worldwide. The 'caliphate upon the Prophetic methodology', as it is often called, is portrayed as a sanctuary for Muslims who are humiliated all over the world. It is a state where the *sharī'a* rules and justice prevails for 'the oppressed, the orphans, the widows and the impoverished', as the Islamic State's spokesperson Abu Muhammad al-'Adnani phrased it. Yet, the caliphate's just rule also has another side, the group emphasises: The adversaries who have disgraced the Muslims over the last decades will be revenged. The Islamic State 'humbles the necks of the enemy', al-'Adnani stated about seven weeks before the Foley video was released.[13] From this perspective, the beheadings were not just a political means of terror; they should also be seen in the context of the Islamic State's perceived religious struggle in defence of the worldwide Muslim community, something Emwazi indirectly points out several times in his statements.[14]

This shows that so-called political and religious factors are strongly entangled in the Islamic State's perspective. As I have argued in my contribution on al-Qaeda in this volume, conceptions of politics and religion have differed across time and place and are the product of particular cultural contexts. For that reason, it is not very useful to ask whether the violence is (primarily) political or religious. Instead, it is more fruitful to examine how Muslim beliefs, texts, symbols and practices are being used to shape and give meaning to violence, as I will do in the remainder of this section.

To grasp the meanings of violence for the actors involved, it is crucial to examine its symbolic form.[15] In the case of the Islamic State's executions, it is important to note that the organisers have selected a means of execution that is established in Muslim tradition.[16] Decapitation can be legitimised by Qur'an verses such as *sūra* 47:4, which states: 'When you meet those who disbelieve, strike [their] necks (*darb al-riqāb*)'.[17] In addition, several traditions narrate that the prophet Muhammad and his companions, as well as his successors, the 'rightly-guided caliphs' (*al- rāshidūn*), ordered or executed the beheading of opponents, as was the case with 700 members of the Jewish Banu Qurayza tribe in Medina.[18]

These authoritative early-Islamic traditions provide important sources for the Islamic State to attribute meaning to its actions. Emwazi repeatedly alludes to the (alleged) Qur'anic sanctioning of beheading by phrasing the executions as 'striking the necks' of enemies.[19] In addition, one day after the release of the first beheading video, the Islamic State-supporting ideologue Hussayn bin Mahmud released a statement entitled 'The issue of beheading' in which he argued that the beheading of hostages is thoroughly Islamic. Bin Mahmud supports his claim by extensively commenting on *sūra* 47:4 and its interpretations, as well as on traditions about Muhammad and the first caliphs decapitating their enemies. He concludes: 'So striking the necks was something well-known, famous and in practice without ambiguity in the time of the Prophet and the rightly-guided caliphs'.[20] Thus, both Emwazi and Bin Mahmud attempt to legitimise the beheadings by claiming continuity with the past. Moreover, in doing so, they present the killings as another example that the Islamic State is based on the 'Prophetic methodology'.

As a related point, through the executions, the Islamic State not only portrays itself as the defender of Islam in the footsteps of Muhammad, but also as a state or, to be more precise, a caliphate that claims authority over all Muslims. Decapitation has a long history as a means of capital punishment and has been used by states to display and authorise their power throughout history.[21] This is also the context in which the Islamic State's executions are presented. Emwazi says to the American government in the first beheading video: 'You are no longer fighting an insurgency; we are an Islamic army and a state that has been accepted by a large number of Muslims worldwide'. Therefore, the Londoner claims, 'any aggression towards the Islamic State is an aggression towards Muslims', and any attempt by Obama to deny Muslims a safe life under the Islamic caliphate will be retaliated against.[22] Through its public executions, the Islamic State signals that it is a legitimate state; a caliphate that is responsible for the Muslims worldwide and has the right to defend itself against outside aggression in accordance with the Prophetic methodology.

This shows that the beheading of captives can be perceived as symbolic acts of violence that express some of the central themes of its message. In addition, the violence expresses and authorises the boundaries between the Islamic State and its opponents. The precise way in which the beheadings are carried out is crucial in this respect, as the next two examples illustrate.

First, through its videotaped beheadings, the Islamic State distinguished itself from its jihadist competitors. Over the last two decades, several jihadist groups in countries such as Chechnya, Egypt, Afghanistan, Saudi Arabia and Iraq have executed opponents by means of beheading. The form of these beheadings often diverged, for example regarding the staging, clothing, weapons and statements, as well as the exhibition of the decapitated bodies.[23] It is striking to note that the beheadings of the four Westerners by the Islamic State strongly resemble the executions by Abu Mus'ab al-Zarqawi's al-Qaeda in Iraq. In 2004 and 2005, al-Qaeda in Iraq had beheaded several hostages, including some Westerners, which it had publicised by means of video recordings that were distributed online. Just like the Islamic State's beheadings, these executions involved hostages in orange jumpsuits sitting or kneeling on the ground with their hands tied behind their backs, masked executioners dressed in black standing behind them, statements by both the executioners and the victims on the motivations for the killings, beheadings by cutting the throat of the victims and exhibitions of the decapitated bodies with the heads placed on the middle of the backs.[24] Hence, the Islamic State has appropriated the structure of its beheadings from the 'sheikh of the slaughterers', as al-Zarqawi is sometimes called, which had proven to be a successful way to attract worldwide media attention and therefore to bring the message of resistance against American policies in Iraq to the fore.

That the Islamic State largely copied the 'signature' of al-Qaeda in Iraq might not seem very remarkable due to historical and ideological bonds between both groups.[25] Yet this observation becomes more interesting against the background of an intra-jihadist argument about videotaped beheadings. In June 2005, namely, Ayman al-Zawahiri, Bin Laden's then-deputy, had written a letter to al-Zarqawi in which he strongly criticised the latter's videotaped beheadings. These 'scenes of slaughter' harm the jihadist cause, al-Zawahiri claimed, since the general audience disapproves of them. 'We do not need this', he wrote, since 'we are in a media battle in a race for the hearts and minds of our *umma*'.[26] By distributing beheading videos that resemble those of al-Qaeda in Iraq, the Islamic State positions itself in this debate, aligning itself with al-Zarqawi against al-Zawahiri, al-Qaeda's current leader. This is a particularly significant in the context of the Islamic State's present conflict with al-Qaeda and its representative in Syria, Jabhat al-Nusra (currently known as Jabhat Fateh al-Sham), which have fought each other both on the battlefield and in the media since the spring of 2013.[27] By releasing al-Zarqawi-style beheadings of Western hostages, the Islamic State reaffirmed its jihadist genealogy and (re)constructed the boundaries between itself and its jihadist competitors.

Second, the form of the Islamic State's beheadings resembles a prominent Muslim ritual: the sacrificial slaughter of animals. Sacrificial animals are killed by cutting the throat from behind with a knife while the animal is lying on the ground, which is precisely the way in which the Western hostages are executed by the Islamic State.[28] Whereas some authors have described beheadings by other jihadist groups as 'sacred actions' because of their resemblance to sacrifices, there are no indications that the Islamic State actually perceived the violence as such.[29] Ritualisation of social practices is not necessarily related to sacredness.[30] Yet research has shown that ritualisation can be seen as a strategy to distinguish certain actions from other ways of acting. By means of characteristics such as formality, fixity and repetition, ritualisation establishes a privileged contrast that differentiates actions as more powerful and significant than other, more quotidian activities.[31] Accordingly, by standardising, formalising and repeating the executions, the Islamic State distinguishes the actions from other acts of violence. The beheadings are highlighted as more important than, for instance, 'ordinary' beheadings of enemies on the battlefield. More importantly, the ritualised nature of the beheadings highlights the contrast between the Islamic State and its Western foes.

As we have noticed, the main reason provided for the executions are the American and British airstrikes against Muslims. From a Western perspective, the US-led airstrikes in Iraq and Syria are usually seen as precise and clean. Their ultimate representation is satellite footage showing high-tech bombs precisely striking their intended targets, an example of which is included in the Foley video.[32] However, according to the Islamic State the bombings are actually indiscriminate acts of 'aggression towards Muslims'.[33] They do not differentiate between armed and unarmed people, as a *Dabiq* article that is attributed to Sotloff himself suggests.[34] The West has murdered 'numerous Muslims in Iraq', the magazine claims, which it illustrates by narrating and depicting the killing of nine women and five children by 'crusader jets' near Sinjar on 15 September 2015.[35] Accordingly, in the eyes of the Islamic State the current campaign of the West fits the war against Islam that it is waging for decades already. 'Millions of Muslims have been killed, punished and expelled', Bin Mahmud writes in his statement on beheading, and 'the honour of thousands of Muslim women has been violated by Americans'.[36]

The contrast between the Islamic State's perception of the US-led airstrikes and its own executions is striking. Instead of high-tech, impersonal bombings, the beheadings involve physical closeness and intimacy between the executioner and the victim.[37] A simple knife and physical force are used to retaliate the advanced airstrikes in a way that is deliberately bloody and shocking. Moreover, in contrast to the alleged indiscriminate killing of Muslims in airstrikes, the victims of the Islamic State are not perceived as random. Rather, they are seen as symbolic representatives of Western societies, as is indicated in the beheading videos.[38] Moreover, these symbolic victims are killed in a highly structured, ritualised manner, which implies a sense of control over chaos.[39] Accordingly, the beheadings represent the caliphate's controlled retaliation for the unjust shedding of Muslim blood. It is the killing 'of a single man with a knife' versus the 'killing of thousands of Muslim families all over the world by pressing missile fire buttons', *Dabiq* summarises the Islamic State's perspective.[40]

The violence thus expresses the contrast between the Islamic State and its Western foes; between manliness and cowardice, justice and hypocrisy, faith in God and reliance on technology, and the guardians of the *umma* and the killers of Muslims. Moreover, it shows that it is now the West that is being humiliated, as is visually illustrated by the orange jumpsuits – an evident reference to the humiliation of Muslim prisoners in Guantanamo Bay and Abu Ghraib. Besides, the four Westerners are killed in a humiliating way; not only because of their humble postures during the ritualised executions, but also because mutilation of the body is often seen as humiliating for the enemy, and therefore experienced as redeeming the honour of the perpetrator. As al-Zarqawi addressed the US government just before he personally beheaded the American Nicholas Berg – dressed in an orange jumpsuit – in 2004: 'We tell you that the dignity of the Muslim men and women in Abu Ghraib and others is not redeemed except by blood and souls'.[41]

In short, by drawing from several sources, including traditions perceived as authentically Islamic, the Islamic State has shaped powerful performances through which they, in Geertzian terms, tell a story about themselves.[42] The beheadings of four Westerners express some of the central themes of the Islamic State's message and (re)construct the boundaries between the Islamic State and its adversaries. Hence, they can be seen as performances of the Islamic State itself: powerful messages that express what the Islamic State is about. About one year later, nine men would improvise on the same story in Paris.

'A RAID IN THE WAY OF THE PROPHET'

On Friday evening 13 November 2015, a series of coordinated attacks rocked the French capital, killing 130 people and injuring over 350. According to the French President, François Hollande, the objectives behind the attacks were quite clear: 'to sow fear in order to divide us and to keep us from fighting terrorism in the Middle East'.[43]

Terrorising the enemy was definitely important for the Islamic State, as the statement in which it claimed the attacks on the next day indicates. The statement explains that 'a group of soldiers of the caliphate' set out to target the 'lead carrier of the cross in Europe – Paris'. And they succeeded, it claims: 'Allah granted victory upon their hands and cast terror into the heart of the crusaders in their very own homeland'.[44] A similar view on the attacks becomes apparent from a video of the Islamic State's media group al-Hayat, which includes the farewell statements of several of the perpetrators of the attacks. In these farewell statements, which were mostly recorded in Syria, the attackers all indicate their intent to sow fear and terror in France. Each of them underlines this threat by executing an alleged 'apostate' (*murtadd*) in front of the camera, after which the fate of the beheaded victims is presented as a chilling warning for Europe's future. 'This will be your fate, God willing', one of the perpetrators states while holding the severed head of the man he just beheaded in his hand'.[45] The rationale behind these scenes is obvious: to cause further shock among the enemy population.

However, just like the beheadings of Westerners discussed in the previous section, the Paris attacks comprised more than a means of terror. These attacks, too, can be seen as performances through which the Islamic State shows what it is about. This becomes evident from taking a closer look the group's media representations about the events.

In accordance with the beheading videos discussed in the previous section, the central theme in the group's publications about the Paris attacks is that the violence should be seen as retaliation for France's bombings in Syria and Iraq. Several articles in the Islamic State's online magazines *Dabiq* and *Dār al-Islām* and twelve videos about the attacks that were released by the Islamic State's 'provinces' (*wilayāt*) all frame the attacks along these lines. The same is true for the perpetrators themselves. 'This is the result of your policy', Abdelhamid Abaaoud (a.k.a. 'Abu 'Umar al-Belgiki') states in his farewell message, while Foued Muhamed al-Aggad ('Abu Fu'ad al-Firansi') claims that 'we will shed blood as you did in the caliphate'.[46] The Islamic State's French-language magazine *Dār al-Islām* summarises: 'I think we cannot be much clearer. It is the bombings of the blind French that are the cause of this threat'.[47]

Whereas the Islamic State particularly emphasises France's air-strikes in Syria and Iraq, it frames the airstrikes as part of the country's general 'war against Islam'. France's military campaigns in Afghanistan and Mali, the 'cursing of the Prophet' by Charlie Hebdo and the humiliation of Muslims in France are repeatedly mentioned as other grievances.[48] The Paris attacks are seen as revenge for France's anti-Islam policies in general. 'Your history is bloodstained', an Algerian fighter in Libya comments on the attacks, so now 'it's our turn to retaliate'.[49] The French perpetrator Ismaël Omar Mostefaï ('Abu Rayyan al-Firansi') states: 'We will repay the suffering of our sisters and brothers (. . .) You will experience the same suffering as we are going through'.[50] The Paris attacks thus express the perception that the Islamic State defends itself against outside aggression. Moreover, they signal that it not only defends the Muslims living inside its caliphate, but that it should be seen as the protector of the entire *umma*.

Relatedly, the attacks are perceived as evidence that the Islamic State fulfils this role successfully. France is represented as one of the most militarily advanced nations on earth, yet the Islamic State emphasises that it was capable of executing several 'simultaneous attacks' against 'precisely chosen targets in the centre of the capital'. As a result Paris was 'shaken beneath the crusaders' feet', the statement of 14 November claims.[51] 'Paris was shocked and awed', a *Dabiq* articles states in an evident reference to the airstrikes. 'The eight [sic] knights brought Paris down to its knees, after years of French conceit in the face of Islam. A nationwide emergency was declared as a result of the actions of eight men armed only with knives and explosive belts'.[52] Hence, whereas the Islamic State might have experienced some setbacks on the battlefields in Syria and Iraq in the previous period, the attacks represent the group's enduring power by showing its capability of striking the enemy in its heart.

In the meantime, according to the Islamic State's media publications, the attacks showed the West's inherent weakness. The perpetrators acknowledge France's military and technological superiority, but, as Ismaël Omar Mostefaï expresses in his farewell message: 'Your equipment will not help you before Allah'.[53] The mujahidin have God on their side, they believe, as they repeatedly emphasise by quoting part of *sūra* 59:2: 'They thought that their fortresses would protect them from God; but God came upon them from where they had not expected, and He cast terror into their hearts'.[54] Therefore, in the eyes of the Islamic State, the Paris attacks not only signalled resistance to France's policies, but they also showed its vulnerability and undermined the government's authority, as it had not been able to protect its very own capital against assaults on multiple places.[55] The violence not only retaliated for the airstrikes, but also symbolised the Islamic State's successful struggle against the world's superpowers.

The above already indicates that, in this case too, the Islamic State perceives its violence as part of an all-encompassing religious struggle. Moreover, particular beliefs, values and practices derived from Muslim tradition provide significant 'tools' to construct the meanings of the attacks. A prominent example in this case is the concept of martyrdom (*istishhād*), which features frequently in the group's publications about the events. The Arabic term for 'martyr', *shahīd* (pl. *shuhadā'*), literally means 'witness', but both meanings of the term are closely related.[56] By their actions, martyrs deliver a testimony about their cause: they draw attention to their belief system and publicly show their preparedness to suffer or even die for it, which adds to its credibility. This makes martyrs powerful advertisers of their cause.[57] This is also the case in the Paris attacks, as I will argue in the remainder of this section. Four points are particularly noteworthy.

First, through their attacks, the 'martyrs' bear witness to the Islamic State's central message that it stands up for the Muslims and retaliates against their enemies in the footsteps of the Prophet. For instance, the attacks are repeatedly labelled as a 'raid' (*ghazwa*), which is the same term that is used for the military campaigns of the prophet Muhammad. By employing this term, the Islamic State emphasises the continuity between both struggles.[58] Likewise, a lengthy article in *Dār al-Islām* explains that the Paris attacks should be seen as 'attacks in the way of the Prophet' (*attentats sur la voie prophétique*). The attacks are fully in line with Islamic jurisprudence, the piece argues, and therefore profoundly Islamic.[59] 'Nine lions of the caliphate (...) raised the word of *tawḥīd*',[60] the al-Hayat video on the Paris incident further underlines that the Paris attackers testified to their belief: 'they lived the verses of the Qur'an by killing the unbelievers wherever they found them'.[61] As these quotes illustrate, the 'martyrs' acted as witnesses to the Islamic State's message through their attacks.

Second, this testimony is particularly powerful because the men showed their willingness to die for it. This is repeated numerous times in the Islamic State's messages about the attacks, for instance by stating that they are 'soldiers who are willing to offer themselves as sacrifices to Allah'.[62] The men 'advanced towards the enemy hoping to be killed for Allah's sake, doing so in support of His religion, His Prophet and His allies', the 14 November statement claims.[63] By showing their willingness to die for their cause, the men demonstrated that they care more about their religion and their fellow Muslims than about worldly affairs. They do not 'cling heavily to earth', as *sūra* 9:38 describes it in a phrase that repeatedly recurs in the Islamic State's media productions.[64] The perpetrators of the Paris attacks even downplay earthly life. In a written testament that is included in *Dār al-Islām*, Abdelhamid Abaaoud advises Muslims: 'Work in the way of Allah, persevere in the construction and development of the caliphate. Give your time, your knowledge, your strength to this and not to the futile affairs of the world down here'.[65] This shows that, through their attacks, the 'martyrs' express that the Islamic State is fully dedicated to its struggle. 'Either victory on earth, or martyrdom in the way of Allah', Abaaoud states.[66]

Third, by emphasising their distancing from worldly affairs, the perpetrators of the Paris attacks underline the difference between the mujahidin and Muslims who have not joined the battle. In the view of the Paris attackers, 'those who claim to be Muslims' are too attached to their earthly lives to make sacrifices for their religion and fellow believers. One of the perpetrators asks the Muslims who have not joined battle: 'What is the matter with you that you cling to earth while the blood of Muslims is being shed?' Another one states: 'You see brothers and sisters being killed and slaughtered, while you live a normal life making wages and receiving financial support'. The cause of their passivity is 'the weakness' (*al-wahn*), Abaaoud indicates: 'love of this life and fear of death'.[67] Hence, the nine men emphasise, Muslims should awaken from their slumber and rise up for their brothers and sisters in need.[68] More than being just a call for mobilisation, these statements indicate that the Paris attacks highlight and reinforce the opposition between the perpetrators' supreme sacrifice and the attachment to earthly life of others. Just as we have noted that the beheadings of the four Westerners established boundaries between the Islamic State and its adversaries, the Paris attacks distinguish the group from the Muslims who have not yet joined the fight.

Fourth, and relatedly, the 'martyrs' personify the honourable nature of the Islamic State's struggle. Whereas the West 'cowardly bombarded' Muslims from their jets and whereas the Muslims are 'sitting there idly' while their brothers and sisters are being killed, the mujahidin are 'brave knights' retaliating for the humiliation of the *umma*.[69] They do not let their religion being disgraced, but restore the honour of Islam by humiliating the unbelievers in return. 'Mujahidin are masters, not slaves', Abaaoud emphasises in his farewell message. 'They live with their heads raised. They fight for the cause of Allah and die with a radiant smile on their faces'.[70] The Paris attackers represent honour and dignity, thus underlining the Islamic State's message that the era of humiliation has ended. The twelfth issue of *Dabiq* emphasises this point by quoting Abu Bakr al-Baghdadi:

> By Allah, we will take revenge! (...) Soon, by Allah's permission, a day will come when the Muslim will walk everywhere as a master, having honor, being revered, with his head raised high, and his dignity preserved (...) So let the world know that we are living today in a new era. Whoever was heedless must now be alert. Whoever was sleeping must now awaken. Whoever was shocked and awed must comprehend. The Muslims today have a loud, thundering statement, and possess heavy boots. They have a statement that will cause the world to hear and understand the meaning of terrorism.

The 'brave knights' of the Paris attacks took revenge, *Dabiq*'s editors subsequently emphasise, as they spilled enemy blood 'in revenge for the religion and the Ummah'.[71] The Paris attacks were not just about the death and destruction they caused. From the Islamic State's perspective, they were also honourable acts in themselves, representing the dawn of a new era in which Muslims rise up against injustice and the honour of Islam is restored.

In short, the Paris attacks reconfirmed the message of the Islamic State and re-established boundaries between the group and its opponents. Like the beheadings of four Westerners about a year before, the Paris attacks can be seen as performances of the Islamic State itself. Yet the attacks not only showed what the Islamic State is about. Like other performances, the attacks also had a performative impact on people directly or indirectly witnessing the actions.[72] They not only represented the group to a worldwide audience, but also contributed to its construction. They defined and authorised the group's identity, created a bonding among its supporters and provided them with a sense of empowerment.[73]

CONCLUSION

As we have seen in this contribution, the Islamic State's dramatic acts of violence comprise more than acts of terror. By focusing on their theatrical, expressive aspects and cultural meanings, we have seen that they can also be approached as performances through which the actors display for others what their caliphate is about.

Just as Clifford Geertz has argued in the case of public rituals, the Islamic State's violence can be seen as both a model *of* and a model *for* reality.[74] On the one hand, the violence is a model *of* reality by providing the audience insights into the Islamic State and its struggle. Rather consistently, the beheadings and the Paris attacks express some of the main themes of the Islamic State's message. They tell the story of a group that successfully retaliates against the Western-led war against Islam, that makes sacrifices to defend oppressed Muslims and that restores the honour and dignity of the first generations of Muslims. In addition, the story told through the actions reconstructs and empowers the boundaries between the Islamic State and others, be it its Western adversaries, its jihadist competitors or the Muslims who have not yet joined its struggle. Thus, the violent performances define and authorise the Islamic State itself, showing to the audience what the Islamic State is about. On the other hand, the violence also offers a model *for* reality. It provides the audience with a way to take action and stand up against the perceived humiliation of Muslims. It offers them an empowering role as members of the caliphate upon the Prophetic methodology and it shows them role models who were willing to sacrifice earthly affairs to revenge injustice and gain victory, either in this world or in the hereafter.

From this perspective, it becomes clear that asking about the role of religion, as an abstract category, does not facilitate the analysis of the Islamic State's violence. Factors that could be labelled as historical, political, social, cultural and religious are strongly entangled and cannot be consistently separated. Instead, this exploration has shown that particular, contextually determined interpretations of, for instance, state and caliphate, slaughtering and raids, humiliation and honour, justice and retaliation, and martyrdom and sacrifice have contributed to countless dramatic acts of violence over the last few years. These acts of violence have been framed as 'religious' actions by specific actors, including the perpetrators in certain contexts. Yet, rather than taking this perspective at face value, we could better ask why they have done so. In the case of the Islamic State, we have seen that the group has benefited from framing the conflict as a religious conflict in certain circumstances. Particularly when addressing its supporters, the Islamic State's message of the worldwide war against Islam and the faithful few defending it has been a powerful message. This message has enabled the Islamic State to legitimate its – sometimes quite innovative – practices by invoking authorities from the past. It has facilitated the group to authorise its struggle and define itself against its opponents, and it has empowered thousands of people from over the world to find purpose and meaning under the banner of the caliphate.

Endnotes

1 Abū Bakr Nājī, 'Idāra al-tawaḥḥush: akhṭar marḥala satamurru bihā al-umma' ['The Management of Savagery: The Most Critical Stage Through which the Umma Will Pass'], n.p., n.d. Original version and English transl. by Will MCants (2006) available at https://pietervanostaeyen.wordpress.com/category/idarat-at-tawahhush, accessed March 2016.

2 Cf. al-Furqān Media, audio statement by Abu Muḥammad al-'Adnānī, *Hadha wa'd Allah* ['This is the Promise of Allah'], 29 June 2014, available at https://pietervanostaeyen.wordpress.com/2014/06/29/the-islamic-state-restores-the-caliphate, accessed March 2015.

3 On the history and ideology of the Islamic State, see Cole Bunzel, 'From Paper State to Caliphate: The Ideology of the Islamic State', The Brookings Project on US Relations with the Islamic World: Analysis Paper No. 19., 2015, at www.brookings.edu/~/media/research/files/papers/2015/03/ideology-of-islamic-state-bunzel/the-ideology-of-the-islamic-state.pdf, accessed March 2016; Charles R. Lister, *The Syrian Jihad: Al-Qaeda, the Islamic State and the Evolution of an Insurgency* (London: Hurst Publishers, 2015); William McCants, *The ISIS Apocalypse: The History, Strategy and Doomsday Vision of the Islamic State* (New York: St. Martin's Press, 2015); Michael Weiss and Hassan Hassan, *ISIS: Inside the Army of Terror* (New York: Regan Arts, 2015).

4 Cf. Abdel Bari Atwan, *Islamic State: The Digital Caliphate* (London: Saqi Books, 2015), 153–164; Jessica Stern and J.M. Berger, *ISIS: The State of Terror* (London: HarperCollins Publishers, 2015), 199–218.

5 Cf. Anton Blok, 'The Meaning of "Senseless" Violence', In Idem (ed.) *Honour and Violence* (Cambridge: Polity Press, 2001) 103–114; Ingo W. Schröder and Bettina E. Schmidt. 2001. 'Introduction: Violent Imaginaries and Violent Practices', In Idem (eds.) *Anthropology of Violence and Conflict*, (London: Routledge, 2001) 1–24.

6   Mark Juergensmeyer, for example, claims that religious violence is 'almost exclusively symbolic, performed in remarkable dramatic ways'. This is understandable, he explains, since public ritual 'has traditionally been the province of religion', which means that performance violence comes 'naturally for activists with a religious background'. Mark Juergensmeyer, *Terror in the Mind of God: The Global Rise of Religious Violence* (Berkeley: University of California Press, 2003²) 127–128 and 220.

7   Cf. Jeffrey C. Alexander, 'Cultural Pragmatics: Social Performance Between Ritual and Strategy', *Sociological Theory* 22:4 (2004), 527–573, at 529.

8   Al-Furqān Media, *A Message to America*, 19 August 2014, downloaded from http://clashdaily.com/2014/08/beheaded-isis-beheads-us-journalist-james-foley-graphic-video; Idem, *A Second Message to America*, 2 September 2014, downloaded from https://leaksource.info/2014/09/02/graphic-video-islamic-state-beheads-american-journalist-steven-sotloff; Idem, *A Message to the Allies of America*, 13 September 2014, downloaded from https://leaksource.info/2014/09/13/graphic-video-islamic-state-beheads-british-aid-worker-david-haines/; Idem, *Another Message to America and its Allies*, 3 October 2014, downloaded from www.youtube.com/watch?v=NCzDa2WBPAA.

9   Al-Furqān Media, *A Second Message to America*, 2:09–2:17.

10   Al-Ḥayāt Media Centre, 'Foreword', *Dabiq* 3, 30 August 2014, 3–4, available at https://azelin.files.wordpress.com/2015/02/the-islamic-state-e2809cdc481biq-magazine-322.pdf, accessed March 2016.

11   Nājī, 'Idāra al-tawaḥḥush', 3.

12   In the fourth video, which shows the beheading of Alan Henning, the next hostage that is being presented is the American Peter (Abdul Rahman) Kassig. However, his execution was not featured in a comparable fifth video. Rather, the video *Although the Disbelievers Dislike It*, which was released on 16 November 2014 and shows the execution of 22 Syrian regime soldiers, including a final scene featuring 'Jihadi John' standing above Kassig's severed head. Why Kassig's death was announced in this particular way is still unknown. For a detailed analysis of this video, see Quilliam Foundation and Terrorism Research and Analysis Consortium, 'Detailed Analysis of Islamic State Video: *Although the Disbelievers Dislike It*', n.d., available at www.quilliamfoundation.org/wp/wp-content/uploads/publications/free/detailed-analysis-of-islamic-state-propaganda-video.pdf, accessed February 2016.

13   Al-Furqān, *Hadha wa'd Allah*.

14   For example, Emwazi phrases the airstrikes against the Islamic States as attacks against 'Muslims', which he also calls 'our people'. Cf. Al-Furqān Media, *A Message to America*, 4:02'; Idem, *A Second Message to America*, 2:12'.

15   Blok, 'The Meaning of "Senseless" Violence', 108; Juergensmeyer, *Terror in the Mind of God*, 124–128.

16   For an overview of decapitation in Islamic scripture and history, see Timothy R. Furnish, 'Beheading in the Name of Islam', *Middle East Quarterly* 12:2 (2005), 51–57.

17 Whereas this passage can be translated differently, leading Muslim scholars have interpreted it as justifying decapitation. See also Q. 8:12, which states: 'I will cast terror into the hearts of those who have disbelieved, so strike [them] upon their necks (*aḍrabū fawq al-aʿnāq*).'

18 ʿAbd al-Malik Ibn Hisham, *The Life of Muhammad: A Translation of Isḥāq's Sīrat Rasūl Allāh*, with introduction and notes by A. Guillaume (Karachi: Oxford University Press, 2004 [1955]), 461–469.

19 Cf. al-Furqān Media, *A Second Message to America*, 2:13'; Idem, *Another Message to America and Its Allies*, 1:08'.

20 Ḥussayn bin Maḥmūd, *Mas'ala qaṭʿa al-ru'ūs* ['On the Issue of Beheading'], 20 August 2014, https://justpaste.it/gran, accessed March 2016. Transl. available at https://justpaste.it/decap3170, accessed March2016.

21 On the history of beheadings, see Frances Larson, *Severed: A History of Heads Lost and Heads Found* (New York: Liveright Publishing Corporation, 2014). On the relationship between power and public torture and executions, see Michel Foucault, *Discipline and Punish: The Birth of the Prison*, transl. from French by Alan Sheridan (New York: Random House, 1977 [1975]).

22 Al-Furqān Media, *A Message to America*, 3:47–4:18'.

23 Cf. Pete Lentini and Muhammad Bakashmar, 'Jihadist Beheading: A Convergence of Technology, Theology, and Teleology?', *Studies in Conflict and Terrorism* 30:4 (2007) 303–325; Dawn Perlmutter, 'Mujahideen Blood Rituals: The Religious and Forensic Symbolism of Al Qaeda Beheading', *Anthropoetics* 11:2 (2005–2006) available at www.anthropoetics.ucla.edu/ap1102/muja.htm, accessed March 2016.

24 The beheadings by al-Qaeda in Iraq and the Islamic State also show some differences, the most important of which are that the al-Qaeda in Iraq videos feature several executioners and show the entire beheading.

25 On the relationship between both groups, see Bunzel, 'From Paper State to Caliphate'; Weiss, *ISIS: Inside the Army of Terror*; Stern, *ISIS: The State of Terror*.

26 Untitled Letter from Ayman al-Zawahiri to Abu Mus'ab al-Zarqawi, 9 July 2005, available at www.ctc.usma.edu/v2/wp-content/uploads/2013/10/Zawahiris-Letter-to-Zarqawi-Original.pdf, March February 2016.

27 The conflict between the Islamic State and al-Qaeda broke out publicly after the Islamic State of Iraq expanded into Syria and announced the establishment of the Islamic State of Iraq and Syria (ISIS) in April 2013. While ISIS claimed to incorporate Jabhat al-Nusra, the latter renounced this claim, in which it was eventually supported by al-Zawahiri. Since that moment, ISIS, which would rename itself the Islamic State in June 2014, has remained in conflict with al-Qaeda and Jabhat al-Nusra, both in the media and on the Syrian battlefield. For a detailed account of the establishment and rise of Jabhat al-Nusra and its conflict with ISIS, see Lister, *The Syrian Jihad*, 51–218.

28 The term '*dhabīḥa*', which is used to denote the ritual slaughter of animals, is also used by the Islamic State to denote the beheading of its enemies.

29   Farhad Khosrokhavar, *Suicide Bombers: Allah's New Martyrs*, transl.
     from French by David Macey (London: Pluto Press, 2005) 68–69; Perl-
     mutter, 'Mujahideen Blood Rituals', 2. Noteworthy in this respect is
     Talal Assad's remarks on suicide attacks as sacrificial violence: *On
     Suicide Bombing* (New York: Columbia University Press, 2007) 42–45.
30   Cf. Barry Stephenson, 'Ritual', in Robert A. Segal and Kocku von Stuck-
     rad (eds.), *Vocabulary for the Study of Religion* 3, (Leiden: Brill, 2015),
     243–249
31   Cf. Catherine Bell, *Ritual Theory, Ritual Practice* (Oxford: Oxford Uni-
     versity Press, 1992), 88–93; Idem, *Ritual: Perspectives and Dimensions*
     (Oxford: Oxford University Press, 1997), 138–169.
32   Al-Furqān Media, *A Message to America*, 1:39–1:49. For an interesting
     illustration of the coalition's representations of its violence, see the
     website of the Combined Joined Task Force – Operation Inherent
     Resolve at www.inherentresolve.mil, last accessed March 2016.
33   Al-Furqān Media, *A Message to America*, 4:02.
34   Al-Ḥayāt Media Centre, 'A Message from Sotloff to His Mother
     Days Before His Execution', *Dabiq* 4, 12 October 2014, 47–51, at 48, avail-
     able   at   https://azelin.files.wordpress.com/2015/02/the-islamic-state-
     e2809cdc481biq-magazine-422.pdf, accessed March 2016.
35   Ibid., 49–51.
36   Bin Maḥmūd, *Mas'ala qaṭ'a al-ru'ūs*.
37   Cf. Ellis Goldberg, 'Sacrificing Humans', *Jadaliyya*, 23 February 2015, at
     www.jadaliyya.com/pages/index/20934/sacrificing-humans,   accessed
     March 2016.
38   It is striking that the statements of all four captives include phrases
     such as 'I as a member of the British public' or 'Am I not an American
     citizen?' Cf. Al-Furqān Media, *A Second Message to America*,
     1:09–1:11; Idem, *Another Message to America and its Allies*, 0:34–0:36'.
39   Cf. Bell, *Ritual Theory*, 174.
40   Al-Ḥayāt, *Dabiq* 3, 3.
41   Quoted in Ronald H. Jones, 'Terrorist Beheadings: Cultural and Strategic
     Implications', Strategic Studies Institute, June 2005, at www.strategicstu
     diesinstitute.army.mil/pdffiles/PUB608.pdf, accessed March 2016.
42   Geertz, 'Deep Play', 448.
43   François Hollande, 'Speech by the President of the Republic Before
     a Joint Session of Parliament', 16 November 2015, available at www
     .diplomatie.gouv.fr/en/french-foreign-policy/defence-security/parisat
     tacks-paris-terror-attacks-november-2015/article/speech-by-the-pre
     sident-of-the-republic-before-a-joint-session-of-parliament,   accessed
     March 2016.
44   'A Statement on the blessed Paris raid against the crusader nation of
     France', 14 November 2015, downloaded from https://justpaste.it/atta
     queParis on 14 November 2015.
45   Al-Ḥayāt Media Centre, *Et Tuez-Les Où Que Vous Les Rencontriez*
     ['And kill them wherever you find them'], 23 January 2016,
     16:55–17:02, downloaded from https://ia601502.us.archive.org/27/
     items/KillThemArabic/kill%20them-arabic.mp4 on 23 January 2016.

46 Al-Ḥayāt, *Et Tuez-Les*, 3:47–3:51 and 7:17–7:21.
47 Al-Ḥayāt Media Centre, 'Introduction', *Dār al-Islām* 7, 30 November 2015, available at http://jihadology.net/2015/11/30/new-issue-of-the-islamic-states-magazine-dar-al-islam-7/, last accessed March 2015, 3–4, at 4.
48 See, for example, 'A Statement on the blessed Paris raid'; Al-Maktab al-I'lāmī li-wilāya Ḥimṣ, *Wa-l-qādim adhā wa-'amr* ['The Coming Is Worse and Commanded'], 18 November 2015, 8:18–8:24, downloaded on 18 November 2015 from https://ia801501.us.archive.org/25/items/limaerit_tmail_135/135.mp4
49 Al-Maktab al-I'lāmī li-wilāya al-Barqa, *Min Barqa ila Bārīs* ['From Barqa to Paris'], 2 December 2015, downloaded on 2 December 2015 from https://ia801503.us.archive.org/3/items/FROMBARQAHTOBARIS.
50 Al-Ḥayāt, *Et Tuez-Les*, 14:53–14:55.
51 'A Statement on the blessed Paris raid'.
52 Al-Ḥayāt Media Centre, 'Foreword', Dabiq 12, 18 November 2014, 2, available at http://jihadology.net/2015/11/18/new-issue-of-the-islamic-states-magazine-dabiq-12%E2%80%B3, last accessed March 2016.
53 Al-Ḥayāt, *Et Tuez-Les*, 13:30–13:36.
54 Cf. 'A Statement on the blessed Paris raid'; Al-Ḥayāt, *Dabiq* 12, 2; Idem, *Dār al-Islām* 7, 3.
55 Cf. Juergensmeyer, *Terror in the Mind of God*, 128–135.
56 The Arabic term is probably derived from the Greek *martys* via the Syriac *sahda*, which also means 'witness', but was used by Christians to refer to their martyrs as well since the second century. In the Quran the term is primarily used to refer to 'witnesses' (e.g. Q. 2:143, 2:282, 22:78, 24:4), although there are also some verses in which it seems designate martyrs (e.g. Q. 3:140, 4:69). Cf. E. Kohlberg, 'Shahīd', *Encyclopaedia of Islam* (Leiden: Brill, 2010²) at www.referenceworks.brillonline.com, last accessed March 2016.
57 David Cook, *Martyrdom in Islam* (Cambridge: Cambridge University Press, 2007), 1–2.
58 See, for example, 'A Statement on the blessed Paris raid'.
59 Al-Ḥayāt Media Centre, 'Attentats sur la voie prophétique', *Dār al-Islām* 8, , 6–38, available at http://jihadology.net/2016/02/06/new-issue-of-the-islamic-states-magazine-dar-al-islam-8, last accessed March 2016.
60 *Tawḥīd* refers to the oneness and absolute unity of God. For the Islamic State, *tawḥīd* not only implies that no one may be worshipped besides God, but also that the upholding of man-made laws is idolatry *(shirk)*. Due to their strict interpretation of the doctrine, they consider many Muslims as *mushrikūn* (those committing *shirk*).
61 This text is shown together with the pictures of the nine Paris attackers in Al-Ḥayāt, *Et Tuez-Les*, 2:05–2:23. The phrase 'kill them wherever you find them', which is also the title of the video, is a quote from Q. 2:191.
62 Al-Ḥayāt, *Et Tuez-Les*, 14:42–14:46'.
63 'A Statement on the blessed Paris raid'.
64 Al-Ḥayāt, *Et Tuez-Les*, 7:34–7:37.

65   Al-Ḥayāt Media Centre, 'Le Testament de Notre Frère Abū 'Umar al-Baljīkī', *Dār al-Islām* 8, 41.

66   Al-Ḥayāt, *Et Tuez-Les*, 3:06–3:10.

67   Al-Ḥayāt, *Dār al-Islām* 8, 41.

68   Al-Ḥayāt, *Dabiq* 12, 2–3; Idem, *Dār al-Islām* 7, 3–4.

69   Al-Ḥayāt, *Dabiq* 12, 2–3; Idem, *Et Tuez-Les*, 6:33–6:52.

70   Al-Ḥayāt, *Et Tuez-Les*, 3:27–3:37.

71   Al-Ḥayāt, *Dabiq* 7, 2–3.

72   On 'performance violence' and its impact, see Juergensmeyer, *Terror in the Mind of God*, 124–128.

73   Cf. Pieter Nanninga, 'Paris through the Eyes of IS Supporters', *The Religion Factor*, 24 November 2015, at http://religionfactor.net/2015/11/24/paris-through-the-eyes-of-is-supporters, accessed March 2016.

74   Clifford Geertz, 'Religion as a Cultural System' (1966), in idem, *The Interpretation of Cultures: Selected Essays by Clifford Geertz* (New York: Basic Books, Inc., 1973) 87–125.

13 Where's Charlie? The Discourse of Religious Violence in France Post-7/1/2015

PER-ERIK NILSSON

INTRODUCTION

In the wake of the brutal attacks in Paris, 7 and 8 January 2015, against the satirical weekly *Charlie Hebdo* and the kosher supermarket *Hyper Cacher*, the hashtag 'I'm Charlie' (*Je suis Charlie*) quickly spread in the news and social media.[1] It soon became a watchword for manifesting adherence to the French national body. On 11 January, a Republican March in Paris saw one and a half million participants and approximately four million nationwide, making it to one of the biggest demonstrations in the country's history. The day after, 'We're all Charlie' echoed throughout the news media. According to one journalist the march was 'a national communion on a par with the liberation of Paris'.[2] In following months French citizens wore the logo 'I'm Charlie' pinned to their clothes, as car stickers and as the profile photo in social media. People who had never read *Charlie Hebdo* paid a subscription and the post-attack edition sold seven million copies, compared to the regular 30,000.

But not everybody wanted to be Charlie, nor was everybody allowed to be Charlie. Those who thought to problematise the *being* of Charlie – a whole palette of French anti-racist organisations, critical sociologists and post-colonial feminists – were quickly criticised. As the aforementioned journalist put it, they were seeking to understand the irrational, legitimising the unlegitimisable, whereas the answer was simple: 'There's a war going on between the West and Islamism'.[3] Yet another journalist accused them of practising *sociologism*, a wicked ideology resulting in their being the gullible puppets of the Islamist onslaught.[4] While not being representative of what was partly a nuanced public debate, statements of this sort epitomise important ideological functions of the nationwide 'I'm Charlie' movement. Thus, when the security alert system (*Plan Vigipirate*) is on highest alert, careful reflection is unwanted; we, the leaders of the Republic, already know what is in play: the enemy of the French people is not just on the doorstep, the enemy is among us. In this moment, you are either with us or against us, with the Republic and against Islam(ism); you are either Charlie or not.[5] And to protect Charlie, exceptional measures are called for. This gives rise to the question: Where was Charlie located post 7/1?

In this chapter I set out to answer this question by analysing what I call the discourse of religious violence.[6] This means understanding how certain statements at a given period, despite being potentially contradictory and paradoxical, share common ontological and epistemological groundwork. It also implies stressing the creative, proscriptive, and disciplinary power of discourse: how discourse targets the production of subjects and the performative dissemination of power through them.[7] As such, the discourse of religious violence during the post-Charlie debate was construed on three interrelated discursive tropes: identification, displacement and expansion.

IDENTIFICATION

The trope identification divides, classifies and proscribes binary identities – we and other, friend and foe, religious and secular. It draws on centuries-old Eurocentric, orientalist and colonial knowledge production that wilfully lends a helping hand in providing the epistemic field of the contemporary articulations of the discourse.[8] The discourse of religious violence should be so called with some caution as the category 'religious' can be misleading, since contemporary articulations of the discourse gather ideological fuel from the image of the Muslim other as villain within the secular order.[9] However, Jews as victims and grievable bodies, were attributed an ambiguous role in the discourse as well. When 'everybody' was Charlie, somewhat symptomatically, few 'were' the Jewish victims at *Hyper Cacher*. Joël Mergui, president of the Israelite Central Consistory in Paris, asked: 'If there had only been the attack against *Hyper Cacher*, would there have been four million people in the streets?'[10]

If *Charlie Hebdo* became the collective symbol for freedom, a white middle-aged man (in)famous for his anti-Muslim writings or cartoons emerged as the individual hero – ranging from the murdered cartoonists to the Swedish artist Lars Wilks, who has made a career of drawing anti-Muslim bigotry.[11] In the post-attack issue of *Charlie Hebdo* the counter image of the heroes of freedom stereotypically portrayed Muslim ragheads as either flaccid penises or rape victims of the Eiffel Tower – imagery of symbolically reclaiming virility and of national pathos.[12]

However, to talk about the depiction of the Muslim other as one-sided during the post-Charlie debate is wrong. It is more accurate to talk about a double-sided image – as the good and the bad Muslim.[13]

In a number of articles in the news media the good Muslim was given voice, as if Muslims as a group had something particular to say about the events. Not only then was the gunmen's Islamic identity given precedence over their French nationality, gender or class, it became an a-prioric interpretative frame for portraying Muslims in general. This is why during the debate countless journalists and politicians reproduced such statements as '*all* Muslims are not terrorists' and 'terrorism is not *really* Islam'.[14] The problem here is that, although these 'Muslims' are French by birth, they were being reduced to their imagined religious-ethnic origin which becomes the determinant factor in how they supposedly think and act.

The bad Muslim, 'the enemy within' to quote former president Sarkozy, was unsurprisingly epitomised by the Kouachi brothers and Coulibaly.[15] Numerous statements made clear that they were merely the tip of the iceberg. The production of this religious other was construed from hearsay, gossip and fabricated stories turned into news by official channels and then taken as fact by public spokespersons and politicians.[16] An essentialist, culturalist and racist understanding of Muslims is what made this possible; facts did not matter since *we* already knew who *they* really were. This imagined truth about the Muslims in France was also what justified patronising and paternalist statements echoing colonial supremacy, like that of renowned scholar and public intellectual Marcel Gauchet. The time had come for the Republic to 'put Muslims in their place', to give Muslims 'a lesson in responsibility'.[17] The binary of the French hero/victim and the Muslim perpetrator turned (white) French citizens into Charlie incarnate while a cultural racist logic forced Muslims into a perpetual renouncement of the attacks, turning any Muslim not conforming to the hegemonic national sentiment into a potential terrorist.

Here, it is important to understand how the discourse of religious violence, building on a Eurocentric and colonial logic of centre and periphery, divides, construes and structures social space in line with the trope of identity.[18] While Charlie was located in central Paris, *Place de la République*, its counterpart was in the suburbs – *la banlieue*. The French suburbs are commonly associated with large-scale housing projects (*cités*), ethnic minorities, poverty, violence and Islam(ism). Often portrayed as a lawless territory in the grip of young gang leaders or Salafists, the suburb is a mythical place where white middle- and upper-class French citizens rarely venture. News media, scholars and politicians have all played their part in thus construing this place.[19]

Partaking in the Republican March was something everybody should do, as PM Manuel Valls declared.[20] However, the reported absence of participants from the suburbs in the Republican March was interpreted as a refusal of *being* Charlie. This was, for example, the conclusion of the renowned historian Benjamin Stora, who expressed worry about the meagre participation of 'youth from the suburbs' and 'second and third generation immigrants from the Maghreb'.[21] If the suburbs were the auto-excluded interior of France, the post 9/11 imagery of screaming and flag-burning men depicted the outraged 'Muslim World'. In the news media, decontextualised and monolithic accounts of 'Muslim outrage' construed the 'Muslim World' into a ubiquitous space that could be reported on without critical reflection, where Boko Haram and the Taliban are on the same level as peaceful demonstrators in Algiers or praying Muslims in Jerusalem.[22] The point here is that the suburb appeared as an objectively culturalised site, the gateway to the foreign Orient in the midst of the Republic.

DISPLACEMENT

The tropes of identification and displacement are the proscriptive inception for the secular nation-state; displacement makes possible the projection of the secular nation-state's exercise of violence onto the religious other. As such, the discourse of religious violence construes secular violence as benign and a necessity to control and discipline religious violence – fanatic, fundamentalist, irrational.[23] In contemporary France, this has been of great importance in the ratification processes of the two laws targeting female Islamic clothing in public schools and in public space – not least by the logic of 'White men saving brown women from brown men'.[24] To undo the intricate interdependence of legitimising *our* violence vis-à-vis d-legitimising *their* violence, it is fruitful to approach the question through Slavoj Žižek's notion of *subjective* and *objective* violence.[25]

Subjective violence refers to acts of violence with a conspicuously identifiable perpetrator and an equally identifiable victim. This violence is obtrusive and disruptive and concerns direct physical violence, such mass murder and terrorism, or conspicuous acts of racism, sexism and incitement.[26] Importantly, 'subjective violence experienced as such against the background of a non-violent zero level', is what interrupts 'the "normal" state of things'.[27] Subjective violence is in this sense deceptive; it feeds on the ostentatious, on the abnormal and seen through the lens of the discourse of religious violence, Islam(ism). The attacks against *Charlie Hebdo* and *Hyper Cacher* are emblematic cases – as if the Hollywood versions of Samuel Huntington's inane clash of civilisation theory had come alive.[28]

The counterpart of subjective violence is objective violence – the violence 'inherent' to the normal order of things. It comes in two forms, *symbolical* (meaning making) and *systemic* (structural).[29] The perpetual workings of objective violence – economic exploitation, social inequalities, patriarchal structures, racist discrimination – are rarely treated as matters of ingrained structures in the secular nation-state. They function on the premise of being neutralised and hidden, and when they surface for the public to see they are rationalised either as pathology or as benevolent, sane and necessary. One example of this is anti-Semitism in France. While numerous studies show that anti-Semitism is on the rise,[30] anti-Semitic acts by (white) French are routinely rationalised while acts by (brown) French citizens are culturalised.[31] As one report states, the major problem in France today is 'imported' anti-Semitism, as part of the supposed religious-cultural essence of North-African immigrants (be it second or fourth generation French).[32] In the news media, post 7/1, a common statement was that French Jews were making *aliyha*, i.e migrating, en masse due to the rise of Islamic anti-Semitism. However, as the aforementioned president of the Israelite Central Consistory, argues, the French take on secularism is one of the most important causes for the emigration.[33]

The ideological problem here is that understanding the acts and biographies of the Kouachi brothers and Coulibaly through the lens of the discourse of religious violence neutralises the French nation-state's potential culpability in the acts. Even by following the logic of the discourse of religious violence, France has been waging a war against terrorism long before PM Valls' declaration post 7/1. During the last thirty years France has been involved in dozens of military operations, either leading – neo-colonial warfare in Central and Northern Africa – or as part of international interventions, as in the US-lead Global War on Terrorism.[34] In warfare, retaliation from the enemy comes as no surprise. It is as if the the Huntingtonian clash of civilisations, driven by states like the USA and France, is backfiring. Moreover, the evidence that at the time of writing has been made public suggests that three gunmen's hatred towards France and the West was less the result of *Charlie Hebdo's* cartoons than the leaked pictures from Abu Ghraib, American-led drone strikes and the French nation-state's objective violence.[35] As four high-school teachers in the Parisian suburb of Auber-villies put it: 'We are also the parents of three assassins'.[36] This should give rise to the realisation that if a war is to be waged against terrorism, where it is to be waged and how it is to be fought is not answered as easily as the discourse of religious violence suggests.

The coming together of the displacement of violence together with spatiality and identity thus legitimises anti-Muslim racism (or Islamo-phobia) at a symbolical level. It appears seductively easy to conclude that Muslims de facto are the source of their own symbolical and systemic ostracism, which is on the rise in France.[37] This is why Muslims are continuously expected to denounce Islam(ism) and confess their love for the secular nation-state. This is a game that cannot be won. Following the logic of the tropes of identity and spatiality, when Muslims denounce subjective violence they are denouncing their own nature, they are thus lying. The most common racist amalgam of sub-jective violence and Muslims today is not just *in vogue*, it is seen as a courageously clear-sighted statement.[38]

EXPANSION

The de-legitimisation of the religious other's violence is not only a question of framing, as Talal Asad suggests; the principle of legality is central to the continued expansion of objective violence.[39] Today, ter-rorism has become a legal category by which distribution and depriv-ation of citizenship and basic human rights are practised.[40] Similar to 9/11, 7/1 became a trigger for measurements awaiting implementation and another step towards strengthening France's pre-emptive counter-terrorism apparatus, as well as making the EU and its member states 'the most surveilled, monitored region in the world'.[41] In this way the discourse of religious violence has come to rationalise, legitimise and expand existing and new repressive disciplinary and penal measures specifically targeting the religious other where the paradoxical logic of undermining democracy and the rule of law in order to save it is guiding these processes.[42]

Even though pre-emptive counter-terrorism measures are intrusive for all citizens, they specifically target certain groups. In this regard the culturalisation of the religious other is crucial. To paraphrase Simon Patrick, even if the Republic is supposedly colour blind, political actors are not.[43] Post 9/11 citizens with an Arab or Muslim appearance were targeted throughout the West by social, legal and political measures.[44] And in Europe, as expressed by Tony Bunyan, 'measures ranging from the draconian to the frankly bizarre have been targeted specifically on Muslim communities across Europe'.[45] It is symptomatic that a discussion took place immediately after the 7/1 attacks concerning the Republic's problem with 'integration', which, in Republican lingua, is best understood as assimilation of foreign bodies into the national secular community.[46] Supposedly, one of the reasons for the gunmen's act was the lack of a proper understanding of French republican values, notably secularism. Minister of Education Najat Vallaud-Belkacem stated that students and teachers needed to be thoroughly educated in the 'Republic's values' and that 'tools for critical reflexion of religion, the state, freedom, and secularism' were necessary.[47] The minister also proposed that one thousand teachers specially educated in secularism would be appointed' that 9 December would be appointed Secularism Day, and that students who put the Republic's values in peril would be systematically reported and subjected to disciplinary sanctions.[48] Numerous intellectuals and public spokespersons also stressed the importance of the school as a site in the 'war against terrorism'.[49] However, the image of the religious other as a backwards other in need of civilisational enlightenment is reproduced at the expense of targeting symbolical and structural causes for why certain citizens choose to attack the Republic and join foreign militant groups such as ISIS. Republican values and especially secularism become tools in a disciplining apparatus targeting the religious other; techniques employed to create a monocultural national body.[50]

One recent measure in policing the religious other is the criminalisation of opinions. For some time now, in France (potential) terrorists have been arrested under the legal heading 'association with wrongdoers' (*association de malfaiteurs*).[51] The term, as Liz Fekete noted, 'is so imprecise, and open to creative judicial interpretation, that all sorts of "conduct", including speech, is prosecutable'.[52] With the new antiterror act, the French security apparatus could add another highly ambiguous term to the judicial toolbox. With 'apology of terrorism' (*apologie du terrorisme*), meaning praise, support, glorification and justification of terrorism, a whole range of conduct can be penalised. Although this measurement exists in the 1881 Freedom of Press Act, in November 2014 Parliament ratified a new anti-terrorism act that brought it within the Penal Code, with a maximum sentence of seven years imprisonment and a 100,000 euro fine.[53] In the aftermath of the attacks, the vagueness of the act was employed by the police and the judiciary to prosecute citizens in flash trials. In just one month after the attacks there had been approximately seventy convictions, of which many concerned verbal threats or glorification of the attacks under the influence of alcohol and/or drugs. In schools, over 200 cases of 'apology' were reported, resulting in police interrogation of teachers and 'Muslim' students, one as young as eight.[54] The ideologically 'neutral' public school became the site for nationalistic reification. In this fashion, similar to how Charlie came to function as a watchword, *apologie* became less a tool against the recruitment of jihadists than a rather vast apparatus in the wake of the attacks to reinforce republican law and to manifest (obligatory) national solidarity – as if freedom of speech for one citizen is turned into an apology for terrorism by the other.[55] Even if President Hollande and other ministers assured that 'all hateful, racist, anti-Semite or homophobic statements' now fall under the Penal Code, judging what is racist and hateful, and towards whom, is coded along the lines of race, ethnicity, religiosity, secularity, gender and so on.[56] There is a risk here that freedom of speech is employed as a tool for neutralising criticism of the secular national body.

Moreover, the apology law opens up for a self-policing panoptical society where every (brown, Muslim) body is potentially a jihadi in disguise and every (white, secular) body a potential state informant.[57] When President Hollande was lobbying for the new surveillance act, ratified 24 June 2015,[58] he was echoing George W. Bush by stating that in the fight against terrorism, everybody had a responsibility, especially French telecom companies, if they 'did not want to be an accomplice to evil'.[59] Here the contours of a secular securitarian order, with potentially devastating effects on the state of 'right' of the very principles it sets out to safeguard, are drawn. It is an order based on a Christian understanding of evil. As Asad explains, this is not a Manichean order of an eternal good versus evil. Evil is here a 'dynamic principle that opposes divine will and is therefore eliminable. Consequently, it is resistance to that will that defines evil, and all virtuous men are urged to overcome it at any cost'. And just as Christ overcame evil through the crucifixion, undermining the state of right appears as a necessary sacrifice, a crucifixion of the Republic, to retaliate and to overcome evil.[60]

CONCLUDING REMARKS

The discourse of religious violence, based on the tropes of identification, displacement and expansion, is as much about the religious other as it is about the secular self. Discursive constructions of identity are most often, if not exclusively, constructed on a negative and parasitic logic.

So, Where is Charlie? Nowhere and everywhere – in the housing projects, at the *Place de la République*, in ISIS territory, in the Élysée Palace, in the mosques and on the streets. However, being omnipresent does not mean that Charlie lends itself to the same lecture on all these spaces. The over determination of Charlie is what made it such a potent statement in relation to the discourse of religious violence. By displacing its contingency onto binary pairs it became a legitimising statement in the epistemic groundwork for contemporary socio-economic structures and the expansion of sovereign power through governmental techniques of surveillance and discipline. To quote Phil Scraton, 'to demonise perpetrators, to represent their humaneness as monstrousness, creates and sustains a climate within which a deeper understanding of historical, political and cultural contexts is inhibited and is replaced by an all-consuming will to vengeance'.[61] Herein lies a great danger for the future development of the rule of law and fundamental liberal-republican values.

Endnotes

1 All translations from French original sources to English are my own.
2 C. Fourest, *Éloge du blaspheme* (Paris: Bernard Grasset, 2015), p. 12.
3 P. Cohen, '7/9: Interactiv', *France Inter*, 30 April, 2015.
4 See P. Val, *Malaise dans l'inculture* (Paris: Grasset, 2015).
5 Islam(ism) refers to the fluid boundaries in public speech between Islam as a category of 'religion' and Islamism as a category of terrorism.
6 Compare to W. T. Cavanaugh, *The Myth of Religious Violence* (Oxford and New York: Oxford University Press). Also see T. Fitzgerald (ed.) *The Religious and the Secular* (London: Equinox, 2008).
7 See M. Foucault, *The Archeology of Knowledge* (London and New York: Routledge, 2002); M. Foucault, 'Governmentality', in G. C. Burchell and P. Miller P (eds.), *The Foucault Effect. Studies in Governmentality* (Chicago: University of Chicago Press, 1991), p. 87–104; M. Foucault, *Sécurité, territoire, population. Cours au Collège de France, 1977- 1978* (Paris: Seuil-Gallimard, 2004).
8 See T. Mastnak, *Crusading Peace. Christendom, the Muslim World and Western Political Order* (Berkeley and London: University of California Press, 2015); T. Masuzawa, *The Invention of World Religions. Or, How European Universalism Was Preserved in the Language of Pluralism* (Chicago: University of Chicago Press, 2005).
9 Cavanaugh, *The Myth*, p. 4.
10 C. Chambraud, 'Entretien: "C'est à chaque citoyen de protéger la démocratie"', *Le Monde*, 17 January 2015, p. 8.
11 See Fourest, *Éloge du blasphème*, 150ff.
12 See *Charlie Hedbo*, n°1178, 14 January 2015

13 See M. Mamdani, *Good Muslim, Bad Muslim: America and the Cold War, and the Roots of Terror* (New York: Pantheon Books, 2005).

14 S. de Larquier, 'Terrorisme, islamisme: la guerre des mots des politiques', *Le Point*, 12 January 2015, www.lepoint.fr/politique/terror isme-islamisme-la-guerre-des-mots-des-politiques-12-01-2015-1895787_20.php (accessed 20 August 2015).

15 V. Vergnaud, 'Les propositions de Nicolas Sarkozy pour lutter contre le terrorisme', *Le Journal du Dimanche*, 12 January 2015, www.lejdd.fr/ Politique/Les-propositions-de-Nicolas-Sarkozy-pour-lutter-contre-le-ter rorisme-712068 (accessed 18 February 2015).

16 See D. Perrotin, '"Charlie, ils l'ont bien cherché": le "témoignage" choc était inventé', *Le Monde*, 29 January 2015, http://abonnes.lemonde.fr (accessed 27 July 2015).

17 E. Levy, 'Entretien: Marcel Gauchet: "Il faut parler claire avec les musulmans"', *Le Point*, February 5 2015, n°2213 [iTunes Store].

18 See J. Samson, *Race and Empire* (New York: Pearson Longman, 2005).

19 See M. Dikeç, 'Voices into Noises: Ideological Determination of Unarticulated Justice Movements', *Space and Polity*, 2015, vol. 8, n. 2, p. 194; L. Mucchielli, 'Immigration et délinquance: Fantasmes et réalités', in N. Nacira Guénif-Souilamas, *La République mise à nue par son immigration* (Paris: La Fabrique, 2006), p. 39–61.

20 AFP, 'Marché républicain à Paris: un dispositif de sécurité excpetion-nel', *Le Parisien*, 10 January 2015, www.leparisien.fr/paris-75/marche-republicaine-dimanche-au-moins-deux-itineraires-transports-gratuits-en-idf-10-01-2015-4435145.php (accessed 20 August 2015).

21 T. Wieder, 'Entretien: "Il faut préserver les principes républicains tout en s'adressant aux minorités"', *Le Monde*, January 20 2015, p. 8; G. Rof 'C'est un complot pour salir les musulmans', *Le Monde*, 17 January 2015, p. 9.

22 AFP (2015), 'Des milliers manifestants dans le monde musulman contre les caricatures de Mahomet', *Le Monde*, 18 January. Accessed 27 July, 2015, at http://abonnes.lemonde.fr.

23 Cavanaugh, *The Myth*, p. 7.

24 See M. Fernando, *The Republic Unsettled* (Durham, NC: Duke University Press, 2014)

25 S. Žižek. *Violence. Six Sideweays Reflexions* (New York: Picador, 2008).

26 S. Žižek. *Violence*, p. 10.

27 S. Žižek. *Violence*, p. 2.

28 S. P. Huntington, *The Clash of Civilizations: And the Remaking of World Order* (New York: Touchstone, 1996).

29 S. Žižek. *Violence*, p. 2.

30 See M. Wieviorka, *The Lure of Anti-Semitism: Hatred of Jews in Present Days France* (Leiden: Brill, 2007).

31 See J. Marelli,'Usages et maléfices du thème de l'antisémitisme en France', in N. Guénif-Souilamas (ed.), *La république mise à nu par son immigration* (Paris: La Fabrique, 2015), p. 133–159; E. Hazan and A. Badiou, *L'antisémitisme partout. Aujourd'hui en France* (Paris: La Fabrique, 2011).

32 In J. C. Rufin. 'Chantier sur la lute contre le racisme et l'antisémitisme', *Minstère de l'intérieur, de la sécurité et des libertés locales*, 19 October 2004, www.ladocumentationfrancaise.fr/var/storage/rapports-publics/ 044000500.pdf (accessed 16 April 2009).

33 C. Chambraud, 'Entretien'

34 See P. Hansen and S. Jonsson, *Eurafrica. The Untold History of European Integration and Colonialism* (New York: Bloombury, 2014).

35 A. Chrisafis, 'Charlie Hebdo Attackers: Born, Raised, and Radicalised in Paris', *The Guardian*, 12 January 2015, www.theguardian.com/world/ 2015/jan/12/-sp-charlie-hebdo-attackers-kids-france-radicalised-paris (accessed August 30 2015).

36 D. Boussard, V. L. Damien, I. Richer and C. Robert, 'Comment avons-nous pu laisser nos élèves devenir des assassins?', *Le Monde*, 14 January 2015, p. 12.

37 CCIF, 'Annual Report' (Paris, 2015), www.islamophobie.net/sites/ default/files/CCIF-Annual-Report-2015.pdf (accessed 25 August 2015).

38 See A. Hajjat and M. Mohammed, *Islamophobie* (Paris: La Découverte, 2013).

39 T. Asad, *On Suicide Bombing*, p. 27.

40 M. Stone, I. Rua Wall and C. Douzinas, 'Introduction: Law, Politics and the Political' in M. Stone, I. Rua Wall, and C. Douzinas (eds.), *New Critical Legal Thinking* (New York: Routledge 2012), p. 3.

41 T. Bunyan, 'Just Over' the Horizon – the surveillance society and the state in the EU', *Race & Class*, vol. 51, n. 3, p. 7.

42 See A. Agamben, *State of Exception* (Chicago: The University of Chicago Press, 2005).

43 M. Baumard, 'Le système "produit des discriminations en se pensent égalitaire"', *Le Monde*, 25 January 2015, p. 10.

44 See S. Razack, 'Imperilled Muslim Women, Dangerous Muslim Men and Civilised Europeans: Legal and Social Responses to Forced Marraiges', *Feminist Legal Studies*, 2004, n. 12, p. 129–174.

45 Bunyan, 'Just Over', p. 8.

46 See G. Noiriel, *Immigration, antisémitisme et racisme (Xixe-Xxe Siècle): Discours Publics, Humiliations Privées* (Fayard, Paris, 2007)..

47 S. Balboa, 'L'école après Charlie: on a mis le doigt dans un engrenage pervers', *Rue 89*, 31 January 2015, http://rue89.nouvelobs.com/2015/ 01/31/lecole-apres-charlie-avons-mis-doigt-engrenage-pervers-257446? imprimer=1 (accessed 2 February, 2015).

48 Ministère de l'Éducation nationale, de l'Enseignement supérieur et de la Recherche, *Grande mobilisation de l'École pour les valeurs de la République* (Paris: La Rèpublique Française), www.education.gouv.fr/ cid85644/onze-mesures-pour-un-grande-mobilisation-de-l-ecole-pour-les-valeurs-de-la-republique.html (accessed 29 August 2015).

49 See C. Halmos, 'Contre les kalachnikovs: l'école', in Collectif, *Nous sommes Charlie* (Paris: Livre de poche, 2015), p. 76–77.

50 Bunyan, 'Just Over', p. 9. See also S. Hennette-Vauchez, and V. Valentin, *L'affaire Baby Loup ou la nouvelle laïcité* (Paris: LGDJ, 2014).

51   See, *Loi n° 92–1336, Legifrance*, 16 December 1992, http://legifrance
.gouv.fr/affichTexte.do?cidTexte=JORFTEXT000000177662   (accessed
29 august 2015).

52   L. Fekete, *A Suitable Enemy. Racism, Migration, and Islamophobia in
Europé* (London and New York: Pluto Press, 2009), p. 55.

53   *Loi n° 2014–1353 du 13 novembre 2014 renforçant les dispositions
relatives à la lutte contre le terrorisme* http://legifrance.gouv.fr/affich
Texte.do?cidTexte=JORFTEXT000000177662 (accessed 29 August 2015).

54   L. Imbert, 'Apologie d'actes terroristes: des condamnations pour l'ex-
emple', *Le Monde*, 13 January 2015, www.lemonde.fr/societe/article/
2015/01/13/apologie-d-actes-terroristes-des-condamnations-pour-l-
exemple_4555102_3224.html (Accessed 29 July 2015).

55   See I. Labarre, 'Apologie du terrorisme. Un lycéen nantais poursuivi
pour un dessin', *Ouest-France*, 17 January 2015, www.ouest-france.fr/
apologie-du-terrorisme-un-lyceen-nantais-poursuivi-pour-un-dessin-
3119401 (accessed July 29 2015).

56   See AFP, 'Au dîner du Crif, Hollande s'attque aux propos "de haine"', *Le
Monde*, 24 February 2015, http://abonnes.lemonde.fr (accessed 14
January 2015).

57   On the effects of US counter-terrorism laws see K. Rygiel, 'Citizenship
as government: Disciplining populations post-9/11', in J. Leatherma
(ed.),   *Discipline and Punishment in Global Politics: Illusions of
Control.* (New York: Palgrave-MacMillan 2008), p. 85–110.

58   See the new surveillance act, *Loi n°2015–912 du 24 juillet 2015, Legifrance*, 27 July 2015, www.legifrance.gouv.fr/affichTexte.do?cidTexte=
JORFTEXT000030931899 (accessed August 15 2015).

59   AFP, 'Des milliers manifestants dans le monde musulman contre les
caricatures de Mahomet', Le Monde, 18 January 2015, at http://
abonnes.lemonde.fr (accessed 27 July 2015).

60   Asad, *On Suicide Bombing*, p. 4.

61   P. Scraton, 'Introduction: Witnessing "Terror", Anticipating "War"', in
P. Scraton (ed.), *Beyond September 11. An Anthology of Dissent*
(London and Sterling, Virginia: Pluto Press), p. 3.

14 Understanding the Threat of the Islamic State in Contemporary Kyrgyzstan

MEERIM AITKULOVA

On July 16, 2015, the usual routine of the day was disrupted by sounds of a fierce firefight and explosions on one of the central streets of Bishkek, the capital of Kyrgyzstan. Being an unusual event for the country – in combination with a lack of explanatory details – triggered various speculations. Later that day, Kyrgyzstan's State Committee for National Security (KSCNS) released an official statement on the incident. According to the statement, this had been an anti-terroristic attack against a local cell of the Islamic State (IS), who, it was said, were planning several terroristic attacks, including one against the Russian military base located not far from the capital, and another during the mass prayer at the end of Ramadan, which was to take place the next day. The two-hour long operation ended with four terrorists killed. Another two had been liquidated earlier at another location in the city, and seven more detained.

Numerous statements from high officials warning about the threat of religious radicalization and alarming media headlines in the same vein appeared to be not so divorced from reality. However, some details that came out later shifted opinions on the part of the population from the originally laudatory assessment of the State's actions that prevented mass casualties, to various emergent speculations on the real causes of the event and doubts about IS's involvement.

The leader of the cell was identified as Amirov, a Kazakh citizen imprisoned in Kyrgyzstan for forgery and illegal border crossing, who had escaped from prison in May 2015. From the perspective of some experts, it was dubious that Amirov could manage to be a leader of the group and plan an attack from prison or in such a short period of time. Three days later a new figure appeared on the stage – Kunakunov, the ex-deputy of the Parliament, was detained at the airport while trying to leave the country. He was accused of being member of the group and sponsoring its actions. It is no secret that criminal groups are influential in the country, and often conspire with politicians to benefit both parties. Since many members of the cell had criminal backgrounds, another set of discussions revolved around the idea that they were a typical bandit group under the protection of Kunakunov, or he had to be removed from the election race on the eve of forthcoming Parliament elections.

For Masylkanova, 'this incident looks more like an operation to capture heavily armed members of a criminal gang who also happen to be religious extremists'.[1] Besides never showing much religious inclination, Kunakunov's persona hardly fits the image of a bloodthirsty religious extremist. Since no more information was forthcoming from the KSCNS, the motivations of the group to initiate attacks also remains quite vague. It was unclear why IS would be interested in recruiting new militants from Central Asia that would carry out mass killings during prayer in a country of moderate religiosity. It is unlikely to be an attractive action even for the most dedicated radicals in the country to see Muslims being killed for no particular reason.

Other speculations based on conspiracy theories often involved the role of both Russia and the United States. Hushed discussions about 150 tons of 'diplomatic mail' that had arrived at US embassy in Kyrgyzstan three months earlier, allegedly construction material needed for the embassy, resumed with renewed vigor. Some recalled that the unrest in Ukraine began after the embassy in Kiev received similar mysterious 'mail', while in Kyrgyzstan, invoking the threat of IS could be advantageous destabilizing the situation. For others, the IS threat could also be advantageous for Russia, after the long contest with United States for military presence in the country: Using the IS bogeyman could strengthen Russia's role in Central Asia and counterbalance the influence of the United States.

Finally, details of the interrogation of captured terrorists were not made public, and probably never will be. This in combination with the above-mentioned speculations provoked a broad public response, resulting in a division among the supporters of the official version and an emerging group of sceptics. On the one hand, given the fact that some citizens actually do leave the country to join IS, it is hard to deny the possibility of religious violence in Kyrgyzstan. On the other, the contradictory information that emerged following the incident made some people ask if raising and maintaining the spectre of such a threat may serve the interests of certain players.

When a quarter of a century ago the country became independent after the dissolution of the Soviet Union, a wave of enthusiasm based on expectations that embracing new values would eventually bring prosperity on par with the Western world swept the country and stimulated hasty transformations in all spheres of public life. For a short period of time, Kyrgyzstan was famous as an 'island of democracy' in the international arena thanks to the country's commitment to the principles of democracy. Due to its open-door policy in the sphere of religious regulation, it is still recognized as the most tolerant among Central Asian governments, although some recent tendencies appear to signal a reversal.

Largely excluded from the communist ideology of the Soviet Union as a relic of the past that hampered progress, religion re-emerged in all its diversity of virtues and new challenges as if there had been no eighty years of atheism. A new liberal religious policy, distinguished by minimum State interference into religious life and freedom of practices, facilitated a revival not only of traditional religions like Islam or Christianity, but also opened the door to the arrival of new and previously unknown religious groups and movements. It is hard to imagine a more expressive picture of communism's failure than a crowd of thousands kneeling down in the name of an unseen abstract deity beneath the statue of Vladimir Lenin in the centre of the capital.

Islam, the dominant religion in Kyrgyzstan professed by 87 per cent of population, is mainly represented by two ethnic groups: Kyrgyz (71 per cent) and Uzbeks (14 per cent).[2] The kind that exists today in the country has important features that developed historically under cultural and traditional values of the Kyrgyz and active cooperation with the larger Muslim world in post-Soviet times.

For centuries, majority of the population living in Central Asia confessed Islam, and yet it did not take deep roots among Kyrgyz tribes. Dating its presence on the territory of Central Asia since the seventh century, Islam started to play a significant role in the life of the Kyrgyz only in the sixteenth and seventeenth centuries. However, it remotely resembled the original Islam disseminated by Arab merchants along the Silk Road and evolved into a form more adapted to local realities. Many historians have pointed to a nomadic lifestyle that greatly hindered the development of Islamic centres like mosques or religious schools where collective practices and the dissemination of knowledge could take place. As a consequence, strong heathen traditions became deeply entangled with Islamic values. Such a form of Islam as conditioned by culture and traditions is still largely followed by the majority of Kyrgyz who acknowledge the fundamental spiritual components of Islam such as belief in a single creator, but otherwise the requirements of the religion are used rather fragmentarily and usually only come to the fore during certain rituals, such as circumcision or prayers during weddings and funerals. Simply put, it is spiritual acceptance of the notion of one God, not the duty to follow a diversity of religious practices, bans and requirements. There is no exact definition for this group of believers. However, in opposition to the rise of alien Islamic movements and practices, they are often referred to as traditional Muslims or secular Muslims. This version of Islam as historically authentic was announced by the government to receive all possible support. Given such superficial Islamic practices throughout the history, and the considerably limited religious practices during Soviet period, the contemporary unprecedented rise of Islamization is the subject of special attention and concern for many, who perceive it as threatening. If traditionally-sedentary Uzbeks had always been more religious, then the active embracing of Islamic values by the Kyrgyz might be associated with a replenishment of historical gaps in Islamic knowledge and practices in the new realties. It might also be viewed as part of the search for national identity and individual self-identification after independence. However, it is not the causes that are being scrutinized, but rather the transformations and threats this process brings to society. Although Christianity, predominantly followed by Russians that make 7.8 per cent[3] of population, also underwent its own process of rise and development in the post-Soviet era, it is less in the public eye and has not attracted the same kind of attention as Islamization.

When liberal religious policy facilitated the unimpeded arrival of all sorts of religious groups, groups that could hardly gain a foothold without significant financial and ideological support from outside the country, the spiritual foundation of traditional Islam has been shaken as a consequence of the onslaught of new religious values brought in from countries where they underwent own reshaping under the cultural and social environment of their own history and environment. Many of the traditional people of Kyrgyzstan appear to be dazzled by activities of new, predominantly Islamic religious groups. Among twenty-one Islamic movements identified by the State Commission on religious affairs,[4] most references in the media and academia are on members of Islamic political party Hizb ut-Tahrir, and religious groups recognized by country of origin – such as the proselytizing groups, Tabligi Djamaat from Pakistan, Wahhabi and Salafi movements from Middle East and, from Turkey, mainly the Hizmet movement of *Fethullah Gülen*. Accordingly, each of these groups has contributed to the revival of Islam, a revival that strikes outsiders in a pronounced visual way: a booming number of mosques that increased from 39 in

1990 to 2,362 in 2014,[5] several higher Islamic institutions, religious schools, a growing number of young women demonstrating commitment to Islam by wearing hijabs and heavily bearded men doing door-to-door preaching or distributing religious literature.

Such visible manifestations of religion cannot proceed insensibly in a small country with 6 million people, where the number of mosques has already exceeded the number of secondary schools.[6] Despite the fact that there is no ban on religious self-expression such as putting on a hijab or wearing a beard, such open demonstrations of religious disposition differs from the mainstream. Thus, it is more becoming an irritant for the secular part of society who see it as alien to local culture and threatening to traditional Islam. In this context, the hijab has turned into a vivid symbol of confrontation between two differing outlooks on the world. Despite the fact that almost 90 per cent of population are Muslims, debates about the head scarf in Kyrgyzstan are as hot as they are in Europe. The secular part of the population appeals to the historical foreignness of hijab for Kyrgyz women; notably, both the President and the Prime minister use this kind of rhetoric when expressing their position on Islamization,[7] while representatives of fundamentalist version of Islam parry with the constitutional right for freedom of religion, which the hijab obviously does not violate. Being the most visible part of Islamization, the hijab endures societal pressure: the critique of the headscarf connotes a wider meaning, implying all alien changes that non-traditional Islam has brought to society.[8]

Perhaps it is not much the external manifestation of unfamiliar forms of Islam, but rather the firmly entrenched fear in the public consciousness of religious radicalization that pops up every time upon seeing people whose appearance speaks of religion. Such fears are rooted in the 'war on terror' in Afghanistan fifteen years ago and, more recently, fears of IS's rise. The tragic events of 9/11 and the following war against Islamic militant groups had a direct impact on Kyrgyzstan. The geographical proximity to Afghanistan turned into a source of potential threats to the security of the country, while such terms as Islamic extremism, religiously inspired violence and international terrorism appeared overnight on everyone's lips. Since narratives about the direct connection between religious extremism and Islamization had not yet dominated Kyrgyz media, and since Islamization had not manifest itself so obviously, the threat was mainly perceived as existing somewhere outside the country. However, the recent phenomenon of IS has not only revived fading threats, but also escalated fears to a new level since the 'enemy' has never been so close.

With appearance of IS and phenomenon of the recruitment of citizens of Kyrgyzstan, the critique of public displays of religious identity and the activities of religious groups only reinforced the opinion that Islamization is dangerous, not only for cultural and traditional values, but also the threat to security. Considering the growing tension already existing in the religious sphere of the country before IS topped the global agenda, it is not surprising that both local media and the State got caught up in the narrative about the IS threat and religious radicalization circulating in the world with very little in the way of critical questioning. The content of the news media embodies a surprising myopia to the complexity of the religious situation in Kyrgyzstan. The activities of religious groups are often considered through the lens of radicalization, regardless of the specifics and aims of each group. Quantitative measures of the rise of Islam cannot be but a source of alarm when one sees religion turned into a kind of 'trendy' topic, with experts from many fields expressing their opinions on situation. On the other hand, recent Parliament elections demonstrated how political parties may easily tone down their critique of religion when votes from 'radical' Muslims ae needed. Seeing the cause of radicalization in enhanced state pressure on religious groups, in a low level of religious education and in socio-economic hardships, reports of international organizations reproduce the same narrative of the rising radicalization of Muslims and the threat of IS. The study of the International Crisis Group, a prominent and respected think tank, indicates the threatening scale of Muslim radicalization in Central Asia and nurtures the core notion that active Islamization inevitably leads to radicalization.[9] However, such discourse is analyzed by many international security analysts and organizations, some of which 'take issue with the attempt to link particular examples of violent extremism with non-violent political Islam'.[10] On the other hand, it is often the case that a small number of incidents in religious arenas are considered dangerous signals of the mass radicalization of non-traditional Muslims. In such situations, it is likely that it is not only ordinary citizens that may find themselves caught up in this kind of reasoning, but also the sources of information themselves, since the same narrative is circulating on all levels of opinion propagation.

However, the actual situation on the ground does not seem to be as hopeless as portrayed. None of the three major events in the modern history of independent Kyrgyzstan – the revolutions of 2005 and 2010, which resulted in change of governments, and the violent ethnic conflict of 2010 – were religiously inspired, nor distinguished by the participation of local or foreign terrorist organizations. Yet, it is common to hear that a third revolution will be Islamic, unless non-traditional religious groups are put under strict control or banned. Members of Hizb ut-Tahrir, Tabligi Djamaat and the Salafi movement have the most exposure to charges of disseminating extremist views – supposedly calling for the overthrow of the regime and supporting IS either by joining it physically or ideologically. In contrast, the primary aim of Tabligi Djamaat, which is, by the way, the second largest Islamic group in Kyrgyzstan after followers of traditional Islam, is to conduct proselytizing activities based on the apolitical nature of the group. Labelled the most dangerous, Hizb ut-Tahrir was banned in 2010 for its aim of building an Islamic Caliphate, while their concept of non-violence for achieving this ultimate goal is almost never mentioned by experts or the government, either for lack of knowledge or by intention.

The Salafi movement is fundamentalist on many matters. However, in relation to the State, it is guided by the hadith of submission to the will of the government, believing that a revolt will cause greater evil. No doubt there are extremists among them, but equating everyone with extremists is only weakly supported by threats implicit in the ideologies of such groups. As for numbers, data on the number of citizens who left Kyrgyzstan to fight for IS is rather contradictory, ranging from 100[11] to 350[12]. Given the background of alarming assertions that radicalization has gripped the entire country, these numbers are hardly proportional to the claimed threat. Besides, if looked at from a regional dimension, then the percentage of participants from the five countries of Central Asia, which are inhabited by 82 per cent of Muslim, comprises the lowest percentage in IS, with the total slightly exceeding the number of recruits coming from France.[13] According to data from the security services of the country, the majority joining IS from Kyrgyzstan are representatives of the Uzbek ethnicity from the southern part of the country. Finding themselves in comparatively disadvantageous conditions after the violent ethnic conflict between Kyrgyz and Uzbeks that took place on the southern part of the country in 2010, it is highly probable that it is not primarily religious zeal which motivates them to leave the country. Given this fact, attributing IS recruitment to religious radicalization is on shaky ground and overlooks the real problem.[14]

Returning to the main question of who would be interested in sustaining the opinion that Islamization means radicalization – manifested in its most extreme form in the appearance of the IS threat on the territory of Kyrgyzstan – our attention focuses on the government, which until recently had distanced itself from religious affairs. For many, the placement of the threat of religious extremism on the top of the agenda during a meeting of country's Security Council in February of 2014[15] appeared to be a disturbing message about the gravity of danger. The announcement of a tough anti-extremist strategy signaled the end of the liberal era in the religious sphere.

Heathershaw and Montgomery (2014) argue that the myth of radicalization is politically influential because it provides the basis for a common threat perception and an opportunity to enhance militant secularism in Central Asian countries with the assistance of the international community.[16] Surrounded by officially democratic and yet authoritarian in neighboring countries, Kyrgyzstan has deserved recognition as an 'island of democracy' for its aspiration to fully transform into a democracy, not only on paper but also in practice. The religious sphere enjoyed greater freedom until recently, largely because it existed beyond the State's interests. However, the recently declared commitment to the struggle against radical Islam and the tightening of control over religious activities that would be more characteristic of the leaders of neighboring countries zealously guarding own regimes may signal a move to enhance the authority of the State.[17] Especially after the two coup d'etats, the lesson for the new leadership implementation of new strategies against any potential threat to their positions. In the context of the State's interests, the destruction of an alleged IS group seems to serve multiple goals. State activities rarely receive positive feedback from the population. By successfully carrying out the operation, the government demonstrated its own potency and ability to ensure security in the face of a global threat. If neighbouring Uzbekistan and Tajikistan have earned the statuses of authoritarian regimes for their ruthless suppression of radical Islamists since independence, then the manipulation of the recent threat of IS enables Kyrgyzstan to deploy militant secularism without much risk for the status of a democratic republic. Taking into account that Islamic values are especially popular among the younger generation that did not grow up under the atheistic regime of the Soviet Union and the fact that the main driving force of two revolutions were young men from rural areas, the pre-emptive strategy of the government is quite understandable. The incident of supposedly suppressing IS played a unifying role, so that even the most critical opposition supported Governmental action. Additionally, the country's ongoing problems in the socio-economic sphere have been overshadowed by a greater threat.

On the one hand, acknowledgement of the fact of an exaggerated threat may call into question the very existence of security bodies. Besides, ample funding for security provision both from the State as well as (primarily) from international organizations have created an army of cadres that must be fed and occupied with work. In the absence of violence committed by terrorists – except for the alleged plans of an alleged local IS cell to impose attacks – it seems that the threat of international terrorism has turned into a mutually beneficial factor for cooperation. For the recipient State, Kyrgyzstan, it is a common practice to use such threats as the basis for applying for extra funds for the support of its own security forces. For the donors, predominantly the United States or Russia, a pretext for having a certain level of presence and control in the country by rendering financial support, trainings and antiterrorism counselling. On the other hand, it is likely that the State indeed believes in such threats, because since independence both local and international experts keep warning about the danger of geographical proximity to Afghanistan and, more recently, the threat of the new phenomenon of religious radicalization due to activities of IS, both inside and outside the country.

A retrospective glance at the early ages of building independent statehood shows that the fulfilment of one of the basic duties of the State – the provision of security provision in a country historically aligned with the anti-Western rhetoric of the Soviet Union – required serious reconstruction and new investments. At this stage, the United States as the main ideologue of democratic transformations for many emergent post-Soviet nations, sponsored Kyrgyzstan with multi-millions in grants for building up the security services and military equipment. However, it was the war in Afghanistan after 9/11 that facilitated an intensive cooperation of security services between the two countries. Sharply increased anti-terrorist trainings and expertise was provided for Kyrgyzstan's security services, along with numerous agreements to fight against international terrorism, and finally the installation of an American military base for the purposes of the 'war on terror' could not help but influence the development of the State's policy towards security issues.[18] In a weak country suffering from a high level of corruption and busy with the constant political confrontations of opposing parties, the operation of a military base gave some sense of security from the troublesome neighbourhood with Afghanistan, while expert and financial support from the United States greatly relieved the burden of enhancing its military capacity with its own resources. It is thus no surprise that, since the 9/11, Afghanistan had played the role of the main threat to security, and the country unconditionally adapted international security discourse in relation to the phenomenon of terrorism. Russia being a constant rival of the United States for the expansion of its own geopolitical influence in

Central Asian region, under the same narrative of the threat of international terrorism they hurried to open their own military base in 2003. Not without difficulties, the country managed to manoeuvre between the ambitions of the two powers and to demonstrate impartiality. However, deteriorating relations with the West against the background of an escalating Ukrainian crisis gave the Kremlin a way to reinforce its own presence in its 'backyard' represented by Central Asian countries.[19] In relation to Kyrgyzstan, an unprecedented donation of military equipment worth 1.1 billion USD was negotiated in 2013 in return for promise not to prolong the rental agreement of the United States's military base that terminated the following year.[20] Additionally, in order to avoid economic hardships in trade and in the larger economic sphere, Kyrgyzstan decided to join regional economic union dominated by Russia. All this was combined with diplomatic pressure from Russia. The longstanding aspiration of Russia to push the United States from the region seems to have been success, at least in case of Kyrgyzstan.[21] The current security situation in Kyrgyzstan reveals the shift of players. If the United States was the main provider of funds and an ideological promoter of the 'Afghan threat', then Russia is playing a parallel role regarding the new threat of IS. The image of a common enemy like IS and the problem of Muslim radicalization in both countries may have an important role in enhancing Russia's position in the region. In this regard, the threat of the attack on Russia's military base attributed to the eliminated IS group in Kyrgyzstan is likely to culminate in the strategy to consolidate its own position, and to provide extra justification for the decision to bomb IS in Syria. Yet the logic of the attack would have some other reason if the 16 July incident happened after Russia had taken such decision. Casey (2015) argues that 'so long as ISIS exists, officials, based in both Moscow and regional capitals, will continue using the group as a convenient canard for increasing their own security measures, no matter the facts on the ground'.[22] Though the United States considerably cut spending on military support of Central Asian governments in recent years, it never downplayed IS's threat in the region.[23] The IS threat for the United States as the background of an unrealized prognosis about Afghanistan's threat, might be as beneficial as it is for Russia. Though leadership in the region has recently been relinquished to Russia, the United States is too big a partner for Kyrgyzstan to ignore in multilateral ongoing projects, including those aimed at counter terrorism.

Summing up the above discussion, the author assumes that the problem of religious radicalization in general and the threat of IS in particular are exaggerated in Kyrgyzstan to suit the security interests of the government and international players. Expert forecasts parroting the same popular international discourses of radicalization without a more detailed analysis of local realities and disregarding the voices of religious people evokes a deja vu feeling of the Afghan threat that was based on the same narrative of the inevitability of the problem. Yet neither the Taliban's nor other terrorist traces could be identified in Kyrgyzstan's major conflicts in the post-Soviet era that thrice violated the peace and stability in the country, namely two revolutions and a bloody ethnic conflict. However, enhancement of the militant secularism of the current authorities and the ambitions of certain international powers to plant their own flag in the country may have far more negative consequences than the Afghan problem since the entire growing religious population is under suspicion.

Endnotes

1 Aidai Masylkanova, *Is the ISIS threat in Kyrgyzstan real?*, August 04, 2015, available at http://thediplomat.com/2015/08/is-the-isis-threat-in-kyrgyzstan-real/.

2 National statistic committee of Kyrgyz Republic. *Population 2015* (2015), available at www.stat.kg/ru/statistics/naselenie/.

3 Ibid.

4 *Государственная политика в религиозной с фере и основные религиозные течения в Кыргызстане* (2015). [State policy in religious sphere and main religious movements in Kyrgyzstan] (2015). Methodological handbook. www.unfpa.kg/wp-content/uploads/2015/03/Binder2.pdf.

5 Franco Galdini, *Islam in Kyrgyzstan: Growing in diversity*, October 22, 2015, available at www.opendemocracy.net/od-russia/franco-galdini/islam-in-kyrgyzstan-growing-in-diversity.

6 Muhiddin Zarif and Behzod Muhammadiy, *More mosques than schools being built in Kyrgyzstan, November 07, 2015*, available at www.voanews.com/content/more-mosques-than-schools-being-built-in-kyrgyzstan/3044830.html.

7 'Hijab is not our clothing, not our culture, we need to understand it and not go to extremes' – President Atambaev's statement during a meeting with students on May 31, 2012, available at www.akipress.com/news:487531/

«Даже самые развитые страны уже не могут противостоять ему в п олной мере. Особенно крепчает религиозный фанатизм. Нам пытаются навязать несвойственные нам традиции, обычаи. Кыргызы никогда не носили паранджу, чалму, дамбалы. Мы должны остановить попытки изменить наши традиции. Да, мы признаем, что наша религия – ислам, но то, что нам навязывают, мы не приемлем» - заявил на коллегии МВД премьер-министр Темир Сариев 24 июля 2015 г.

['Even the most developed counties cannot oppose it. Especially religious fanaticism is becoming stronger. There are attempts to impose unusual traditions, customs. Kyrgyz people have never wore paranjas, turbans, dambals. We should stop the attempts to change our traditions. Yes, we do acknowledge that Islam is our religion but we do not accept that what is imposed upon us'] – Prime Minister Sariev's statement during a panel with representatives of the Ministry of internal affairs on July 24, 2015, available at http://24.kg/obschestvo/16722_temir_sariev_kyirgyizstan_doljen_vyis tupat_protiv_togo_chtobyi_nashih_lyudey_odevali_v_chalmu_dambalyi_ i_hidjab_/.

8 Ibid.

9 International crisis group, *Syria calling: Radicalization in Central Asia, policy briefing, 2015, available at* www.crisisgroup.org/~/ media/Files/asia/central-asia/b072-syria-calling-radicalisation-in-cen tral-asia.pdf.

10 John Heathershaw and David W. Montgomery, The myth of post-soviet Muslim radicalization in the Central Asian republics, *Chatam House,* 2014 p.2. available at www.chathamhouse.org/sites/files/ chathamhouse/field/field_document/20141111PostSovietRadicaliza tionHeathershawMontgomery.pdf.

11 Anna Dyner, Arkadiusz Legiec and Kasper Rekawek, Ready to go? ISIS and its presumed expansion into Central Asia, *Polish Institute of International Affairs,* 2015 p.11. available at www.isn.ethz.ch/ Digital-Library/Publications/Detail/?ots591=0c54e3b3-1e9c-be1e-2c24-a6a8c7060233&lng=en&id=192428.

12 ГКНБ: В Сирию из Кыргызстан уехали 350 человек. (27 июля 2015) [Kyrgyzstan's State Committee for National Security: '350 left Kyrgyz-stan to Syria'] (July 27, 2015), available at http://rus.azattyk.org/arch ive/ky_News_in_Russian_ru/20150720/4795/4795.html?id=27154381.

13 Anna Dyner, Arkadiusz Legiec and Kasper Rekawek, Ready to go? ISIS and its presumed expansion into Central Asia, *Polish Institute of Inter-national Affairs,* 2015 p. 15 available at www.isn.ethz.ch/Digital-Library/Publications/Detail/?ots591=0c54e3b3-1e9c-be1e-2c24-a6a8c7060233&lng=en&id=192428.

14 Rebekah Tromble, Securitising Islam, securitising ethnicity: the dis-course of Uzbek radicalism in Kyrgyzstan, *East European politics.* 30:4, 2014, pp. 526–547, available at www.tandfonline.com/doi/abs/ 10.1080/21599165.2014.950417.

15 Президент Кыргызстана об исламе и народных традициях, радикали-зации, хиджабе (2014). [President of Kyrgyzstan about Islam and trad-itions, radicalization, hijab] (2014), available at www.islamsng.com/ kgz/report/8308.

16 John Heathershaw and David W. Montgomery, The myth of post-soviet Muslim radicalization in the Central Asian republics. *Chatam House,* 2014, available at www.chathamhouse.org/sites/files/chathamhouse/ field/field_document/20141111PostSovietRadicalizationHeathershaw Montgomery.pdf.

17 Ibid.

18 Rebekah Tromble, Securitising Islam, securitising ethnicity: the discourse of Uzbek radicalism in Kyrgyzstan. *East European politics.* 30:4, 2014, pp. 526–547, available at www.tandfonline.com/doi/abs/10.1080/21599165.2014.950417

19 Michel Casey, *Russia continues inflating the ISIS threat in Central Asia*, September 24, 2015, available at http://thediplomat.com/2015/09/russia-continues-inflating-the-isis-threat-in-central-asia/.

20 Stephanie Ott, *Russia tightens control over Kyrgyzstan*, September 18, 2014, available at www.theguardian.com/world/2014/sep/18/russia-tightens-control-over-kyrgyzstan.

21 Jacob Zenn, What options for US influence in Central Asia after Manas? *The Central Asia – Caucasus Analyst*, March 08, 2013, available at www.cacianalyst.org/publications/analytical-articles/item/12668-what-options-for-us-influence-in-central-asia-after-manas?.html.

22 Michel Casey, *Russia continues inflating the ISIS threat in Central Asia*, September 24, 2015 available at http://thediplomat.com/2015/09/russia-continues-inflating-the-isis-threat-in-central-asia/.

23 In November 2015 for the first time in the history of visits of US State Secretaries to Central Asia (CA), John Kerry visited all five countries of the region within one tour. On one of the main discussion topics – the IS problem. Kerry assured them that the US Government shares concerns of the CA countries and is ready to render all possible support to eliminate the threat.

15 Terror and the Screen: Keeping the Relationship of Good and Bad Virtual

CHRISTOPHER HARTNEY

24

Zero Dark Thirty
(dir. Kathryn Bigelow, 2012)

American Sniper
(dir Clint Eastwood, 2014)

Moby-Dick; or, The Whale
(author: Herman Melville, 1851)

In this chapter, I do not try to provide an historical overview of all terror and all violence as it appears on our screens in relation to religion in the tightest sense. But I do want to seriously problematise how we approach such a subject in light of the work of the recent methodologies developed by thinkers like Fitzgerald, Cavanaugh, and Sloterdijk. That is, I seek to examine terrorism and violence in relation to themes I have discussed elsewhere as regards the state, and identify some key problems that emerge in the crossover between reality and narrative as they relate to terror and religion. I show here that terror depicted on our screens in narrative structures reinforces wider mythic understandings of our worldview and the processes by which we conceive of its defence and act to defend it.[1] The 'crossover' point, I will argue, highlights some very dubious political agendas and demonstrates that the relationship between terror, politics, and religion can never be clear-cut within a modernistic milieu that seeks to confuse narratival and mythic conceptions of the other with 'our' reality – and then obfuscate further that confusion through extremely tight definitions of religion.[2] To demonstrate this in a limited but hopefully effective way, I have chosen to focus on a small number of very popular recent examples of terror which are, I believe, extremely telling examples. These include the Hollywood films, *Zero Dark Thirty* and

American Sniper, and the popular television series 24. To begin this discussion, I suggest that these examples make a fascinating comparison with a classic work of literature that sits at the heart of the textual (and more recently cinematic) experience of the United States: Melville's *Moby-Dick*.[3] But I argue here that the comparison between these 'terror' narratives and the great American novel is fascinating for all the wrong reasons.

In 1851, Herman Melville finished *Moby-Dick; or, The Whale*. It remains one of the cornerstones of North American literature in part because it offers us no clear heroes.[4] It is a tale of obsession and pursuit leading to mutual destruction. As Captain of the Pequod, Ahab pursues his cetaceous adversary (which in a previous confrontation had ripped off his leg) with an epic obsession. One that is described as a complete self-obsession.[5] During his pursuit of the monstrous whale, Ahab himself is revealed as monstrous. Perhaps he is more monstrous than his prey because unlike the instinct-driven whale, the human (Ahab) has the capacity to know better. But is the whale *really* innocent? In a point that will become telling with the examples below, David Dowling demonstrates how, as film adaptations of the novel continue to multiply, the whale becomes increasingly an agent of mayhem and revenge. He argues that this attitude in the cinematic *mis-en-scene* of *Moby-Dick* adaptations overshadows the real power of the novel – which rests within the tensions between the humans on the Pequod.[6] This ability to lay evil intent on the whale in the screen world comes in part from its monstrous *voicelessness*. We are given no chance to empathise with a monster who suddenly and unspeakably appears from the depths. This voicelessness is something to chart when the cultural, religious, and national 'other' is presented in the stories we tell about ourselves. In fact the essential question in examining terror and religion on screen has to be *who gets to speak, and who gets to speak over and silence others?*

There is another obsession at work in *Moby-Dick*, and it is one of verisimilitude. Here I refer to the manner in which Melville, through the overtly-descriptive account of the narrator of the story, Ishmael, seeks to convince the reader of the 'true reality' of the account that he delivers. This narratival quest for absolute verisimilitude includes exacting lists of whale types, particular details regards the whaling industry, whaling boats, and the processes of whale hunting and processing. In fact, the extensive details provided by Ishmael on the Nantucket whaling industry are drawn from Melville's own experiences on passenger and whaling ships from 1839–1841. One imagines it would be a simple thing to rebuild the entirety of the mid-century, Northeast whaling industry simply by replicating the encyclopaedic and ethnographic details provided in the pages of the novel. This desperate need to convince us that what is taking place is 'real' is an atmosphere deeply shared by the following examples as well.

The final enlightening element in the comparison between Melville's masterwork and the examples I have chosen is its 'epic' nature. Most commentators discuss epic solely as a literary genre.[7] But it is time to take the 'atmosphere' of thought and behaviour behind that which is epic into our late-modernist world as a modality of action that, in some readings, seems all-pervasive to our Western, and specifically Anglophone, culture. Handbooks on the epic, such as the one produced by Cambridge University Press, see no point in defining the genre in an introduction. Rather this particular book leads with examples, starting with *Gilgamesh* and ending with Walcott's *Omeros*. In doing this, it avoids any essentialising questions regarding what the epic precisely is. Distilling some of these examples, however, we can say that epic as I adapt its use here, is marked by heroics, including extreme journeys (often to the underworld or an otherworld), and the confrontation of the non-human (the monstrous). The epic often speaks of a national or group destiny, which the hero both defines and defends. Thus Aeneas must found Rome, the Greeks must find unity in their obliteration of Trojan civilisation and, mock-epic or not, Harold Bloom must get through his day and in so doing delineate the quintessence of Irishness as he goes. Similarly, there is a national essence at play in *Moby-Dick*. As Christopher N. Phillips has highlighted in his study of the epic in America, the Romantics, Transcendentalists, and other formative white authors seek to emphasise the epic nature of the American project.[8] This underlines the central pillars of the United States: (1) as a promised land with its own destiny – (it is both God-given and Edenic), (2) as a land of individuals of Protestant outlook who (3) hold authority over the products of that land and the rewards that come from this if they are willing to labour. In these myths, the validity of an individual rests upon how they respond to the divine injunction to derive profit from the land.[9] Liberty is enshrined to overshadow communal moral compulsion and emphasise choice. This is then connected with a moral perfectionism that can be achieved in following these ideals and which the American philosopher Stanley Cavell has sought to define.[10] All these themes are hard at work in Melville's work as Dean Mendell notes,

Ahab's desire to kill Moby Dick is ethically justified by God's pledge to Noah and its reiteration in the eighth Psalm: 'The fear of you, and the dread of you shall be upon every beast of the earth, and upon every fowl of the air; upon all that moveth upon the earth, and upon all the fishes of the sea: into your hand are they delivered' (*Gen.* 9.2) ... But there is one difference between Ahab's attitude and the attitudes of all other Christian sailors in *Moby-Dick* and in other works. The pledge is always linked to the principles of the Protestant work ethic ... professional and religious obligations are analogous; that to be industrious and contribute to the material prosperity of one's ship is to achieve goodness and earn God's grace ... Starbuck pleads with Ahab to act morally – by killing [whales] for profit, not vengeance.[11]

What then remains a distinct threat to this epic America are societies that are represented as being more collectivist, where the individual quest for freedom and individuality is subsumed within some more socially cohesive attitude, and where the freedom to pursue profit as a demonstration of divine election is of a much less central concern. During the Cold War, global Communism served as a perfect foil to this America. Since the fall of the Wall, the threat of religious violence and terrorism serves instead as the foil against which American exceptionalism can shine.[12]

'24'

At first glance, it seems as though the successful television series *24* [8 seasons 2001–2010] is not all about Islam and Muslims as the mortal enemies of the United States. In fact, the connections between Islam and terrorism emerge most intensely as a theme only in various episodes of seasons 4, 6, and 8. Sometimes American Muslims and non-American 'Arabs' support the hero Jack Bauer [Kiefer Sutherland] in his quest to hunt terrorists, sometimes they act as stooges to Russian operatives, sometimes they are 'evil' in and of themselves. The producer of *24*, Joel Surnow, admits some racial problematic in all this. '*24* [Surnow] acknowledged, has been criticised as racially insensitive, because it frequently depicts Arab-Americans as terrorists'.[13]

In many publications, Jack Shaheen has reasonably argued that American visual culture, and Hollywood in particular have long established the Arab and the Muslim as a less-human other.[14] *24* plays into this hegemonic and Orientalist representation. To focus, however, on the presence of Islam and Muslims in *24* as the only indicator of a link between religion, violence, and screen narrative is to miss a more profound investigation of one of the significant and unique influences *24* has had on the war against terror. *24* uses the 'ticking time bomb' plot line. It is the *raison d'être* of the show. Bauer works for a US blackops office the Counter Terrorism Unit, and he finds on regular occasions that he only has minutes to get information out of men and women of evil intent. If the information is not forthcoming, thousands, perhaps millions, will die. So he tortures them. And the torture works.

> Although the ticking time bomb has been exposed as a 'million-to-one scenario' and 'so exceptional it is all but mythical,' it has been firmly lodged in the public debate as likely and common.[15]

The perpetuation of this myth is perhaps the foundational error of the programme.

Yet the salvational mechanism it suggests (torture a few to immediately save millions) enables an heroic and epic mentality to play itself out. What may seem to be moments of normal life in and around Los Angeles suddenly become the testing points for the preservation of the United States itself. Jack Bauer must, in every minute that the screen-clock in *24* ticks on, rise himself to heroic outcomes.

Additionally the 'ticking time bomb' conceit allows Bauer to come face-to-face with monsters who perpetuate terrorism. They refuse to talk. So Bauer makes them talk using pain. Here we find an answer to who talks and who is allowed to speak. Bauer guides what his torture victims can and cannot say through the shootings, electrodes, truth serums, beatings, and psychological torture at his disposal. The words that come out are not determined by what the 'evil' Muslims, Russians, traitors, and others would like to say. They cannot really explain their own experiences or outline their own sense of justice. Bauer just wants them to reveal details on the looming attack; that is, to follow the script. The 'ticking time bomb conceit' demands that they 'divulge', which means they say exactly what the American government wants them to say. Once they have said what Bauer needs them to say, the plot moves on without them.

Enjoyable as this kind of drama might be, the 'ticking time bomb' conceit is absurd. Surely the point at which terror suspects are most likely to *not* tell an interrogator exactly what they need to know is in the hours leading up to an attack. Moreover, as we will see below, torture produces confessions that are in the main useless. Yet this absurd plot conceit in the first instance made *24* a compendium of various torture techniques that seemed effective and viable. The question of what influence this had on the Bush administration dealing with the aftermath of the 9/11 attacks seems unfortunately clear.

In an article for *The Slate*, Dahlia Lithwick traces some of the source evidences that demonstrate the influence that the show had on the White House under Bush:

> According to British lawyer and writer Philippe Sands, Jack Bauer – played by Kiefer Sutherland – was an inspiration at early 'brainstorming meetings' of military officials at Guantanamo in September of 2002. Diane Beaver, the staff judge advocate general who gave legal approval to 18 controversial new interrogation techniques including water-boarding, sexual humiliation, and terrorizing prisoners with dogs, told Sands that Bauer 'gave people lots of ideas.' Michael Chertoff, the homeland-security chief, once gushed in a panel discussion on 24 organized by the Heritage Foundation that the show 'reflects real life.'[16]

Even if we take these details with a little salt, it is true that 24's debut just months after 9/11 provided a fictional space where Americans could play out their fantasies of revenge and swift justice. The sort of motivations that Pape has discovered drives suicide bombers.[17] This attitude of retribution was enunciated clearly by the producer of the show Joel Surnow, and those around him,

> Surnow and Nowrasteh [a close friend of Surnow and fellow producer] regard '24' as a kind of wish fulfilment for America. 'Every American wishes we had someone out there quietly taking care of business.' [Nowrasteh] said. 'It's a deep, dark ugly world out there. Maybe this is what Ollie North was trying to do. It would be nice to have a secret government that can get the answers and take care of business – even kill people. Jack Bauer fulfils that fantasy.'

The question remains, however, how real was the 'fantasy'? In her *New Yorker* feature article on the programme, Jane Mayer recorded the arrival on set (i.e. 2006) of U.S. Army Brigadier General Patrick Finnegan, the Dean of the United States Military Academy Westpoint. He was not there as a fan.

> Finnegan and others had come to voice their concern that the show's central political premise – that the letter of the American law must be sacrificed for the country's security – was having a toxic affect ... 'They should do a show where torture backfires.'[18]

Finnegan found he was having trouble instructing military officers on their constitutional obligations, and on obligations for interrogating captured enemy combatants because of 24. But the essential point of 24 is that torture must always remain effective when carried out by an insightful hero such as Bauer. This is not simply because various megalomaniacs are attempting to blackmail, or destroy the world (as is the case with examples of the James Bond franchise) but after 9/11 there was a perceived dichotomy between the 'homeland' as the United States became in official nomenclature at this time, and a threatening Islamic world. In summing up the whole 24 project in 2014, Ian Crouch concluded,

> '24' seemed to carry water for the Bush government by endorsing the Administration's sense of the world as a set of binaries, pitting the U.S. against an enemy so unscrupulous that our own scruples must be considered a hindrance to safety.[19]

And that enemy was ostensibly Muslim. This takes us into themes of the development of the concept of the 'sphere' as it has been developed by Peter Sloterdijk. For him a sphere represents the conceptualisation of group cohesion. This provides a fascinating way to examine how nations adhere. Furthermore in *The Shadow of Mount Sinai*, Sloterdijk speaks of a phobocracy, or rule of fear that underwrites the concept of a total membership As we move into a late-modernity, the responsibility.[20] Additionally, the rise of the modern nation changes our basic attitudes to the other.[21] Our martial intent is to protect our sphere at all costs – not to conquer the other and add him/her to our empire – but to severely retard or obliterate that other – to poison her or her atmosphere.[22] The response of the citizen must then be self-transformation into a more efficient defender of the sphere and Sloterdijk makes this most clear in his book *You Must Change Your Life*.[23] But more of this paradigm below.

The epic atmosphere that is developed between those within the sphere who seek its protection and are responsible for it, and those forces who are against the sphere or simply excluded from it (refugees help in this) sets in train a dramatic dichotomy. An essential battle between the truly good and the truly evil rest on those who are 'inside' and those who are 'outside'. Muslims specifically, and Islam in general, fit well into this good/evil divide in fictional structures such as 24. But in the case of 24, that fiction became palpably real.

> For all its fictional liberties, '24' depicts the fight against Islamist extremism much as the Bush Administration has defined it: as an all consuming struggle for America's survival that demands the toughest of tactics.[24]

Finally, once the viewer has accepted that the 'ticking time bomb' scenario is not ridiculously rare, but regularly possible, 24 and its ticking clock become enmeshed in a reality that sucks Bush administrators, lawyers, conservative think tanks, and Westpoint students into its maw. This occurs not necessarily because 24 goes out of its way to stress the reality of its stories, but because it makes the reality of the need for torture self-evident if the homeland (the home sphere) is to be protected. It is the political influence of the programme, which we can chart, that makes the phenomenon of 24 so unique. In the two following cinematic examples we will see that the immediate political effects are much less palpable, this is perhaps why they must stress their documentary nature far more than 24. They do this by claiming their own journalistic and or television news atmosphere.

AMERICAN SNIPER

In 2012 U.S. Navy Seal Chris Kyle wrote (to quote the front cover) 'American Sniper: The Autobiography of the MOST LETHAL SNIPER in U.S. Military History'.[25] By 2014, Hollywood had produced a film version with Clint Eastwood directing. It was to prove this actor-director's most successful film.

Perhaps the real story of Chris Kyle's life is not the recounting of his military daring but the fact that he, like so many of his fellow citizens, was shot dead not in a warzone but in his home state, and by fellow citizen and fellow soldier Eddie Ray Routh in 2012. Routh 'worshipped Chris Kyle' Corporal Corey Smalley told the *Daily Mail*.[26] Additionally, Routh's family suggested that Veteran's Affairs had failed Routh in his struggles with PTSD.[27] This part of the story Eastwood glides over. Scenes that refer to Kyle's relationship with his wife and family as he becomes increasingly affected by the war are glossed over, and as the credits roll we see grainy footage of Kyle's funeral. The procession of his body takes place along roads lined with his fellow Texans. This footage is confirmation that the film, starring Bradley Manning as Kyle, is more like a documentary than a dramatic film. It accords seamlessly with the 'real' events of Kyle's life.

Kyle's book opens with a note that states, 'The events that happened in this book are true, recounted from the best of my memory'.[28] This frames the autobiography as a personal *remembered* account. In contradistinction the directorial decisions that Eastwood makes is to tell the film's story is done in a style that centres upon Kyle's experience, but which is not heavily narrated in such a way as to make it clear that it is a single witness's account. In this way the film conflates its documentary-like reality presentation with the fact that it is the account of one person. As Alderton and I have shown elsewhere, the witness accounts of soldiers can be used to create an epic atmosphere particularly in state rituals we have studied such as the dawn service of the Australian ANZAC Day.[29] These military 'witnessing' accounts relate heroic actions, pain suffered, list extreme emotions, and tell of extreme journeys, but their usefulness to the state also lies in the fact that they cannot put the war in a wider context. In Eastwood's *American Sniper*, Kyle sees the twin towers fall, and very soon after he is deployed to Iraq as though his deployment is a natural and rational consequence of the homeland being attacked. Using Kyle's first-person account to create a third-person narrative of what *really* happened avoids all the questions about the legitimacy of the war that soldiers and citizens may have had. Nevertheless it still presents a 'reality' in the film that is dressed up as larger than just one man's 'witnessing' of the war.

The dichotomy of good and evil is portrayed starkly by Kyle in his own account of his first kill. He shoots a woman running at some marines with a grenade. Although she may have been defending her homeland, perhaps even her actual home, Kyle can only see her actions through a good/evil paradigm.

> My shots saved several Americans, whose lives were clearly worth more than that woman's twisted soul. I can stand before God with a clear conscience about doing my job. But I truly, deeply hated the evil that woman possessed. I hate it to this day.[30]

Eastwood develops this thematic by doing what so many Hollywood depictions do, and that is keep the 'other' (Iraqis and Muslims both the good and the evil) as voiceless and distant figures of monstrous intent. The above scene in the book becomes one of the most tense in the film as Kyle [Bradley Manning] must summon the gumption to kill a woman who has a child close to her. The film plot then rotates around Kyle's several tours of duty between trying to live a suburban life and building a family on one hand, and working as a professional killer, albeit one who operates through a long-distance gun-sight. The process of keeping the enemy silent and distant in the film had some interesting effects on the audience during its cinematic release. Homeland crowds cheered the kills. This worried the filmmaker and commentator Robert Greenwald, who saw the film as a Neocon fantasy. He added,

What this movie will achieve will be more Americans believing and cheering for more wars and then more veterans being injured – more veterans losing arms and legs and their families destroyed ... [watching *American Sniper*] tore my guts apart, [and I was] particularly sickened by how people in the movie theater were cheering after every time an Iraqi got shot.[31]

Most cheers were saved for the climactic scene of the film when Kyle takes out 'Mustafa' an enemy sniper who had a track record of American kills. Of Kyle's 160 confirmed kills, this seems the sweetest. Again we know nothing about Mustafa except that we see him setting up and doing something very similar to Kyle, but from the other side. Of course there is no justification for why he might be doing this, no sign that Mustafa himself has a family and a community to defend, a wife and family at home. Like the woman Kyle shot, this sniper is monstrous and evil because of his silence. It is this lack of complexity in a film about the war experience *as a whole* that makes *American Sniper* as epic as a text such as *Gilgamesh*: unspeakable monsters are disposed of, great and testing journeys are made. Whilst as this happens particular political agendas remain unchallenged.

ZERO DARK THIRTY

Academy award-winning screenwriter Mark Boal wrote and Kathryn Bigelow directed *Zero Dark Thirty* [ZDT]. The film was released at the end of 2012 and dramatised the decade-long manhunt for the world's most dangerous man, Osama Bin Laden. In exacting documentary-like scenes (the film is 157 minutes long), we get to see how Americans discovered Bin Laden. The film contains at its start a more than thirty-minute long torture scene, which produced the information that begins the discovery process. This cinematic experience seemed to conclusively prove the premise of *24* – torture works, it just takes more time than Jack Bauer would expect for it to bear fruit. Boal, who had already won two Oscars for his script for *The Hurt Locker*, was also nominated for *ZDT*, centring this film at the heart of the Hollywood production experience. It is a rousing, yet detailed examination of torture and its effectiveness and of the investigation that went into the discovery of the whereabouts of Bin Laden – the mastermind behind the 9/11 attacks.

The film commences in darkness with calls made by those trapped in the World Trade Centre on the 11th of September 2001. Their screams then segue into the screams of an Islamic detainee who is being tortured by the heroes of the film Maya [Jessica Chastain] and Dan [Jason Clarke]. Again we face the situation where, when the homeland is under attack, any means of retribution are valid. As Matt Taibbi reminds us,

> By graphically depicting the sexual humiliation ('You don't mind if my female colleague sees your junk?' Clarke says, ripping the suspect's pants down as he hangs by his wrists), the walking around of suspects in dog-collars Lynndie-England-style, the putting of people in boxes, the waterboarding and the flat-out punching in the face (which Maya resorts to later, with help from another interrogator), Bigelow made it clear that she wasn't making any half-assed Rumsfeldian claim that what went on after 9/11, in thousands of grimy rooms around the world with thousands if not tens of thousands of people, somehow wasn't torture.[32]

He starts by congratulating Bigelow for showing as it is, but then ends by condemning her film's lack of attitude on the issue. The torture is perhaps made morally simpler by the fact that the torture centre is not in the United States where human rights monitoring may interfere with the inquisitorial techniques. In this way, *ZDT* is a strong cinematic argument for torture and it certainly demonstrates how torture is effective.[33] The film continues to follow Maya in her exacting work to discover the name of Bin Laden's courier. Playing out the cliché of many police procedurals, she must battle with her obsession for the truth against the intransigence of her superiors. In another well-worn trope, a side plot shows how her colleague Jessica [Jennifer Ehle] is killed in a suicide bomb attack trying to seek further information. Despite this deathly game, Maya prevails. The CIA operatives get to brief a number of Navy Seals on the exact location of Bin Laden. The film then climaxes with an operation to land helicopters next to Bin Laden's compound, storm his house, execute him, and retrieve whatever information, computers, et cetera might be in the compound. Once this is done, a call is made to the President to let him know that America's number one enemy is dead.

This, of course, accords with real life events from May 2, 2011 when, after receiving the telephone call confirming the death of Bin Laden, Barak Obama made the following public statement,

> Tonight, we are once again reminded that America can do whatever we set our mind to. That is the story of our history, whether it's the pursuit of prosperity for our people, or the struggle for equality for all our citizens; our commitment to stand up for our values

abroad, and our sacrifices to make the world a safer place. Let us remember that we can do these things not just because of wealth or power, but because of who we are: one nation, under God, indivisible, with liberty and justice for all.

The President, with these words, confirms that the killing of Bin Laden was a completely American project. What is also interesting is that in the rhetoric of the President, the killing of Bin Laden certifies the American ideals of fortitude, prosperity, and equality. One might argue that the invasion of a sovereign state (Pakistan) and the summary execution of a disabled man asleep in his bed (Bin Laden) is a twisted way to justify the greatness of the United States, but reason here is not the point. Breann Fallon is right to highlight the sacred dimensions of this slaughter for the confirmation of the principals of the American Civil Religion.[34] In their representations of the killing, both Obama and Bigelow are working from the same script. In the epic battle between good and evil, it is Americans who finally get to tell the story of how significant America is and how America triumphs. The unspeakable beast is killed and we do not get to hear his or her side of the story, nor do we get detailed explanations in this film from non-Americans about the process of finding Bin Laden.

And so, as with my other examples in this chapter, we need to judge this film from the voices that it excludes. Fallon is emphatic when she states

> It is imperative to note that this film tells the story of Osama Bin Laden's death from an entirely White-Western, and particularly American viewpoint. Bigelow does not allow any other opinions besides that of the pro-American, anti-terrorist to enter her film.[35]

This is perhaps our clue into the exact operation of the film. It remains one-sided and thus operates as entertaining propaganda. It fits into an Orientalist paradigm in presenting non-Westerners as incomprehensible, quick to violence, and exotic unspeaking operatives.[36]

The propaganda dimensions of both Obama's words, and Bigelow's film were even more starkly revealed in May 2015 when respected journalist Seymour Hersh published his investigative article on the real facts behind the killing of Bin Laden. Hersh suggests that, for many years, Osama Bin Laden was a prisoner of the Pakistani Secret Service. He was being kept under house arrest in Abbottabad, a township that was a major operations base for the Pakistani military. Osama Bin Laden was already an unarmed prisoner when the Seal team assassinated him.

More interestingly, all the general studies on torture as an ineffect-ive way of gathering information are confirmed in Hersh's article because torture did not reveal Bin Laden's location. Rather, someone just walked in off the street and told the Americans where he was

> It began with a walk-in. In August 2010 a former senior Pakistani intelligence officer approached Jonathan Bank, then the CIA's station chief at the US embassy in Islamabad. He offered to tell the CIA where to find bin Laden in return for the reward that Washington had offered in 2001. Walk-ins are assumed by the CIA to be unreliable, and the response from the agency's headquarters was to fly in a polygraph team. The walk-in passed the test. 'So now we've got a lead on bin Laden living in a compound in Abbottabad, but how do we really know who it is?' was the CIA's worry at the time, the retired senior US intelligence official told me.[37]

It seems as though the Pakistanis were keeping Bin Laden as a bargain-ing chip to play off in future deals with the United States. The walk-in revealed their asset. Hersh speaks of deals done between ISI (the Paki-stani Secret Service), the Pakistani administration, and the White House to set the scene for a clean execution of Bin Laden. On the night of the planned American attack on his one-man prison, Bin Laden's prison guards were dismissed and the electricity to the area was cut off. The Seals had permission to enter Pakistani airspace (Bigelow's film suggests that they had to get in and get out before the Pakistanis realised they were invading their airspace). The noble America-justifying execution of Bin Laden was in fact the murder of an unarmed and disabled prisoner locked in his prison cell. As with *American Sniper*, homeland audiences cheered as the Seals shot the old imprisoned man. As a good American son records the experience,

> And when they dragged the big prize with its blood-soaked beard back into the copter and flew off, well – the triumph the characters felt at that moment exploded into the theater, there were gasps and patriotic applause, and even I got caught up in it. The only thing I can compare it to was seeing *Rocky* or *Star Wars* in theaters as a kid, the way the crowds went wild over the ass-kicking ending.[38]

Yet if Hersh's words are true, then they confirm that procedures of law and justice that have evolved since the days of witch hunts, inquisitions, and trials by fire and water, are the best that we have in obtaining truth, and that torture does not work. In fact Taibbi argues that the disinformation generated by torture provided a delay in finding Bin Laden, and created false facts that were used to justify the second invasion of Iraq.[39]

The uselessness of torture and the CIA's Enhanced Interrogation Techniques (EIT) is confirmed in the work of Senator Dianne Feinstein. The Democratic senator from California was a relentless supporter of the CIA throughout her long federal career, and between 2009 and 2015 was Chairman of the Intelligence Committee. It was from 2006, however, that she began to react badly to the briefings from the CIA on their interrogation activities. Once she became Chairman of the committee that had oversight on the CIA, she was able to ask for a full report on its EIP activities. With strange timing, the 6700 page report was completed in the same month as *ZDT* was released. A much redacted 500 page report was subsequently released to the public. There were 20 findings of the report and these include:

#1 The CIA's use of its enhanced interrogation techniques was not an effective means of acquiring intelligence or gaining cooperation from detainees.

#2 The CIA's justification for the use of its enhanced interrogation techniques rested on inaccurate claims of their effectiveness.

#3 The interrogation of CIA detainees were brutal and far worse than the CIA represented to policymakers and others.

#5 The CIA repeatedly provided inaccurate information to the Department of Justice, impeding a proper legal analysis of the CIA's Detention and Interrogation Program.

#20 The CIA's Detention and Interrogation Program damaged the United State's standing in the world, and resulted in other significant monetary and non-monetary costs.[40]

One wonders how Jack Bauer would react.

CONCLUSIONS: OR BACK TO THE WHALE

The epic genre is a flexible modality of story telling. As one side battles the other, a great pathos can be evoked when we are allowed into the lives of those fighting on both sides. In *The Iliad*, the Greeks defeat the Trojans not by greater valour, but by the trick of the wooden horse. Virgil picks up on this in his epic on the founding of Rome. In *The Aeneid*, Aeneas flees burning Troy only to battle his way towards the founding of Rome. Perhaps the greatest threat to him as he takes his

epic voyage is not the monsters he must face, but Queen Dido of
Carthage who falls in love with him, and who burns herself to death
as he flees her bed. Similarly Dante weeps when he sees those of his
colleagues who have been committed to hell.[41] What we face in these
types of epic are a complexity of characters battling to achieve great
things and go on extraordinary journeys. The other modality of epic still
relies on great national enterprises and bringing heroes and heroines to
prominence. It still includes great journeys, but instead renders the
'other' voiceless, that is provides them with a status that is more
whale-like than human. More whale like than human. Taibbi picks up
on this in his reaction to *ZDT*,

> No, this was a straight-up 'hero catches bad guys' movie, and the
> idea that audiences weren't supposed to identify with Maya the
> torturer is ludicrous. Are we really to believe that viewers aren't
> supposed to be shimmering in anticipation for her at the end, as
> she paces back and forth with set-fans whooshing back her
> beautiful red hair, waiting for her copter to come in? They might as
> well have put a cape and a Wonder Woman costume on her, that's
> how subtle that was.[42]

Through the examples I have provided here, we have to wonder that in
the basic voiceless presentation of the 'terrorist other' against which she
struggles, America must not only conquer her foes, but also render them
completely inhuman. The victory over the foe is, in reality, nothing
more complex than the slaying of whales.

When we come to consider the motivations for this, Sloterdijk's
concept of spheres again aids us in understanding the present modern
state's need to obliterate the other in order to defend its own sphere. In a
democracy where every citizen becomes responsible for the sphere, the
anxiety to protect plays itself out in culture. So much so, in fact, that as
we saw with *24*, this culture encourages ideas that may do more harm
than good. Together with the Bush administration, *24* promoted the
idea that America's own scruples regards humans rights and the rule of
law needed to be suspended to exact revenge after 9/11 and protect the
homeland at all costs. Yet as the Senate report on torture makes clear,
not only was this an ineffective course of action, it was an action that
damaged the very values upon which America argues for its
exceptionalism.

Finally we come to considerations of how precisely religious all this
violence is. This is a significant consideration because the constants in
all the three examples I have provided here, and many other cultural

examples besides, are the presence of voiceless Muslim operatives who seek to do harm to America for immediate reasons that (because of their enforced voicelessness) remain obscure. Because of this obscurity ultimate motivation for their violence must rest on the one thing we know about them – that they are Muslim. It follows then that there is something inherently violent in Islam itself.

Timothy Fitzgerald has done much to show how 'religion' is a false category used by the academy and elsewhere to divorce a specific discourse and a particular human behaviour from the political and economic spheres of human activity.[43] I do not rush to wholeheartedly agree with Fitzgerald, but nor is he completely wrong. Similarly, Bruno Latour in his investigations of 'modernity' shows how we moderns have sought to divide up the field of knowledge in very particular ways, but we do so asymmetrically – that is without examining ourselves and the assumptions behind why such things as 'politics', 'religion', and 'science' become the categories they do.[44] Both these authors back up the strong argument found in William Cavanaugh's examination of religious violence where, in Chapter Two of *The Myth of Religious Violence*, the author successfully debunks a whole range of definitions that seek to define 'religious' violence. It cannot be done. So if we seek to find the 'religious terrorist' or the 'perpetrator of religious violence' in recent history and culture, we need to ask, 'why is it that we only consider the *other* to be religious'. Cavanaugh argues that this is because 'we' in the White Western world only exact a reasonable violence and only do so to counter the irrational and religious violence that is perpetrated against us.

But what happens when a Senate enquiry reveals that our violence is not rational at all, and could have more to do with a need to protect our sphere at all costs, and do, as Jack Bauer does – whatever it takes. And what happens if an enquiry like the Chilcot Enquiry in the United Kingdom reports that a former Prime Minister, in supporting the second invasion of Iraq, is a war criminal? And that, by consequence George W. Bush and others supporting the invasion were equally war criminals?[45] How do we maintain that our violence is rational and their violence is religious?

It follows then, that when we go searching for terrorists, enactors of violence, and perpetrators of religious violence, we must not make our study asymmetrically. We cannot *only* study them. We cannot only count Muslims in films and television who act violently. Instead we have to view the entire cultural complex within which we operate. And when we do we find that there is something sick about the stories we

tell ourselves. We not only enjoy the ticking time bomb scenario of *24*
we *believe* in it. It becomes a policy outcome of administration. We not
only see a sniper at work, we *believe* that he must kill the evil he sees
around him, and we cheer in the audience when he does. And we cheer
too when an old man is summarily executed in his prison cell in the
middle of the night. We *believe* he had to die unspeaking and without
justifying his actions to us. All these points are acts of belief and
certainly not rational examples of the administration of violent justice.
So if we do not administer violence rationally, nor record its rational
administration in our culture, does that mean that we too are perpetrators of religious violence? This seems to be the case.

Endnotes

1   Christopher Hartney, 'Why Muslims Kill Themselves on Film: From
    Hollywood's Racism to Girard's Victimage Mechanism,' in *Sacred Sui-
    cide*, ed. James R. Lewis, Ashgate New Religions (Farnham Surrey,
    England; Burlington, VT: Ashgate, 2014).

2   For a wider examination of this academic sleight-of-hand see: Christo-
    pher Hartney, 'Indigenous or Non-Indigenous: Who Benefits from
    Narrow Definitions of Religion?,' in *Constructing the Indigenous: First
    Peoples and the Study of Religion*, ed. Christopher Hartney and Daniel
    J. Tower (Leiden: Brill, 2016).

3   Orson Welles, John Houston, and a range of Hollywood luminaries have
    worked on or in cinematic adaptations of *Moby Dick*. This year Ron
    Howard directed *In the Heart of the Sea* examining the fate of the
    whaling ship Essex, which inspired Melville in the penning of his novel.

4   Herman Melville, *Moby-Dick, Or, The White Whale*, Everyman's
    Library 40 (London: Everyman's Library, 1991).

5   Mortimer J. Adler, ed., *Great Ideas: A Synopticon of the Great Books of
    the Western World* (Chicago, London, Toronto: Encyclopaedia Britan-
    nica. Inc., 1952), 1052.

6   David Dowling, ''Revenge Upon a Dumb Brute': Casting the Whale in
    Film Adaptations of Moby-Dick,' *Journal of Film and Video* 66, no. 4
    (Winter 2014): 50–63.

7   See, Catherine Bates, ed., *The Cambridge Companion to the epic*,
    Cambridge Companions to Literature (New York: Cambridge Univer-
    sity Press, 2010).

8   Christopher N. Phillips, *epic in American Culture: Settlement to
    Reconstruction* (Baltimore, Md: Johns Hopkins University Press,
    2012).

9   These significant thematics are dealt with subtly in the American
    instance by Stanley Cavell, *The Senses of Walden*, An expanded ed.,
    [3. Dr.] (Chicago: Univ. of Chicago Press, 1997). And more generally
    the link from the Reformation to an insidious and extreme heroic
    individualism can be found best enunciated in Brad S. Gregory, *The*

Unintended Reformation: How a Religious Revolution Secularized Society (Cambridge, Mass: Belknap Press of Harvard University Press, 2012).

10 Stanley Cavell, *Cities of Words: Pedagogical Letters on a Register of the Moral Life*, 1. Harvard Univ. Press ed (Cambridge, Mass.: Belknap Press of Harvard Univ. Press, 2005).

11 Dean Mendell, 'Pious Ahab: The Conduct of a Christian in Melville's "Wicked Book"', *C.E.A Critic* 76, no. 3 (November 2014): 278.

12 Seymour Martin Lipset, *American Exceptionalism: A Double-Edged Sword* (New York: Norton, 1997).

13 Jane Mayer, 'Whatever It Takes: The Politics of the Man Behind "24"', *New Yorker*, February 19, 2007, 14, www.newyorker.com/magazine/2007/02/19/whatever-it-takes.

14 Jack Shaheen, 'Reel Bad Arabs: How Hollywood Vilifies a People,' *Annals of the American Association of Political and Social Science* 588 (July 2003).

15 Sara Brady, *Performance, Politics, and the War on Terror 'Whatever It Takes'* (Houndmills, Basingstoke, Hampshire; New York: Palgrave Macmillan, 2012), 119, http://public.eblib.com/choice/publicfullre cord.aspx?p=1016556.

16 Dahlia Lithwick, 'The Bauer of Suggestion,' *The Slate*, July 26, 2008, www.slate.com/articles/news_and_politics/jurisprudence/2008/07/the_bauer_of_suggestion.html.

17 Robert Anthony Pape, *Dying to Win: The Strategic Logic of Suicide Terrorism* (New York: Random House, 2006).

18 Mayer, 'Whatever It Takes: The Politics of the Man Behind "24"', 5.

19 Ian Crouch, '"24" Drones On,' *The New Yorker*, May 19, 2014.

20 Peter Sloterdijk: *In the Shadow of Mount Sinai*, Cambridge, Polity, 2015.

21 Benedict R. O'G Anderson, *Imagined Communities: Reflections on the Origin and Spread of Nationalism*, Rev. ed (London; New York: Verso, 2006).

22 Peter Sloterdijk, *Terror from the Air*, trans. Amy Patton and Steve Corcoran (Los Angeles: Cambridge, Mass: Semiotext(e); Distributed by the MIT Press, 2009).

23 Peter Sloterdijk, *You Must Change Your Life On Anthropotechnics.*, trans. Wieland Hoban (Cambridge, UK: Polity, 2013).

24 Mayer, 'Whatever It Takes: The Politics of the Man Behind "24"', 2.

25 Chris Kyle et al., *American Sniper: The Autobiography of SEAL Chris Kyle, (USN 1999–2009), the Most Lethal Sniper in U.S. Military History* (New York: HarperCollins, 2012).

26 Laura Collins, '"My Brother Marine Eddie Ray Routh Was Not a Monster: He Hero-Worshipped Chris Kyle" Comrade Speaks in Defence of American Sniper's Killer as Murder Verdict Nears', *The Daily Mail*, February 25, 2015.

27 Ibid.

28 Kyle et al., *American Sniper*, i.

29 Zoe Alderton, Christopher Hartney, Daniel J. Tower: 'Fieldwork on Anzac Day: A Performance Analysis of the Dawn Service and Other

Rituals, 25 April, 2015.' in *Fieldwork in Religion*, vol 11, no. 2, pp.170–198.

30   Kyle et al., *American Sniper*, 4.

31   Josh Feldman, 'Filmmaker: "Neocon Fantasy American Sniper Gets People Cheering for More War"', *Mediaite*, January 19, 2015, www .mediaite.com/tv/filmmaker-neocon-fantasy-american-sniper-gets-people-cheering-for-more-war/.

32   Matt Taibbi, '"Zero Dark Thirty" in Osama Bin Laden's Last Victory Over America', *Rolling Stone*, January 16, 2013.

33   Glen Greenwald, 'Zero Dark Thirty: CIA, Hagiography, Pernicious Propaganda,' *The Guardian*, December 15, 2012. Tim Kroenert, 'Evil Is Relative in the Hunt for Bin Laden,' *Eureka Street*, 2013. Simon Cooper, 'Enlightened Barbarism,' *Arena* 122 (2013): 54–55.

34   Breann Fallon, ''Zero Dark Thirty' (2012) and Girard: The Fortification and Veneration of American Civil Religion in Film,' *Literature and Aesthetics* 24, no. 1 (June 2014): 29–46.

35   Ibid., 29–30.

36   Edward W. Said, *Orientalism* (New York: Vintage Books, 1979).

37   Seymour Hersh, 'The Killing of Osama Bin Laden,' *London Review of Books*, May 21, 2015, 4.

38   Taibbi, '"Zero Dark Thirty" in Osama Bin Laden's Last Victory Over America.'

39   Ibid.

40   United States and Dianne Feinstein, eds., *The Senate Intelligence Committee Report on Torture: Committee Study of the Central Intelligence Agency's Detention and Interrogation Program* (Brooklyn, NY: Melville House Publishing, 2014), 3–22.

41   Frances Di Lauro, *Between Heaven and Hell: Faces of Iniquity and Surrender in Dante Alighieri's 'La Divina Commedia'* (Saarbrücken, Germany: Lambert Academic Pub., 2012).

42   Taibbi, '"Zero Dark Thirty' in Osama Bin Laden's Last Victory Over America'.

43   Timothy Fitzgerald, *Discourse on Civility and Barbarity: A Critical History of Religion and Related Categories* (New York: Oxford University Press, 2007).

44   Bruno Latour, *We Have Never Been Modern* (Cambridge, Mass: Harvard University Press, 1993).

45   Nicholas Watt, 'Tony Blair Makes Qualified Apology for Iraq War Ahead of Chilcot Report', *The Guardian*, October 25, 2015.

16 Understanding Falun Gong's Martyrdom Strategy as Spiritual Terrorism

JAMES R. LEWIS AND NICOLE S. D'AMICO

> **Terrorism**: Premeditated, politically motivated violence perpetrated against noncombatant targets by subnational groups or clandestine agents.[1]

The above definition, originally taken from a piece of US legislation, is often referred to in discussions of terrorism. However, this definition and related definitions are clearly deficient in that they exclude acts of state terrorism, which are arguably far more lethal than the violent acts perpetrated by groups like AUM Shinrikyo and the Black September organization. Nevertheless, academic scholarship,

> has concentrated almost exclusively on sub-state terrorism, specifically al-Qaida but extending to the Taliban, Hezbollah, Hamas and other Islamic paramilitaries. Virtually no attention has been paid to state terrorism, either before or since 9/11, in spite of the fact that state terrorism has been massively more costly in terms of lives and human well-being.[2]

This imbalance has often been criticized,[3] but is not likely to change in the near future. With the exception of the Islamic State, which the international community refuses to recognize as a proper nation, the bulk of mainstream terrorism research will almost certainly continue to focus on sub-state groups – though so-called rogue nations (which, not coincidently, are never Western nations) have been accused of sponsoring terrorism in other countries.

One also sometimes finds that oppressed groups from within certain nations will accuse their respective governments of conducting campaigns of terror against their members. Thus, for example, followers of Falun Gong (aka Falun Dafa) – the Qi Gong group banned in China in 1999 – have taken up the accusation of state terrorism against the People's Republic of China (PRC). Although individuals other than participants in Falun Gong sometimes accuse the PRC of conducting a campaign of state terrorism against Falun Gong,[4] most of the voices leveling this accusation are either individual practitioners,[5] or groups obviously created by practitioners, such as the World Organization to Investigate the persecution of Falun Gong.[6] Thus, for example, in a presentation given in October of 2001 at a Falun Gong-sponsored forum, 'China's State-Run Terrorism: The Persecution of Falun Gong', Shiyu Zhou, a practitioner as well as a Professor of Information and Computer Sciences at the University of Pennsylvania, stated that,

> Today, under the rhetoric of 'social stability,' China's Communist regime terrorizes tens of millions of its own people – which include those who practice Falun Gong, their families and associates, among others. The government terrorizes them through violence, propaganda, brainwashing, and extortion of money and goods. These are the characteristics of 'a regime that resorts to state terrorism' – as was said in a statement by the International Education Development organization at the United Nations in August of 2001.[7]

Given the proximity of these remarks to the 9/11 attacks – which had taken place only the month before – it is clear that Zhou's rhetoric about terrorism was intended to associate the PRC with al-Qaeda in the minds of his listeners.

On the surface, this accusation seems fair enough if one takes seriously Falun Gong's version of its conflict with the Chinese government – a version of events echoed in many stories published outside of China. However, while most non-specialists think of Falun Gong as a peaceful spiritual exercise group, unjustly persecuted by Chinese authorities, it has a little-known history of forcibly silencing anyone outside of China who challenges its perspective. Additionally, unknown to all but a handful of specialists, the group's ongoing conflict with the PRC is driven by an esoteric theory of karma which prompts practitioners of Falun Gong to actively seek persecution and martyrdom. However, before turning to an analysis of this hidden side of the movement, it will be useful to provide a backdrop by laying out a thumbnail sketch of Falun Gong and its conflict with the PRC.

FALUN GONG AND CHINA

Qi Gong is the generic name for a complex of techniques for physical and spiritual well-being, with a tradition in China predating the Christian era.[8] It has sometimes been referred to as Chinese yoga. Although spiritual and religious activities in general are and have been viewed with suspicion in the PRC, in the latter part of the twentieth century the government began to actively promote Qi Gong and other traditional practices such as acupuncture as part of 'traditional Chinese science'. This eventually led to the so-called Qi Gong Boom of the eighties and nineties, involving hundreds of Qi Gong organizations, with perhaps as many as a hundred million total practitioners. Although the initial impetus from the government was based on an understanding of such practices as scientific and medically beneficial, the growth of the movement was accompanied by an increasing emphasis on Qi Gong's traditional folklore and spiritual philosophy, as well as by the emergence of charismatic, self-designated 'grandmasters' as cultural and even political leaders.

The largest, but by no means the only, such Qi Gong group was Falun Gong. Its founder, Li Hongzhi, established his peculiar brand of Qi Gong in 1992. The core of Falun Gong practices are five key exercises involving movements of the arms and the legs, in some ways reminiscent of Tai Chi practices. The number of participants in Falun Gong grew rapidly, in part because Master Li, as he was often called, taught the practices without charge. Li came from a humble social background; before becoming involved in Qi Gong practices, his first career was as a trumpet player in the People's Liberation Army. Li's early hagiographies, however, paint him as a child prodigy who trained under a series of exalted spiritual masters, and who furthermore acquired supernatural powers.[9] As he saw the political atmosphere in China begin to change from a favorable to an unfavorable attitude toward some of the more sensational claims made by certain teachers of Qi Gong, Li moved permanently to the New York City area in 1998 and, despite later claims to the contrary, continued to direct the Falun Gong movement's eventual resistance against the Chinese government from outside the country.

There were people in China's scientific and political leadership who were never comfortable with opening the door on these traditional practices. Over time, researchers failed to find hard scientific support for the claimed health benefits of Qi Gong. As a consequence, critical voices denouncing many schools of Qi Gong as pseudoscience grew steadily more persuasive. Additionally, many of the leaders of Qi Gong groups seemed to set themselves up as independent authorities who could, it was thought, potentially challenge the authority of the government. This led to what was at first a gradual withdraw of official support for Qi Gong. Eventually, however, the mass practice of Qi Gong was prohibited, some Qi Gong clinics and hospitals were forced to shut down, and Qi Gong organizations such as Zhong Gong and Falun Gong were targeted as superstitious and reactionary by a press campaign. Unlike other targets of this campaign, Falun Gong responded by staging demonstrations, including a demonstration involving 10,000 members outside Beijing's Zhongnanhai, the residence of China's top leaders, on 25 April 1999. This was viewed as a direct threat, as well as an echo of the 1989 Tiananmen Square demonstrations. The leadership was especially taken aback by the failure of its intelligence service to provide information about the pending demonstration beforehand.[10] It has also been said that the nation's top leaders were surprised by both the large size of the movement, and by the fact that, upon investigation, it was found that more than a few mid-level political and military leaders were practitioners.

The group was officially outlawed on 22 July 1999. The government accused it of 'spreading fallacies, hoodwinking people, inciting and creating disturbances, and jeopardizing social stability'.[11] On 29 July, Chinese authorities issued an arrest warrant for Master Li. The government initially arrested hundreds – later thousands – of Falun Gong practitioners. Petitioned by practitioners residing in the United States, the US House and Senate unanimously passed resolutions on 18 and 19 November 1999 that criticized the Chinese government for this crackdown. Additionally, the rapid proliferation of Falun Gong websites and other information on the Internet supporting Falun Gong quickly helped shape international opinion about the conflict. However, it should be realized that – with the encouragement of Master Li – practitioners left out certain essential items of information about the movement, items of information that paint a very different picture of Falun Gong and the group's conflict with the PRC.

THE HIDDEN FACE OF FALUN GONG

One of the group's early videos, *Falun Gong: The Real Story*, which was generally available by late 1999, contains several important inaccuracies: In the first place, the video denies that practitioners ever refuse to consult regular medical doctors. This, however, is not accurate. Rather, 'within the Falun Gong community there is considerable social pressure on practitioners to abandon conventional medicine'.[12] Thus, for example, in his field research, Gareth Fisher translated and transcribed one informant who recounted an illness she had at around the time she first became acquainted with Falun Gong:

My eyes became red as though I was catching a cold. I had several bouts of diarrhea ... The elder sister who introduced me to Falun Gong asked me: 'How about going to see a doctor?' I said: 'I don't think so. The books say that I should experience the cleansing of my body.'[13]

Her sister took her to see a doctor anyway, who in turn told her to 'go to the hospital to have an operation'. She refused, and eventually healed on her own. The informant's purpose in recounting this story was, of course, to testify to the healing powers of Falun Gong practice. However, it also provides a concrete example of a practitioner refusing medical treatment because of something said in the founder's books. Unfortunately, there were apparently many similar scenarios in which the outcome was tragic rather than miraculous. Furthermore, Falun Gong distanced itself from such failures, claiming that those 'who became ill or died after Falungong practice had only themselves to blame, since they ... practiced Falungong incorrectly'.[14]

Three or four minutes into *Falun Gong: The Real Story*, the video also denies that Falun Gong even has leaders – though by implication they clearly acknowledge the more general *spiritual* leadership of Li Hongzhi, the movement's founder. The assertion of having no leaders seems to be based on the fact that the group has a non-traditional organizational structure. (Li explicitly instructs his followers to tell outsiders that, 'Falungong has no organization, but follows the formless nature of the Great Tao'.[15]) However, the Falun Gong organization nevertheless has people at all levels functioning as leaders.[16]

In contrast to the assertion that the founder was never in day-to-day control of the movement, Master Li could mobilize thousands of practitioners, seemingly overnight, for massive demonstrations in China prior to the crackdown.

The network of practice site supervisors was activated to mobilise the practitioners to react against any criticism through public actions directed at media and government offices. The resistance, anchored in public displays of bodies in movement, was spectacular. Thousands of disciplined adepts appeared at strategic times and places, 'clarifying the facts' and demanding apologies, rectifications and the withdrawal of offending newspapers from circulation. Such had never been seen in Communist China: a network of millions of potential militants from all social strata and geographic areas, which did not hesitate to display its power on the public square and confront the media.[17]

At least one other theme misrepresented in the program is Master Li's apocalypticism. In the later part of *Falun Gong: The Real Story* (about 25 minutes in), there is a place where someone is translating Li Hongzhi as he speaks, denying that he had ever taught anything apocalyptic. However, given Master Li's 'unabashedly apocalyptic' pronouncements,[18] this is also markedly inaccurate. Thus, for example, he proclaimed:

> At present, the universe is undergoing momentous transformation. Each time this transformation occurs, all life in the universe finds itself in a state of extinction ... all characteristics and matter which existed in the universe explode, and most are exterminated.[19]

In an early lecture in the United States (well before the group was banned in China), Master Li asserted that (1) the ultimate cause of these catastrophes was immorality, and then described, at some length, (2) the current period of immorality, including such specifics as:

> The change in human society has been quite frightening! People would stop at nothing in doing evil things such as drug abuse and drug dealing. A lot of people have done many bad deeds. Things such as organized crime, homosexuality, and promiscuous sex, etc. None are the standards of being human.[20]

This implies, of course, that humanity is so corrupt that we are on the verge of experiencing a new apocalypse. And this apocalypticism was a part of his teaching almost from the beginning, years before the crackdown. Many people who were at one time Falun Gong's friends subsequently distanced themselves from the group after critics began calling attention to Master Li's pronouncements against homosexuality, feminism,[21] rock music and 'race mixing'.[22] Some former admirers also became adverse after learning about his exotic conspiracy theory regarding shape-shifting space aliens who capture human beings for use as pets back on their home planet,[23] and who are planning to take over our planet via their false, immoral religion of science[24] – an idea which appears to arise out of Li's resentment at the accusation of Falun Gong's being a pseudoscience. San Francisco legislators withdrew their nominations for Li Hongzhi to receive the Nobel Peace Prize after being informed about his pronouncements on homosexuality and race.[25]

The aspect of Li's teachings that speak more directly to this chapter's purposes is the part of his teaching that encourages his followers to seek persecution, if not outright martyrdom.

Falun Gong adepts are fearless of persecution and even seem, by their provocative acts, to deliberately seek it: persecution validates their doctrine and brings them closer to the salvation promised by Li Hongzhi.[26]

In her study of Falun Gong's conversion patterns, Susan Palmer (not to be confused with the Sinologist, David Palmer) points out that involvement in the group eventually 'requires participation in public demonstrations against the PRC government's persecution of Falun Gong practitioners'.[27] Resistance in the face of oppression builds up one's *xinxing*, or spiritual energy. The theory of how this works rests on a quasi-physical interpretation of karma. Li Hongzhi teaches that what other spiritual systems might call 'good karma' is a white substance referred to as *de*; 'bad karma', on the other hand, is a black substance Li refers to as *karma*. How this works out in a confrontation with police and other oppressors is a kind of spiritual vampirism:

> Virtue or Merit (*de*), according to Li Hongzhi, is a form of white matter which enters our body each time we do a good deed or are victimized by others. Bad karma, on the other hand, is a kind of black matter which penetrates us when we commit an evil deed. Thus, if someone insults you, the aggressor's white matter will pass from his body into yours, while your black matter will be absorbed by his body. Therefore, even though you may appear humiliated, the real loser is the aggressor, because he took your black matter and gave you his white matter.[28]

This esoteric view of the karmic process motivates practitioners to *actively seek* oppression: at the unseen spiritual level, what is actually happening is that practitioners are attacking policemen rather than the opposite. This is the covert meaning of Falun Gong's 'Forbearance'. As for followers who die while forbearing, Li Hongzhi assures those 'who martyred themselves to the cause could be expected to receive instant "cultivation" or enlightenment, the goal toward which every adherent struggles'.[29] A first-person account on a (now defunct) Falun Gong website provides a concrete sense of this positive acceptance of martyrdom:

> When I walked out of the door, the scene in front of me shocked me. The courtyard was full of prisoners on the ground being tied up by police. A white board with a name and the accusation was hung on their chests. I was treated the same way. At that moment, I had righteous thoughts: 'do not be afraid; whatever happens will be

helpful to improve my *xinxing*'. It also reminded me of Jesus being nailed on a cross in those days. It would be my pleasure to be able to sacrifice myself for Dafa.[30]

During her imprisonment, this practitioner was given the opportunity to sign a statement saying she would abandon Falun Gong. Had she done so, she would have immediately been set free. She refused, but was nevertheless unconditionally released one month later – a release that she subsequently attributed to the strength of her practice. This was not, however, to be the fate of many other practitioners, who were imprisoned or sent to forced labor camps.

As already mentioned, when it became evident that the government was on the verge of banning the movement in 1998, Li Hongzhi and his family escaped China and relocated permanently in the United States. Then from the safety of his new home, Master Li encouraged his followers left behind in the PRC to continue to demonstrate against the Chinese government, even if it meant dying for the cause. At a large gathering in Montreal a few years after the crackdown began that was attended by Susan Palmer, Li Hongzhi,

> congratulated the martyrs of Tiananmen Square who have 'consummated their own majestic positions' and presumably earned a posthumous enlightenment, or a crown of martyrdom: 'Whether they are imprisoned or lose their human lives for persevering in Dafa cultivation, they achieve Consummation'.[31]

Palmer discusses the philosophy of karma and martyrdom behind these protests, and rightly notes that, 'While Western politicians, journalists and human rights groups respond to social justice arguments, for the practitioners themselves, it is spiritual and apocalyptic expectations that fuel their civil disobedience'.[32]

In other words, it was Master Li's encouragements to practitioners to confront persecutors which had ultimately invoked government repression. Li Hongzhi not only encouraged followers to confront media whose portrayals of Falun Gong were judged inaccurate, but also government authorities – as in the case of the Zhongnanhai protest, which was likely undertaken under Li Hongzhi's personal direction.[33] Alternately, he could, of course, have instructed his followers to continue their practice in secret, and, if necessary, deny that they were practitioners. Instead, he held this kind of cautious approach up for criticism; e.g., 'There are also many new practitioners who practise in hiding at home, afraid of being discovered by others. Just think: what type of heart is that?'[34] This admonition to continue practicing in public appears to have been part of Li's larger strategy for using his followers to keep up the pressure on the Chinese government. This strategy was implicit in Li's 'issuing threatening statements [hinting that his millions] of followers might rise up' against the government shortly after the crackdown started.[35]

Furthermore, the authorities were willing to immediately stop subduing individuals and let them go free if they would just sign a statement (as mentioned earlier); in other words, the abuse, imprisonment and consignment to work camps was mostly avoidable. In the meanwhile, however, the leader who was encouraging his followers to resist and to embrace martyrdom was well out of harm's way. In David Ownby's words, 'Li scorns those practitioners – even in China, where stakes of resistance are high – who lack the courage of their convictions, [and] seems to ask that his followers make sacrifices that he himself has not made'.[36]

Instead of focusing on standing up for religious freedom, practitioners are and have been primarily focused on building up their *xinxing* by spreading the message about their victimage at the hands of security officials – officials who, they had been taught, are '"evil beings" devoid of "human nature"'.[37] As early as December of 2000,

> Li posted a message to the FLG website: 'When this test concludes, all bad people will be destroyed by gods. Those Dafa disciples who are able to come through the test will leave through Consummation. Those people who'll be left behind will have to eradicate sins by paying with horrible suffering.'[38]

FALUN GONG'S MEDIA CAMPAIGNS

The less pleasant aspects of Falun Gong discussed in the preceding section are virtually unknown outside of a small circle of specialists. A major background factor at work influencing perceptions of the conflict between Falun Gong and the PRC is a generalized negative stereotype about the Chinese government found in Western societies – a stereotype that predisposes Western audiences to accept Falun Gong's version of events over the PRC's version. Additionally, the movement has been quite effective at broadcasting its side of the story. Thus in addition to their strong Internet presence, practitioners have created sophisticated news outlets such as *The Epoch Times* (www.theepoch

times.com/) and New Tang Dynasty TV (www.ntd.tv/) that propagate the Falun Gong perspective whenever relevant events are covered. Furthermore,

> The Western media get most of their international information about Falun Gong from press releases from the Rachlin media group. What we are not told is that this group is essentially a public relations firm for Falun Gong, managed by Gail Rachlin – one of Li's most avid disciples who is also spokesperson of Falun Dafa Information Centre.[39]

Additionally, Falun Gong has actively worked to silence its critics. As an example of the movement's efforts to suppress critical voices, in 2001, the Canadian *La Presse Chinoise* (*Chinese Press*)[40] published a critical piece based around the testimony of a former practitioner. In that case, the newspaper was sued for libel. Four years later, Quebec's Supreme Court decided against the plaintiff. The ruling included a statement that, 'Falun Gong is a controversial movement which does not accept criticism'. Similarly, in response to a condemnatory statement published in the *Chinese Daily* newspaper in Australia, Falun Gong filed a defamation lawsuit in 2004. Two years later, the New South Wales' Supreme Court ruled in favor of the *Chinese Daily*.[41]

There have been a number of other lawsuits, but in most cases practitioners rely upon different tactics – though often using the implied *threat* of lawsuits as part of their overall strategy. Thus, for example, in response to an AP piece in 2005, 'Chinese Show off Repentant Falun Gong',[42] practitioners staged a protest at AP headquarters and demanded that the report be withdrawn. And to refer to one more example, in 2008, the *New York Times* published an article, 'A Glimpse of Chinese Culture That Some Find Hard to Watch',[43] critical of a program that had been promoted as a Chinese cultural event, but which was actually a heavily politicized attack on the PRC by the Falun Gong. Movement websites responded with dozens of pieces attacking both the newspaper and the article's author.

As a background to these attacks on Western media, one should realize that, prior to its being banned, Falun Gong had been highly successful at intimidating news media in China:

> Li preached that members must defend the *fa* (way or principle as outlined in his teachings) whenever it was attacked. Practitioners relentlessly protested any negative media reports, initiating over 300 protests between April 1998 and mid-1999, forcing dismissals of reporters and receiving public apologies.[44]

These early protests were successful because in China, 'the media are free only as far as they facilitate social stability ..., so when Falun Gong threatened civil unrest, media managers were quick to capitulate to their demands'.[45]

For a concrete example, on the 24th of May 1998, Beijing Television Station aired a story on the movement which, in addition to mostly positive information,

> also contained an interview with physicist and Marxist ideologue He Zuoxiu, who called the group an 'evil cult' that propagated dangerous and unscientific practices and ideas. Falungong responded vigorously to the attacks: five days later more than a thousand practitioners demonstrated in front of the television studio, until its director apologized, aired another report favourable to Falungong, and fired Li Bo, the journalist who had interviewed He Zuoxiu.[46]

As David Palmer makes clear in his section on 'Falungong Militancy' in *Qigong Fever*,[47] Falun Gong vigorously pursued this strategy of repeated massive protests as a way of silencing criticism in China before the crackdown. (For anyone who wants to understand why Falun Gong was eventually banned in the PRC, the latter sections of Palmer's book are essential reading.)

The events that set the stage for Falun Gong's suppression also involved an article published in a Chinese academic magazine, the *Science Review for Youth*.[48] An important step leading up to the Zhongnanhai protest was,

> a critique of Falun Gong in an obscure academic magazine, describing Li's teachings as superstitious and a health hazard. The article might have been forgotten, except that six thousand Falun Gong protestors occupied the University for three days, demanding a retraction. The editors refused, responding that academic publications do not print retractions. Police broke up the protest, arresting 45 people.[49]

The pivotal protest event (mentioned earlier in our background summary) that eventually set the crackdown in motion was subsequently held in Beijing in response to this police action. Despite the abysmal failure of the Zhongnanhai event – which evoked the opposite of its intended result – Li Hongzhi continued to push his followers to repeat the same disastrous actions over and over again, as if he expected a different result. Practitioners from all over China – as well as from abroad – were encouraged to travel to Beijing to protest the crackdown, only to be arrested and thrown into jail. As we have already seen, rather than being dismayed by the effects of his failed strategy, Master Li subsequently congratulated Falun Gong martyrs, whether they were imprisoned, sent to forced labor camps or died at the hands of the police. At the time (this statement was made in 2001, only a couple of years after the group was banned), he continued to disparage followers who practiced the techniques in secret. Furthermore, Li laid out new instructions that shifted the focus of the movement from individual practice to intensified political involvement. In Susan Palmer's words, reporting once again on Li Hongzhi's 2001 public talk in Canada:

> First, he said the aim of 'cultivation' is no longer *individual* 'improvement' or even spiritual enlightenment (referred to as 'consummation'). Second, he reminded his students they were living in the '*fa*-rectification' period (when the *fa*, or Universal Law, triumphs over the force of evil in a vast cosmic struggle). Third, he insisted that the appropriate action for all disciples is to engage in the *collective* work of activist protest against [former President] Jiang Zemin's persecution of Falun Gong, saying, 'we Dafa disciples ... have been entrusted with a great historic mission ... to safeguard the Fa ... expose the evil.'[50]

How should we understand these quixotic marching orders?

As unrealistic as this might seem from the outside, it appears that – at least during the first few years after the crackdown began – Master Li believed it was still possible to influence the PRC so that Falun Gong would once again be accepted as a legitimate movement on the Chinese mainland. In China, as we have already seen, Li had repeatedly been able to influence news outlets to change their stories from critical to positive during the years immediately prior to the banning of the movement. Those past successes apparently led him to believe that he could once again accomplish the same change of direction – only this time, at a national level. However, rather than exerting pressure directly on the Chinese government, the goal would be to influence world public opinion, which would, in turn, exert pressure on the PRC to change its policy and embrace Falun Gong. It is as if Li Hongzhi had an intuitive understanding of the basic principles of moral panic theory, and then decided to apply them in a naïve attempt to change the minds of Chinese authorities.

The original version of moral panic theory is concisely described in Chas Critcher's introduction to his anthology of readings on moral panic theory[51]:

> Moral panic is a concept [that] specifies the common characteristics of those social problems which suddenly emerge, cause consternation among powerful institutions and seem to require exceptional remedies. Cohen's massively influential version [*Moral Panics and Folk Devils*, originally published in 1972] concentrates on the processes a moral panic passes through as the threat emerges, is caricatured and disseminated by the mass media, seized upon by moralists, dissected by experts and eventually resolved through the adoption of special measures.[52]

Other concepts central to the moral panic notion are 'folk devils', which refers to the person or group caricatured as the threat, and moral entrepreneurs,[53] who are the crusaders that take up the struggle against the perceived threat. For the case at hand, folk devils are readily available in the guise of the leaders of the PRC (such as Jiang Zemin, who practitioners had pictured as a toad demon[54]). In Cohen's articulation of this notion, it is primarily journalists who are moral entrepreneurs, as an extension of the news media's tendency to 'devote a great deal of space to deviance: sensational crimes, scandals, bizarre happenings and strange goings on'.[55]

The initial confrontation between Falun Gong and the PRC was itself newsworthy enough to attract significant media attention. However, public interest eventually waned. Subsequently, at Li Hongzhi's urging, practitioners outside of China acted as moral entrepreneurs who took it upon themselves to further encourage news agencies all over the world to cover the suppression of the movement in China. These activities were undertaken over and above followers' creation of new movement websites and setting up their own news outlets focused on protesting the attack on the 'human rights' of practitioners.

In her analysis of the emergent qualities of the movement in 2001, Susan Palmer describes Falun Gong as having developed into a 'two-tier' movement, combining 'an *exoteric* movement (the rational, respectable pursuit of human rights expressed in the international arena) with an *esoteric* movement (an apocalyptic ideology and ethic of martyrdom)'.[56] Furthermore, Master Li explicitly instructed his followers NOT to tell new students – and, by extension, people outside of the movement – about the teachings 'that are too high-level. Just talk about what's on the surface, like how to improve your *xinxing* and how to get well and stay healthy'.[57]

> The inevitable outcome of keeping Li's teachings secret and passing the apocalyptic religion off as a healthy exercise plan, is that practitioners are left unable to explain why Falun Gong is illegal in China. Unable to say that Falun Gong was banned because Li's divine claims and other unusual teachings were considered to be a threat to public safety, and his ability to mobilise large numbers of protesters was a political threat, they tell reporters, that they are 'mystified' by the ban. 'It was not possible to make truthfulness, compassion and tolerance illegal,' one practitioner exclaims disingenuously.[58]

In addition to presenting Falun Gong as a peaceful spiritual exercise group, the other prong of the media campaign encouraged by Master Li has been to promote the spectacle of practitioners being brutalized by police. As we made clear earlier, Li's teachings about karma actually encourage followers to seek out this kind of repression.[59]

Thus while practitioners feel they are benefiting spiritually from such actions, the spectacle of their brutalization forwards what appears to be Li Hongzhi's strategy of evoking international outrage. Furthermore, if some practitioners subsequently die in an act of martyrdom, then so much the better – both for these individuals' 'Consummation' as well as for making the spectacle that much more compelling for consumption in the global media arena.

CONCLUSION

From a broad structural perspective, the parallels between what we might term Falun Gong's 'martyrdom operations' and Islamist martyrdom operations turn out to be quite close. The goal of a suicide bombing is less the actual infliction of casualties than it is a spectacle,[60] designed to make a powerful statement and to evoke terror in the bomber's audience. From the perspective of a radical Islamist group's leadership, a martyrdom operation is, among other things, a political-military tactic. Thus, for example, the 2004 Madrid train bombings, which took place three days before a general election, helped lead to a change in government and Spain's subsequent withdraw from the coalition occupying Iraq.[61] Comparatively, Li Hongzhi's campaign aims to change the situation in China, leading to a political atmosphere more favorable to his movement.

The victims are, of course, quite different – at an overt level. In a suicide bombing, the tactical goals are to kill enemies, but more importantly to 'strike fear into the hearts of the unbelievers'. The dramatic death of the bomber blowing him/herself up is also part of the terrifying spectacle, demonstrating to the enemy that 'mujahideen love death rather than life'.[62] In contrast, a Falun Gong practitioner who sets him/herself up to be brutalized and potentially killed by police offers him/herself as an apparently innocent victim, which is similarly terrifying for outside observers. However, we should always keep in mind that, at an unseen spiritual level, practitioners *believe* they *are* creating harm: their spiritual 'bomb' drains white substance (*de*) from the police while the practitioners' black substance (*karma*) figuratively 'explodes' onto the police. Thus at an esoteric level, what is actually happening (from the perspective of the practitioners themselves) is that Falun Gong members are assaulting policemen – not vice versa. Furthermore, at an individual, spiritual level, it is these same practitioner-martyrs who are winning, while the police are losing.

One final point of comparison is that both the bomber and the practitioner are being encouraged to undertake their respective radical actions, in part, by being promised a post-mortem reward. In the Islamic tradition, one who dies as a martyr fighting for his/her religion instantly goes to heaven, despite his/her other failings as a good Muslim.[63] And in Falun Gong, as we have seen, the practitioner's reward is 'Consummation', which is the movement's equivalent of enlightenment. In both cases, the assurance of divine compensation after death appears to provide part of the motivation for offering up one's life for the cause.

Endnotes

1   From the 'Glossary' on the US State Department webpage, under the heading 'Diplomacy in Action'. This definition was taken from a piece of legislation (22 USCS 2656) directing the State Department to collect statistics on incidents of terrorism.
    www.state.gov/j/ct/info/c16718.htm.
    Accessed: 21 April 2016.
2   Richard Jackson, Eamon Murphy and Scott Poynting, eds. *Contemporary State Terrorism: Theory and Practice* (Milton Park, Abingdon, Oxon: Routledge, 2010), p. xi.
3   E.g., Richard Jackson, 'Knowledge, Power and Politics in the Study of Political Terrorism'. In Richard Jackson, Marie Breen Smyth and Jeroen Gunning, eds. *Critical Terrorism Studies: A New Research Agenda* (Milton Park, Abingdon, Oxon: Routledge, 2009), pp. 66–83; Jacob L. Stump and Priya Dixit, *Critical Terrorism Studies: An Introduction to*

Research Methods (Milton Park, Abingdon, Oxon: Routledge, 2013), pp. 119–140.

4   E.g., The human rights lawyer, Karen Parker, who accused the PRC of 'State terrorism in the form of Government terror against its own people … in its treatment of Falun Gong' in a UN hearing. http:// sgforums.com/forums/2707/topics/267391. Accessed 21 April 2016.

5   E.g., Chin-Yunn Yang, 'The Perfect Example of Political Propaganda: The Chinese Government's Persecution against Falun Gong'. www .globalmediajournal.com/open-access/the-perfect-example-of-political-propaganda-the-chinese-governments-persecution-against-falun-gong .pdf. Accessed 21 April 2016.

6   E.g., WOIPFG Statement Regarding the Terrorist Act of of Shooting Falun Gong Practitioners in South Africa. www.upholdjustice.org/ node/105. Accessed 21 April 2016.

7   Shiyu Zhou, 'The "610 Office": The Primary Mechanism in Jiang Zemin's State Terrorism Against Falun Gong'. http://en.minghui.org/ html/articles/2001/10/14/14689.html. Accessed 21 April 2016.

8   There are currently a number of good scholarly treatments of Falun Gong in English. David A. Palmer's *Qigong Fever: Body, Science, and Utopia in China* (New York: Columbia University Press, 2007) is essential reading for understanding the Qi Gong 'Boom' and the early Falun Gong movement in China prior to the 1999 crackdown. David Ownby's *Falun Gong and the Future of China* (New York: Oxford University Press, 2008) is a good general treatment. Benjamin Penny's *The Religion of Falun Gong* (Chicago: University of Chicago Press, 2012) is exceptionally good on analyzing Falun Gong as a religion. Finally, James W. Tong's *Revenge of the Forbidden City: The Suppression of the Falungong in China, 1999–2005* (New York: Oxford University Press, 2009) is a detailed study of the suppression of the Falun Gong movement on the mainland.

9   Benjamin Penny, 'The Life and Times of Li Hongzhi: "Falun Gong" and Religious Biography.' *The China Quarterly* 175 (2003), pp. 643–661.

10 Tong, *Revenge of the Hidden City*, p. 6.

11 Cited in Kam Wong, 'Policing of Social Dissents in China: The Case of Falun Gong'. Paper presented at the annual meeting of The Law and Society Association, Renaissance Hotel, Chicago, Illinois, 27 May 2004. (Abstract).
    http://citation.allacademic.com/meta/p_mla_apa_research_citation/ 1/1/7/3/5/p117354_index.html. Accessed 22 April 2016.

12 Susan J. Palmer, 'Healing to Protest: Conversion Patterns Among the Practitioners of Falun Gong.' *Nova Religio: The Journal of Alternative and Emergent Religions* 6:2 (2003), p 353.

13 Gareth Fisher, 'Resistance and Salvation in Falun Gong: The Promise and Peril of Forbearance.' *Nova Religio: The Journal of Alternative and Emergent Religions* 6:2 (2003), p. 299.

14 David A. Palmer, *Qigong Fever: Body, Science, and Utopia in China* (New York: Columbia University Press, 2007), p. 264.

15 Ibid., p. 264

16 Yuezhi Zhao, 'Falun Gong, Identity, and the Struggle over Meaning Inside and Outside China.' In *Contesting Media Power: Alternative Media in a Networked World*, eds. Nick Couldry and James Curran, 209–226 (Lanham, MD: Rowman & Littlefield Publishers, 2003), p. 216.

17 Palmer, *Qigong Fever*, p. 252. As an example of his unquestioned authority over the Falun Gong organization, Li Hongzhi was able to instantly dismiss 'the chief assistant of the Beijing Falungong General Training Station [one of the group's local *leaders*] for having stayed at home rather than taking part in a demonstration.' Ibid., p. 254.

18 Palmer, 'Healing to Protest,' p. 349.

19 Li Hongzhi, cited in Palmer, *Qigong Fever*, p. 226.

20 Li Hongzhi, 'Lecture in Sydney' (1996). www.falundafa.org/book/eng/lectures/1996L.html. Accessed: 4 June 2016.
Master Li reserves his strongest expressions of disdain for homosexuality. Thus, for instance, in *Zhuan Falun, Volume II*, he asserts that 'the irrationality of our times is reflected in the filthy psychological abnormality that is repulsive homosexuality.' Cited in Penny, *The Religion of Falun Gong*, p. 102.

21 David A. Palmer. 'Falun Gong: Between Sectarianism and Universal Salvation.' *China Perspectives* 35 (2001), p. 8. http://hub.hku.hk/bitstream/10722/194523/2/Content.pdf?accept=1. Accessed: 7 June 2015.

22 Li Hongzhi, 'Teaching the Fa in New York City' (23 March 1997). https://falundafa.org/eng/eng/lectures/1997L.html. Accessed: 4 June 2015.

23 Palmer, 'Falun Gong.'

24 William Dowell, 'Interview with Li Hongzhi,' *TIME-Asia* (10 May 1999). http://content.time.com/time/world/article/0,8599,2053761,00.html. Accessed: 27 May 2015.

25 Sarah Lubman, 'A Chinese Battle on U.S. Soil: Persecuted Group's Campaign Catches Politicians in the Middle.' *San Jose Mercury News* (23 December 2001).
www.culteducation.com/group/1254-falun-gong/6819-a-chinese-battle-on-us-soil.html. Accessed: 4 June 2015. We should be careful to note that Li Hongzhu is not exactly racist in the way in which that term is usually used. Rather, on this topic, his aversion is not to other races but to race-mixing, which he sees as a symptom of degeneration as well as one of the causes of the imminent catastrophe; e.g., 'as humankind's morality decays, all matter is rotting. In other words, it has become tainted. At present, the cultures of humankind are in a muddle – they are messy combinations of all sorts, and human races are becoming more and more mixed. These have indeed driven humankind to slide to a very dangerous stage – this is certain. As we said, catastrophes happen because humankind is depraved.' Li Hongzhi, 'Lecture at the First Conference in North America' (29–30 March 1998). https://falundafa.org/eng/eng/lectures/19980329L.html. Accessed: 7 June 2015.

26 Palmer, 'Falun Gong', p. 17.

27   Palmer, 'Healing to Protest', p. 354.

28   Palmer, 'Falun Gong', p. 8.

29   Helen Farley, 'Falun Gong: A Narrative of Pending Apocalypse, Shape-Shifting Aliens, and Relentless Persecution'. In *Controversial New Religions*, eds. James R. Lewis and Jesper Aa. Petersen, 241–254. (New York: Oxford University Press, 2014), pp. 249–250. There might be a connection between this line of thinking and a Chinese tradition that connects sacrality and self-inflicted violence. In this regard, refer to Jimmy Yu, *Sanctity and Self-Inflicted Violence in Chinese Religions, 1500–1700*. New York: Oxford University Press, 2012).

30   Cited in Fisher, 'Resistance and Salvation', p. 302.

31   Palmer, 'Healing to Protest', p. 356. Though she was at the meeting in Montreal on the 19th of May 2001 where Master Li made these statements, in her article Susan Palmer also refers to a now defunct webpage containing the text of his lecture: Li Hongzhi. 'Towards Consummation', 17 June 2000. For a discussion of Falun Gong's notion of 'Consummation,' refer to the discussion in Penny, *The Religion of Falun Gong*, especially chapter Six. www.clearwisdom.net/eng/2000/Jun/17/JingWen061700.html.

32   Palmer, 'Healing to Protest', p. 349.

33   David Ownby, 'In Search of Charisma: The Falun Gong Diaspora.' *Nova Religio: The Journal of Alternative and Emergent Religions* 6:2 (2003), p. 109. Given the fact that Master Li had flow to Beijing in the days leading up to the demonstration, some sources assert that he was obviously involved in the planning of that protest (Palmer, *Qigong Fever*, p. 267), despite later denials (Ibid., p. 271).

34   Cited in Palmer, *Qigong Fever*, p. 253.

35   Ibid., p. 272.

36   Ownby, *Falun Gong and the Future of China*, pp. 118–119.

37   Palmer, 'Healing to Protest,' p. 357.

38   Cited Patsy Rahn, 'The Chemistry of a Conflict: The Chinese Government and the Falun Gong.' *Terrorism and Political Violence* 14:4 (2002), p., 56.

39   Heather Kavan, 'Print Media Coverage of Falun Gong in Australia and New Zealand.' In Peter Horsfield, Ed., Papers from the Trans-Tasman Research Symposium, 'Emerging Research in Media, Religion and Culture'. Melbourne: RMIT Publishing, 2005.

   http://falunfacts.blog.com/2010/03/30/print-media-coverage-of-falun-gong-in-australia-and-new-zealand/. Accessed 27 May 2015.

40   www.chinesepress.com/.

41   James R. Lewis, 'Sucking the "*De*" out of Me: How an Esoteric Theory of Persecution and Martyrdom Fuels Falun Gong's Assault on Intellectual Freedom'. In the *Alternative Spirituality and Religion Review* 7:1 (2016).

42   Associated Press, 'Chinese Show Off Repentant Falun Gong' (2005). www.washingtonpost.com/wp-dyn/articles/A26902-2005Jan21_2.html. Accessed: 5 June 2015.

43   Eric Konigsberg, 'A Glimpse of Chinese Culture That Some Find Hard to Watch.' *New York Times* (26 February 2008).

www.nytimes.com/2008/02/06/nyregion/06splendor.html?scp=1&
sq=A+Glimpse+of+Chinese+Culture+That+Some+Find+Hard+to
+Watch&st=nyt. Accessed: 5 June 2015.

44 Kavan, 'Print Media Coverage.'

45 Heather Kavan, 'Falun Gong in the Media: What Can We Believe?'
ANZCA08 Conference, 'Power and Place', Wellington, NZ, July 2008,
p. 3.
www.equinehospital.co.nz/massey/fms/Colleges/College%20of%
20Business/Communication%20and%20Journalism/ANZCA%202008/
Refereed%20Papers/Kavan_ANZCA08.pdf. Accessed 27 May 2015.

46 Palmer, *Qigong Fever*, p. 252.

47 Ibid., pp. 251–256.

48 Lao Cheng-Wu, *Refutation and Analysis of Falun Gong* (Bloomington,
Indiana: iUniverse, 2012), p. 195.

49 Kavan, 'Print Media Coverage'.

50 Palmer, 'Healing to Protest', p. 349.

51 There have been a number of developments in scholarship on moral
panics over the years, as discussed, for instance, in the introduction to
Charles Krinsky, *The Ashgate Companion to Moral Panics* (Franham,
Surrey: Ashgate, 2013), pp. 1–14.

52 Chas Critcher, *Critical Readings: Moral Panics and the Media* (Maiden-
head, UK: Open University Press, 2006), p. 2. The full reference to
Cohen is: Stanley Cohen, *Folk Devils and Moral Panics: The Creation
of the Mods and Rockers* (Oxford, UK: Blackwell, 1972).

53 A notion originally articulated by Howard S. Becker, in: *Outsiders:
Studies in the Sociology of Deviance* (New York: The Free Press, 1963).

54 'What Shanshan Saw in Other Dimensions (IV)' (25 May 2001)
www.clearwisdom.net/emh/articles/2001/5/25/10373.html.
Accessed: 27 May 2016.

55 Stanley Cohen, 'Deviance and Panics'. In Critcher, *Critical Readings*,
p. 35.

56 Palmer, 'Healing to Protest,' p. 355.

57 Li Hongzhi, 'Touring North America to Teach the Fa'. (March 2002)
http://en.minghui.org/html/articles/2002/4/14/33952.html.
Accessed: 28 April 2016.

58 Kavan, 'Print Media Coverage'.

59 To repeat the basic idea: 'Li says that "When one throws punches at
someone else, he also throws out his white substance [that is *de* or
virtue] to the other person, and the vacated area in his body will be
filled with the black substance [that is *karma*]". This is important as
it goes some way to explaining why Falun Gong practitioners have
been apparently so willing to go to public places in China and do
things that will get them arrested and, as they claim, brutal-
ised. If a policeman were to beat you up, he is actually passing on his
de to you and that space in him is taken up by *karma*! You win – he
loses.' [Brackets in Penney.] Benjamin Penny, 'The Past, Present and
Future of Falun Gong.' Lecture at the National Library of Australia,
Canberra (2001).

www.nla.gov.au/benjamin-perry/the-past-present-and-future-of-falu n-gong. Accessed: 3 June 2015.

60 Jenny Hughes, *Performance in a Time of Terror: Critical Mimesis and the Age of Uncertainty* (Manchester: Manchester University Press, 2011).

61 Mary Habeck, *Knowing the Enemy: Jihadist Ideology and the War on Terror* (New Haven: Yale University Press, 2006), p. 158.

62 Ibid., p. 125.

63 '[A]waiting them in paradise are rivers of milk and honey, and beautiful young women. Those entering paradise are eventually reunited with their families and as martyrs stand in front of God as innocent as a newborn baby.' Walter Laqueur, *The New Terrorism: Fanaticism and the Arms of Mass Destruction* (New York: Oxford University Press, 1999), p. 100. Note, however, that the promise of a post-mortem reward is not always a motivator in suicide bombings, as Peter Schalk makes clear in his study of LTTE insurgents in this collection. Also refer to Mattias Gardell's discussion of how the great majority of Palestinian suicide bombers are not religiously motivated, in 'So Costly a Sacrifice Upon the Altar of Freedom: Human Bombs, Suicide Attacks, and Patriotic Heroes,' In James R. Lewis and Carole M. Cusack, eds. *Sacred Suicide* (Farnham, UK: Ashgate, 2014).

Index